JANE KENYON

JANE KENYON

The Making of a Poet

DANA GREENE

UNIVERSITY OF
ILLINOIS PRESS
Urbana, Chicago, and Springfield

Cataloging data available from the Library of Congress
ISBN 978-0-252-04538-7 (hardcover)
ISBN 978-0-252-05498-3 (ebook)

For Richard
forever and forever

CONTENTS

A WORD OF GRATITUDE

Many people seem to think that art is a luxury
to be imported and tacked on to life. Art
springs out of the very stuff that life is made
of . . . out of the fullness and richness of life.
—Willa Cather

Reading the poetry of Jane Kenyon led me to explore how, as Willa Cather observes, Kenyon's art comes out of her life. My intent in writing this biography was to comprehend this complex, talented, and ambitious woman, track how she became a poet, and link her creative work with the fullness and richness of her life. The goal of biography is understanding, which is a middle way between adulation and censure. The failings and limitation of a person must be woven together with her achievements. My hope is that as Jane Kenyon comes alive for you, the reader, you come to understand her and grow in an appreciation of her art.

I have an immense sense of gratitude for the many people who sustained me through the long process of completing this book. This includes family and friends who cheered me on, the many people who offered their insights into the life and work of my subject, and those who extended their skills, talents, and time to help bring this work to completion. I am grateful for their intellectual and personal hospitality.

This biography is built on Kenyon's own writing, published and unpublished, the critique of scholars, and the reminiscences of Kenyon's friends who allowed me to interview them. People loved Kenyon and were eager to share their memories of her and to comment on her legacy. Only in a very few cases were interviews declined. While I benefitted from all the comments, the views I express are ones for which I alone am responsible.

While writing an earlier biography of the English poet Elizabeth Jennings, I was in contact with Donald Hall, who had been a friend of Jennings in Oxford in the 1950s. When I approached him about this biography of his wife, he was enthusiastic and shared with me the names and contact information of important informants. However, a few months prior to his death, he closed the Kenyon archive at the University of New Hampshire, and it remained closed for a protracted period. When it finally opened, I was allowed access to the archival material, but then the COVID-19 pandemic closed it again. The staff of the Milne Special Collections and Archives, especially Bill Ross and Emeline Dehn, were helpful in securing materials. Thanks to Wendy Strothman of the Strothman Agency for granting permission to quote from the archives, Jeff Shotts of Graywolf Press for allowing me to quote Kenyon's poetry, and Alison Syring of the University of Illinois Press for shepherding this manuscript to completion.

I am especially grateful to Kenyon's dear friends—Alice Mattison and Joyce Peseroff—for sharing their reminiscences and correspondences, to Chad Wriglesworth for his transcription of their correspondence, to Reuel Kenyon for his insights and photographs of the Kenyon family, and to Mary Lyn Ray for memories, photographs, a tour of the Eagle Pond farmhouse, and her leadership in preserving the Wilmot, New Hampshire, home shared by Jane Kenyon and Donald Hall (see www.ateaglepond.org).

I had the great good fortune to interview friends and acquaintances of Kenyon and Hall, including Mary Baron, Victoria Clausi, Kendel Currier, Larry Goldstein, Marie Howe, Linda Kunhardt, Alice Ling, Wesley McNair, the late Mike Pride, Larry Russ, Tree Swenson, David Tucker, and the late Jean Valentine and Virginia Higgins.

For personal hospitality I am grateful to Emily and Herb Archer and Susan and Lewis Greenstein. For her eagerness to share her interest in Kenyon's poetry, I am grateful to the late Marion Torchia, and for her editorial comments, I thank Missy Daniel.

I am also grateful for my family and friends who endured years of conversation about Kenyon, especially my beloved husband, Richard Roesel, who is my dearest friend, first reader, and computer wizard, and our four daughters—Justin, Kristin, Lauren, and Ryan, whose love and support count for so much.

JANE KENYON

PROLOGUE

[F]or all the modern talk about keeping an author's work and life separate, all the schoolroom injunctions against mistaking art for autobiography, there are some works that life electrifies with meaning, some sayings only action authenticates.

—Christian Wiman

The snow-covered ground on this cold, dark Saturday evening is typical of New Hampshire in January. The sole light came from near the door of the white clapboard Wilmot Town Center, illuminating the entrance where an audience was already gathering. The New York film crew had arrived earlier and had set up equipment. Since seating on the hard, wooden benches was already scarce, extra chairs were hauled in and placed along the walls to accommodate the overflow crowd. Neighbors and friends, bundled in heavy sweaters and bulky coats, had come in mid-winter 1993 to hear two local celebrities read their poetry. This was no ordinary reading but one that PBS would televise and make available for millions of viewers. Clips from the evening's program would be used in "A Life Together" to be shown on *Bill Moyers Journal*.[1] This was an occasion to honor Donald Hall and Jane Kenyon, but the gathered local community that had nurtured these two poets for decades would be celebrated, too. Many of the poems read would reflect the residents and the culture of rural New Hampshire.

As Hall, always a witty, charming performer and ebullient personality, read his poems, there was laughter and a shared camaraderie. His comments were peppered with down-home yarns dear to the hearts of his audience.

He was one of them and they loved him for it. Kenyon offered a contrast to her husband both in her person and her poetry. Her erect posture projected a seriousness of purpose; her pearls, earrings, and feminine gestures signaled a certain elegance, and her long, abundant hair reflected freedom and sensuality. She was both reserved and independent. It was evident that she was a complex and vulnerable woman, one who was in touch with some primal inner force that inhabited her body and gave authenticity to her words. There was an immediate attraction between the audience and the poet.

During the evening Kenyon, taking turns with Hall, read several poems including her longest, "Having It Out with Melancholy." Here, in front of people who knew her, she revealed her lifelong depression and how it ravaged her and how she survived. As she read, her pauses and the sound of her voice gave evidence of how difficult it was to speak the truth about depression and its crippling consequences. The audience gave full attention as this calm, gentle woman offered a gift of companionship to those who suffered the same malady. At evening's end people swarmed around her expressing their gratitude for her self-revelation.

Moyers's "A Life Together" would present Hall and Kenyon to a national audience and give them and their poetry increased visibility. But it would also frame a life story that while containing truth also distorted. Framing stories are valuable in that they give direction and purpose to a life, help explain it, and give inspiration. This story was Hall's, developed from his childhood, one in which Kenyon became embedded. It was a story that would involve place, love, suffering, and devotion to what Hall called "the third thing," poetry. It was structured around two married poets living in rural New Hampshire in his ancestral farmhouse. Theirs was a "house of poetry" in which they shared a "double solitude" and lived creative, productive lives. They were called "the Brownings of America."[2] Their story was irresistible, and people wanted to believe it.

According to Hall, their story would continue to evolve over their marriage, making a harmonious life, "the best marriage I know about."[3] They became "a single soul."[4] Yet, while it is true that they both needed and loved each other, the story does not reveal what an unequal couple they were, nor does it reveal how Kenyon had to resist this merger of identities to realize her authentic poetic voice. For years after her early death, Hall writing about her life and work maintained the myth of their oneness.

This biography is Jane Kenyon's story, an attempt to unlock that which was tightly woven together, to penetrate her full poetic gift, and to show how it came to be. It begins with her childhood of isolation; her *amor mundi* (love of the world); her discovering poetry; her purposelessness as a young adult; her unlikely marriage to her teacher, an established poet who was nineteen years her senior; her move to his rural home; her joining his ancestral church and community; her growing acclaim; her affliction with depression; and her death from leukemia. Donald Hall cannot be excluded from this story—they were married for twenty-three years, and he was instrumental in her success—but here Kenyon will be moved to the foreground and Hall to the background.

Understanding Kenyon's life is hindered not only by its being embedded in Hall's life story but also by a form of hagiography that has grown up around her because of her vulnerability, openness to spiritual insight, sense of wonder, and ability to empathize. Such "canonization" limits and locks her into another rigid and unrealistic frame. Kenyon was a complex person who was pleasure-loving, sarcastic, stubborn, raunchy in her humor, sensual, determined, erotic, and deeply sad. She was a constellation of contrary characteristics. The truth of a life matters, and this biography is focused on uncovering and understanding the fullest truth possible.

The meaning of a life depends on who survives to chronicle it. This is particularly true in Kenyon's case. Understanding her life is hampered by the limits of available source material.[5] Her early life is largely undocumented except for her late-life reflections. Although her brother, Reuel, who was older, served as an interviewee, he was not close to Jane until they were adults.

Once Kenyon married Hall, it was Hall who described their lives together. After her death he curated her archive, which while appearing ample, does not contain extensive autobiographical material. There are few journals, the collected letters from others only very indirectly illuminate Kenyon's concerns, and most of the folders consist of multiple draft copies of her poems and prose. Fortunately, many persons who knew her were available to be interviewed, but these late-life friends knew Kenyon and Hall as a couple. Kenyon was a private person who gave access to her inner life principally through autobiographical elements of her poetry. Her life was the seedbed of her art. Her life and her work are intimately tied together. As she attested, "art comes out of your life."[6]

It was from Kenyon's difficult and complex life that her luminous poetry was born. That life, anchored in what she called "the great goodness," was the incubator in which her poems were germinated and brought forth. While her poetry made her life memorable, her life made her poetry possible. As Christian Wiman attests, the life and the work are intertwined, and in Kenyon's case the one "electrifies" the other with meaning. Two things are certain: Jane Kenyon was saved by poetry, and her poetic vocation was to be an "advocate for the inner life."

1

TURNING INWARD

Turning and turning
until it flared to the limit
was irresistible. . . . The grass and trees,
my outstretched arms, and the skirt
whirled in the ochre light
of an early June evening.
And I knew then
that I would have to live,
and go on living: what a sorrow it was;
and still what sorrow burns
but does not destroy my heart.
—Jane Kenyon

Jane Kenyon disclosed a few memories of her childhood, but the memory of her first knowing that she would live with burning sorrows was a striking exception. She recalled having it during what would appear to be a joyful moment, twirling on a June evening with outstretched arms as her yellow skirt flared into a perfect circle. But this was not a moment of ecstasy. Rather, it was the moment when she felt sorrow that she would have to live and go on living but also certainty that the effort would not destroy her. Kenyon's writing offers little to explain this experience. She did not write much about her childhood and rarely discussed it with others.[1] What evidence there is points to an unnamed hurt and simultaneously a joy and pleasure in life and a determination to live. These dual experiences of joy and sorrow were there in her earliest recollection and came to define her life and poetry.[2]

Kenyon was convinced that the seedbed of her vocation as a poet was in her youth, but there are few sources for the reconstruction of this earliest period of her life. Her autobiographical poetry written later in life and one extant journal from 1961 and 1962 provide limited detail.[3]

Three aspects of her early life stand out. She lived in her imagination and frequently escaped to the solitude of the natural world. She experienced submerged anger, which was expressed when it exploded in her journal. And she felt she was weirdly unlike other children.

To others, her parents seemed to the outside world as a typical, hard-working, midwestern couple with a family who lived on a one-acre plot in rural Ann Arbor Township. Polly (Pauline) and Reuel Kenyon married late. Polly had a brief first marriage, and Reuel may have had one, as well.[4] Their son, Reuel, was born in 1944, and Jane Jennifer followed on May 23, 1947, when Polly was thirty-four and Reuel Sr. forty-three.

Jane's father's parents, George Washington Kenyon, a butcher, and his wife, Dora Baldwin Kenyon, lived in Ann Arbor. When George Kenyon died in 1951, he left his seventy-year-old wife to support herself. Although Jane had almost no recollection of her grandfather, her grandmother Dora was to have a significant emotional impact on her, mostly negative. Her father's sister, Geraldine, and her husband, Paul, lived at a distance and had almost no interaction with the family.[5] Her maternal grandfather was a Methodist minister; her maternal grandmother, a socially engaged, beautiful woman who lived in California, was uninvolved in the Kenyons' lives. Jane had only a hazy recollection of a single visit with her when Jane was seven.[6]

Reuel Sr. and Polly Kenyon had jobs that provided modest incomes. Reuel quit high school to play jazz piano and toured Europe playing in a dance band. When he married Polly in 1943, he returned to Ann Arbor, where despite his fragile health. he worked several jobs to make ends meet. During the day he served as a purchaser of sheet music in a bookstore in downtown Ann Arbor, dressed in suit, tie, and pocket handkerchief. In the evenings and on weekends, he either gave piano lessons or played at social and civic clubs. He loved music and the artistic life and often had gigs in other cities. He also was a union member, serving as president of the local branch of the American Federation of Musicians. But he had greater aspirations. In the late 1940s he studied in the School of Architecture at the University of Michigan, but his efforts went nowhere. Jane treasured a precise drawing he made of her stroller, a token of his skill as a draftsman.[7]

But he remained caught between a desire for an artistic life and the pressing financial demands of a family.

Polly and Reuel met in Chicago when she was singing at the city's nightclubs. A year after their marriage, when Reuel Jr. was born, Polly ended her singing career and opened what became a very successful downtown business as a seamstress, producing clothing for the upscale female clientele of Ann Arbor, who were quite taken with her. At one point she had three employees. She also gave sewing lessons at home and managed family life. Both parents worked hard and had minimal social interaction outside the family. While traditional in many ways, they retained a bohemian orientation rooted in their entertainment careers.

The Kenyons lived in a large, white house at 2896 Newport Road in rural Ann Arbor Township, Michigan, on an unpaved road across from a working farm four miles outside the city. Before the house was renovated, it had two bedrooms, a wraparound porch, and room enough for two pianos. In the 1950s the Ann Arbor population was about forty-eight thousand, the city's economy dominated by the university.

FIGURE 1. Polly, Reuel Jr., Reuel Sr., and Jane Kenyon, circa 1951. Courtesy of Reuel Kenyon.

FIGURE 2. Jane Kenyon's childhood home, 2896 Newport Road, Ann Arbor. Michigan. Courtesy of Reuel Kenyon.

Music was something the family shared. It streamed from both pianos and a record player. Reuel and Jane would go to sleep listening to an eclectic array of music ranging from classical pieces by Hayden and Mozart to the blues or the jazz of Fats Waller. Jane's piano lessons trained her ear, but her musical interests would come to be subsumed in the soundscapes of her poetry. Many art and literary books were in the house, but Jane recalled interest in only a few. She was charmed, however, by a translation of Chinese poetry, *The Jade Mountain*, by Witter Bynner, because the poems were short and full of feeling, and over time she grew to like the poems of Ogden Nash and E. E. Cummings.[8]

Young Jane had a dog, Lydia; rode a horse named Lucky; and liked to swim.[9] She occasionally mentions acquaintances but no strong friendships. She was happiest in nature. At a stream on the Kenyon property feeding the nearby Huron River, she found solace in the long grasses of sumac near the river where she created an imaginary world, a secret spot that became a home.[10] She learned to pay attention to frogs and fireflies and to see "the inwardness of things."[11] Lying in the grass, she at times experienced an exquisite joy "so violent it was difficult to separate it from pain."[12]

She loved playing sports, being outside, and wearing comfortable clothes, and she wanted to be a boy because boys got excuses made for them, whereas girls did not.[13] It seemed unfair that her brother had fewer limits and greater admiration. Reuel was permitted to ride off on his bike for hours to explore the world, but her mother admonished, "It's different for girls."[14] When comparing her artwork to Reuel's, her mother left the impression that his was superior.[15]

Jane's childhood was dominated by a pervasive, burning sorrow that was relieved by a few happy memories, such as going to a baseball game with her mother or out with the family to a movie. These are in striking contrast with Reuel's memories of family life.[16] He remembered having regular moments of family fun, working together in their larger kitchen garden, making puns, talking politics around the dining table, doing jigsaw puzzles, and sharing popcorn while watching TV.[17] Jane's experience of family was dominated by the combination of midwestern reserve and parental moodiness, or depression left her feeling emotionally flat. And grievances in the family never seemed to be discussed.[18]

FIGURE 3. Jane Kenyon and brother, Reuel Kenyon Jr. Courtesy of At Eagle Pond Inc.

Even though both parents each had depressive tendencies,[19] Jane had a warmer relationship with her father than with her mother. She recalled with affection how, as a four-year-old, she would wait for her father to return from work to untie the laces of his shoes.[20] She seemed to intuit that he was thwarted in his desire for more intellectual and artistic opportunities; but he had faith in her. Jane's relationship with her austere and pragmatic mother was more complicated. She described her mother's depression as a distancing from her. Jane only *appeared* to belong to Polly.[21] Jane felt as if she were "losing" her mother,[22] and in an early poem Jane worried that when her mother went downtown, she would not return.[23] Later, Jane summed up their fraught relationship: "My mother was a manic-depressive, and I had a terrible childhood because of it."[24] Yet, her mother loved her very much, Jane was sure, and she loved her mother very much, even though she did not act like it; she claimed to hurt people she liked more than those to whom she was indifferent.[25]

Her mother's mood swings help explain one source of Jane's unnamed hurt, but she also attributed a good portion of her misery to her conflicted relationship with her widowed grandmother. She had a fondness for Dora, who was kind to her but who was also totally preoccupied with apocalyptic Christianity and judgment by an angry God. Jane came to understand that the "central psychic fact of that time [in her life] was Grandmother's spiritual obsession, and her effort to secure me in her religious fold."[26]

Jane was raised Methodist, but her grandmother's religiosity was an extreme version, as she was totally preoccupied with the "last things." Humans were sinful, hell was real, sinners were burned. Obedience to the law was primary, and the consequences for flouting it were severe. Jane clearly remembers the day her grandmother announced to her "that the body is the temple / of the Holy Ghost."[27] Dora delineated the sins of the body—wearing shorts, dancing, committing adultery, drinking alcohol; all were particularly egregious.[28] If Dora's God was vengeful, he was also capricious. Her grandmother reminded Jane of the biblical story of the two women grinding corn. One would be taken and the other left. The only explanation for this injustice was that "God's way was not our way."[29]

Dora's depressive personality had a major influence on Jane. Her impact might have been mitigated if they had had less contact, but that was not the case. After the death of her husband, Dora supported herself by running a rooming house for university students at 925 South State Street.

When Jane's parents were away, Jane and Reuel stayed with Dora, and Jane frequently helped her clean student rooms. Religious indoctrination was constant; Jane later referred to the days she spent at her grandmother's as "religious retreats."[30] When she slept at her grandmother's, Jane sometimes had nightmares.[31]

If family life was depressed, school gave no reprieve. Jane entered a kindergarten class of four students at Foster School Number 15 Fractional in 1952 and remained there through the fifth grade. This white clapboard, one-room school was a two-mile walk from her home along a dirt road. Its amenities included a flagpole and a swing set. Her recollections of her early school experience were uniformly negative. In her 1961 journal she records only one classmate, Priscilla, and mentions a few others elsewhere.[32] Kenyon recalled one incident in which she cursed at a classmate who made her angry and then felt she would suffer in hell for all eternity.[33]

She also recounted repeated conflicts with teachers. In one she walked out of school over a teacher's actions Jane perceived as unjust and then changed her mind, only to be punished upon returning. The teacher had "broken her," and she "had neither the courage to rebel nor an obedient heart."[34] In another instance, she recalled stifling feelings that the teacher

FIGURE 4. Foster School Number 15 Fractional, Ann Arbor, Michigan. Courtesy Reuel Kenyon.

was wrong to ask her to read aloud passages from a book that conflicted with the book's illustrations.[35]

But her "decisive school experience" occurred in a math class.[36] In the late 1950s Russia's launching of Sputnik made math and science increasingly important in American education. Jane was not studious, and math was particularly difficult for her. One day when she did not understand how to proceed with a math assignment, she asked a classmate for help. This was perceived by the teacher as cheating, and Jane was marched off to the furnace closet as punishment. While she sat there, she "hardened [her] heart against authority."[37]

Although the principal was kind to her, some of her teachers thought she was "bitter." She confessed that she was a "negative thinker" and liked to make people feel like worms, but she added that she was not really cruel and that deep inside she was sure there must be some good in her.[38] She admitted that she used her journal to let go of her anger and quipped that she was not yet ready to be put away by men in white coats.[39] Other entries yield an unrelenting litany of her negative feelings. She claimed she was the "black sheep of the family" and that she was "warped." She longed to be herself, but she felt lost, depressed, disgusted, angry, and sad. She felt as if the whole world was closing in on her and admitted that her mother did not know what was wrong with her, and neither did she. She wanted to rebel and did not want to grow up and accept responsibility.[40] Jane's anxiety and alienation are evident in a later poem in which she recalls imagining her body floating above other students, watching and listening. Yet, none knew she was not where she seemed to be.[41]

Contemporaneously in her journal and retrospectively in her autobiographical poetry, Kenyon painted a picture of a sorrowful childhood characterized by the absence of friends, limited family intimacy, miserable school experience, and religious pressures. Whether these were causes or effects of her youthful sense of loss, alienation, and rejection, Kenyon subsequently understood them as related to "the bile of desolation pressed into every pore" in her infancy that continued to dominate her early life, bewildering her and her family.[42] She later wrote:

When I was born, you waited
behind a pile of linen in the nursery,
and when we were alone, you lay down

on top of me, . . .
And from that day on
everything under the sun and moon
made me sad—. . . .
You taught me to exist without gratitude.
You ruined my manners toward God:
"We're here simply to wait for death;
the pleasures of earth are overrated."[43]

It was in this same childhood, however, that a spirit of joy and delight took form, nurtured by her exploration of the natural world, her experience of the "inwardness of things" and of solitude. In her earliest memory, sorrow and joy were intertwined and came to characterize both her life and her art. In her youth Jane Kenyon turned inward for self-protection and privacy. But she would soon find a way forward, enlivened by a discovery of poetry, that "crazy impulse" fulfilling a "wish to connect with others, on a deep level, about inward things."[44]

2
ENLIVENED BY POETRY

For me poetry's a safe place always, refuge, and
it has been since I took it up in the eighth grade.
—Jane Kenyon

After completing Forsythe Junior High School at fourteen, Kenyon entered Ann Arbor High School on Stadium Boulevard.[1] Unlike her previous schools, this one was immense, serving nine hundred students. Many were children of university faculty. When her ninth-grade English teacher assigned writing a poem to the class, Kenyon was elated by the opportunity to express her intense emotions. She was not particularly able in either mathematics or science, and she focused on arts and letters and enrolled in chorale. She found poetry increasingly alluring.

Not particularly attracted to academics, she needed and was eager to earn money. She did not care about money, but she wanted to travel and do something fascinating in a challenging place.[2] She babysat, cleaned houses, and found employment as a salesgirl in Leidy's, a downtown china-and-crystal store on East Liberty Street, where she worked throughout high school and college. The savings she accumulated were used to sponsor her participation with the Michigan Youth Chorale's sixty-day trip to several European countries in the summer of 1965. She was one of the sixteen singers from her high school to join with participants from other Michigan schools, which must have helped her relieve her sense of being on the "periphery" of social life. During high school Jane wore thick glasses and

FIGURE 5. Jane Kenyon.
Courtesy of At Eagle Pond
Inc.

had skin pockmarked from acne. She was often moody and depressed, and her weight ballooned to 165 pounds.

After her unhappy experience with her grandmother's efforts at religious indoctrination, Jane announced to her parents that she would no longer attend the Ann Arbor First Methodist Church, where they were members. She thought she could not be a Christian and an intellectual simultaneously. She asserted that nature would be her god and that she could be a good person without religion. Her Methodist youth pin was deposited in the bottom of her jewelry box.[3] She did not share this decision with grandmother Dora.[4] When her brother, Reuel, took her to see Egyptian antiquities at the University of Michigan, this corroborated for her that other civilizations had alternative understandings of life after death. Her reading of Jean-Jacques Rousseau on the noble savage sealed her adolescent contempt for religion. At one point she attended the Unitarian Church but ended that experiment by claiming she was not "a joiner,"[5] a claim she would continue to make. But she insisted later she never doubted the existence of God.[6]

Kenyon entered the University of Michigan in fall 1965. During her first semester she failed a biology course, which prompted her to drop out of the university, return home, and take up her sales position at Leidy's. The next year she reenrolled as a French major. For a time she lived in the French House on campus where her roommate was Dawn Selvius, a literate and cheerful transfer student, who would later marry Jane's brother, Reuel.[7] During her university years, Jane and Reuel got to know each other better, a marked change from their youth when both had lived in independent worlds.

The University of Michigan was a hotbed of student activism of all sorts during Kenyon's undergraduate years from 1965 to 1971: civil rights, antiwar, free speech, and feminist protest. Students for a Democratic Society (SDS) was launched there, and the campus roiled with sit-ins and demonstrations on a regular basis. The counterculture was deeply entrenched as a part of student life. Radical student activism colored everything. But Kenyon seemingly was untouched by it. She may have participated in an occasional antiwar march,[8] and she later confessed to writing antiwar slogans on cars with soap,[9] but she lacked the depth of commitment of many of her contemporaries. As she said, she was not a "joiner"; and she continued on the social periphery. This may also have been partly due to her depression. But she did have friends, was freed from religious pressure, and during her last two years had an academic focus, poetry.

In spring 1969 she enrolled in "Introduction to Poetry for Non–English Majors," a huge lecture course of 140 students taught by Donald Hall, a charismatic professor, who often inspired students to a lifelong dedication to poetry. In this class Kenyon was just one among many students, but she enjoyed the class and her love of poetry deepened. She changed her major to English and decided to compete for a place in Hall's creative-writing course, English 429, to be offered in the fall semester. Since fifty students applied, she must have been delighted to be one of the twelve accepted. She submitted the requisite five poems, one of which was "The Needle," a poem she had written a few years earlier. It caught Hall's attention and gained her admission to the class. "The Needle" describes an unsuccessful visit to an ill grandmother, which concludes,

> I hated coming here.
> I know you can't understand me.
> I'll try again,
> like the young nurse with the needle.[10]

The seminar was Hall's favorite class, and the students enjoyed it tremendously. As Hall admitted, he was a "showoff," a performer. Quick, bright, humorous, he wanted to be and was the center of attention. He attracted students because he loved poetry. His students considered it a privilege to have been selected to participate in the seminar. They all took seriously the craft of poetry and worked hard at it. There were levity, comradery, and competition among them. They met every Tuesday night for three hours in Hall's living room, where lively discussion was fueled by beer. Students felt at ease with each other in and out of the classroom. They met casually for meals and played volleyball together. Drugs were readily available to anyone who wanted them.[11]

Kenyon was remembered by her classmates as serious, thoughtful, reserved, funny, fair-minded, and tough. Some classmates sensed her moodiness and depression might be anger turned inward on herself. She was known to have a negative self-image. Although she was not a leader in the class, she did participate fully. In it she found a small community of likeminded friends with whom she flourished and felt liberated.[12]

The class gave Kenyon confidence to submit her poetry for the university-sponsored Avery and Jules Hopwood Award, an honor that brought with it a prize of $750 for the best poem. She submitted several poems, including "The Socks" and "The Shirt," two short, edgy poems with a feminist twist. "The Socks" spoke of rolled socks that were like "tight dark fists," and "The Shirt" alluded to the "lucky shirt" that goes down into a man's pants, perhaps an allusion to her several romantic affairs of this period.[13] Judges for the Hopwood Award were Robert Bly and X. L. Kennedy. They selected Kenyon as winner of a Minor Hopwood; winners donned denim jackets with "Poet" inscribed in yellow on the back. Hall's jacket read "Coach."[14]

Hall brought his many notable poet friends to the university to interact with students, including Bly, Gary Snyder, Louis Simpson, and Galway Kinnell. Bly, dressed in a serape, electrified the students. Kenyon found him especially magnetic and thrilling, sensing he was in touch with some sublime power. Later she described him: "There is no one else on earth like Robert Elwood Bly. He is a cross between William Blake, Ralph Nader, and Mr. Magoo, and I love and revere him endlessly."[15] Bly considered Kenyon intelligent, generous, disciplined, and very stubborn.[16] He would come to play an important role in her artistic development. His claim that "poetry is a public moral force, or can be, and not only a path into the individual human soul" would have a strong impact on her.[17]

Kenyon received her bachelor of arts with honors in May 1970 and stayed on as a graduate student in the master's program in English. She probably attended neither graduation.[18] In the fall semester, she enrolled in a student-teaching program to secure a teaching certificate.[19] Teaching may have seemed a safe choice for a female at the time, but when she later had a brief teaching opportunity, it proved to be a complete disaster.[20]

Kenyon remained in touch with seminar participants and with Hall. She had lovers at the time and lived with the most serious of them, John Briggs, a Vietnam veteran, who worked as a projectionist at a local movie theater.[21] They seemed ill-matched, and their relationship ended after six months when Briggs took another girlfriend.[22] Kenyon was devastated and felt angry and vulnerable. Later she referred to this relationship as her "first marriage."[23] At this point she wrote many angry and depressive poems that never were published.[24] The emotional impact of the ending of this affair was worsened when she learned of her father's diagnosis of cancerous colon polyps. Her misery spurred her to seek psychological help.

When Hall heard in 1971 about Kenyon's breakup, he invited her to dinner. As he remarked, at that time an invitation to dinner always included an invitation to breakfast.[25] He admittedly was boozing and promiscuous and still in turmoil over his divorce five years earlier.[26] Both he and Kenyon were in great psychic need, shared a love of poetry, and gave each other solace in and out of bed.

3

DONALD HALL, "ROCKSTAR"

For better or worse, poetry is my life.
—Donald Hall

During his years at the University of Michigan, Donald Hall drew students to him. He was a tall man, physically imposing and authoritative in speech, who once hoped to be an actor. Now the classroom and poetry readings provided an alternative platform to the stage. His energy, ambition, sense of humor, generosity, and quick intelligence made him an attractive teacher. He was a connector of people, loyal to friends, family, and place, and, above all, to poetry. He believed in hard work and later announced that he was proud of the fact that he wrote 365 days a year, even on Christmas.[1] Work gave him pleasure, but it was also a distraction from what he did not want to consider. Hall was frank, had no filter, and said what he thought. He had a huge capacity for not knowing.[2] Jane Kenyon would later call him "the Charles Atlas of Denial."[3] Constant work and showing off distracted him from extensive self-reflection.

Hall's early life had an important impact on the person he became. Born in 1928, in Hamden, Connecticut, he was an only child and grandchild who was pampered and given every opportunity. His mother, Lucy, doted on him during his earliest years. But when he was about seven or eight, she became distant. Hall later suspected that she had an undiagnosed nervous mental disease, but the sudden change left him with a sense of loss as a child. His father was a thwarted man who worked for the family business, the Brock-Hall Dairy Company, in Hamden, Connecticut. He hated his work and urged his son not to do anything except what he wanted to do. This admonition would shape Donald Hall's life.

Although not wealthy, the family was prosperous. Initially, Hall attended the public high school in Hamden, but in his third year he transferred to Phillips Exeter Academy, in Exeter, New Hampshire, where he was miserable and reclusive. As a young man he showed interest in poetry, especially the work of Edgar Allan Poe, and at age fourteen he decided to become a poet. At sixteen he published his first poem and attended the Bread Loaf Writers Conference in Vermont, where he lost his virginity to a twenty-four-year-old married woman and met Robert Frost.[4]

Beginning at age six, Hall's life was enriched by his summer visits to the home of his maternal grandparents, Wesley and Kate Wells, whom he adored. They lived on a farm in Wilmot, New Hampshire,[5] in a house built in 1803 and the birthplace of both Hall's mother and grandmother. As a boy he preferred being with older people and so enjoyed summers in Wilmot. His grandfather was for Donald a model human being, his hero. As a teenager, Hall spent his summer mornings in his grandparents' home reading and writing poetry and in the afternoon haying with his grandfather. Wesley Wells was a consummate storyteller, imparting memories of the ancestors and neighbors and creating a love of stories in his young grandson. Wells harvested maple syrup and raised sheep and chickens and milked cows. It was for Hall an Edenic world of family—lots of cousins were in the area—in church and the community. Appreciation for their hard work, loyalty, and belonging was deeply instilled in him, as was a love of the Wells homestead.

Hall matriculated at Harvard University, where his classmates would become some of America's preeminent poets: Bly, Kenneth Koch, Frank O'Hara, and John Ashbury and Adrienne Rich, who attended nearby Radcliffe College. Hall worked on the collegiate literary magazine *The Harvard Advocate*, wrote an honors thesis on William Butler Yeats, and graduated magna cum laude and Phi Beta Kappa in 1951. At Harvard he was happy among like-minded friends. After graduation, with the support of a Henry Fellowship, he enrolled in Christ Church College, Oxford University, for two years, gained a second undergraduate degree, and made friends with contemporary British poets. He was president of the Oxford Poetry Society, was featured in the important Fantasy Press series on new poets, and served as literary editor of *Isis*. He was distinguished by being the first American to win the prestigious Sir Roger Newdigate's Prize for poetry. These kudos were extraordinary for an American student in hallowed Oxford University. The Korean War was underway, but Hall's father, who was on the Selective Service Appeals Board in New Haven, arranged his exemption from military service based on his having won the Newdigate Prize. Donald Hall led a charmed life.

In the early 1950s Hall married a twenty-year-old Radcliffe undergraduate, Kirby Thompson. They were married for sixteen years and had two children, Andrew and Philippa. Immediately after their wedding they sailed for England on the Queen Mary. When they returned to the United States, Hall went to Stanford University, where he studied with poet and literary critic Yvor Winters for a year, and then he returned to Harvard as a Junior Fellow in the Society of Fellows. This three-year appointment required only that he read and write poetry. He began to build a reputation, winning the Lamont Poetry Award and the Edna St. Vincent Millay Award; writing for the *New Yorker*; publishing *Exiles and Marriages*, a very successful book of poems that was a finalist for the National Book Award; assuming the poetry editorship of the *Paris Review*; and editing, along with poet Robert Pack and Louis Simpson, the acclaimed anthology *New Poets of England and America*.

These stunning achievements made it possible for him to secure a position as assistant professor at the University of Michigan in fall 1957, where he helped make the study of poetry a major draw for the institution.[6] Students were attracted to Hall and the poets he brought to campus. Memorable blockbuster poetry events were organized with his gregarious colleague Bert Hornback, and Hall created the Poets on Poetry series and established a master of fine arts program. Later, on leave from the university, Hall returned to England where he episodically worked for the BBC and did interviews with T. S. Eliot and Henry Moore, subsequently writing a biography of the sculptor.[7] While there, he also wrote *String Too Short to Be Saved*, a nostalgic memoir of his days in rural New Hampshire and his longing for the lost agrarian life. As he said, "My mother instilled New Hampshire in me. . . . I was created to love New Hampshire."[8] By the mid-1960s, Hall was a recipient of a Guggenheim Fellowship. He became a celebrity who brought luster and prestige to the university during its golden age of poetry.

Although professionally successful, Hall's personal life fell into disarray. He separated from his wife in 1967, and they divorced in February 1969, and for the next five years he drank heavily and was increasingly promiscuous.[9] His book of love poems, *The Yellow Room: Love Poems*, traces a romance with a nameless creature surrounded by all things yellow; yellow became his favorite hue.[10] One of his students, a married woman about to be divorced, wrote in her memoir how Hall served as a "lifeline" for her and their "closeness went beyond the bounds of student and teacher."[11]

At a low point in his life, Hall sought out a psychoanalyst.[12] He was concerned over his fear of commitment and inability to genuinely love a woman. Simultaneously, he lost his enjoyment of university life, feeling that his colleagues ignored him and no longer appreciated his ten years' work. Increasing factionalism in the English department was repellent, and he resented demands for additional committee assignment and expectations for leadership. He felt stuck, miserable, and uncreative.

Teaching, which allowed him not only to be an evangelist for poetry but the center of attention as well, did remain enjoyable. At this juncture Jane Kenyon enrolled in his creative-writing seminar. Hall recalled that Kenyon did not stand out among her fellow students and was not particularly physically attractive.[13] After the seminar ended, she continued to visit him in his office to discuss her poems. He was dating three or four women a week, and Kenyon had her own romantic involvements so there was no immediate romantic interest. He claimed it was only when he learned about her depression and her breakup with her boyfriend that he contacted her to offer comfort. Both Hall and Kenyon were needy and searching for solace.

MARRIAGE BY DEFAULT

Everyone longs for love's tense joys and red delights.
—Jane Kenyon

During spring 1971 Jane Kenyon took graduate courses, worked part-time in the English department to support herself and pay down her college debt, broke up with John Briggs, and moved out of their apartment to 539 Packard Street. Fixated on the end of their affair, she suffered feelings of worthlessness, anger, and suicide.[1] Initially, this was the focus of her conversation with Hall, but soon he confided in her about his own misery. He, too, was adrift. Sessions with his psychoanalyst, M. M. Frohlich, helped him deal with his fear of commitment and his conviction that he could not love a woman.[2] Soon Kenyon and Hall were spending several nights a week together, resulting in reduced attention to his other paramours. In some cases, Kenyon likely insisted on it. One lover, Jean Feraca, Hall's friend, recalled: "During the year I was away while she and Don were becoming intimate, Jane had discovered our history and decided that I was a potential threat that needed to be eliminated. She had forbidden any further contact between us, 'either by letter or by meeting,' and Don had agreed." Feraca was sure Kenyon was jealous.[3]

Hall's relationship with Kenyon was no secret. They went to dinner together, played volleyball with former students, and attended faculty cocktail parties together, and he introduced her to his children. An assignment on the West Coast physically separated them for several months in the summer of 1971, but they kept in close contact and were happily reunited upon his return. Hall insisted they were "unromantic lovers," they were not passionate, and they gave each other only "light pleasure."[4] This was a far cry from the "tense joys and red delights" Kenyon later characterized as the desire of Madame Bovary and that she likely wished for herself.

Although they did not say they loved each other, they offered comfort and dreaded separation.[5] According to Hall, they discussed the possibility of marriage several times but consistently rejected this option. Their principal concern was the implications of their nineteen-year age difference.[6] And there were substantial disparities in social background, education, professional achievement, and personality that would have been challenging regardless of any age gap.

There are no records from the period of Kenyon's reflections on marriage. She did record wanting to do something adventurous.[7] Certainly, her relationship with an older, accomplished, and creative man was such an adventure. Later, Kenyon admitted she never felt comfortable with men her age.[8] "I needed a man capable of complexity. I enjoy Don's human wisdom and I admire it. It would be very rare indeed in someone younger."[9]

For Hall's part, the relationship with Kenyon might have offered an opportunity to experiment, to see if he could commit to someone. Like Kenyon he was clearly at loose ends. At midlife he claimed to be "petrified of marriage,"[10] but he was willing, nonetheless, to consider new life options, some entirely unrealistic. For example, during March 1972 he left for Florida to try out for a place on the Pittsburgh Pirates baseball team, a truly hopeless undertaking for a physically unfit, 250-pound, forty-three-year-old academic. Perhaps, this was merely a stunt, preparing him to write about baseball, a sport he loved.

Hall maintained that an argument propelled them to marry. On Christmas Day 1971, in a furious disagreement of an undisclosed nature, they separated. But then they hurriedly reunited fourteen hours later after realizing that they could not be apart again.[11] They shared a love of poetry, frequent sex, and cats, and their relationship provided them deep comfort. They soon decided to marry. There is no evidence that Kenyon's parents weighed in on her decision. Although they had sent her to college, they did not seem to have any expectations for their daughter, even though she was about to marry a divorced man with two children who was nineteen years her senior.

A civil wedding was planned for April 17 at Ann Arbor City Hall, a date when Hall's son, Andrew, would be home from college. A small group—her

FIGURE 6. Jane Kenyon and Donald Hall at their wedding reception at the Gandy Dancer, Ann Arbor, April 17, 1972. Courtesy Reuel Kenyon.

parents; his children; her brother, Reuel; and Dawn Selvius, Kenyon's former roommate—assembled in the judge's chambers for the brief ceremony. Afterwards, they all gathered for dinner at the Gandy Dancer, a first-rate seafood restaurant. No friends, except Dawn, attended the wedding or the dinner.[12] Kenyon wrote nothing about her wedding day besides noting that Grandmother Dora gave her a gift of a white leather-bound copy of the King James Bible.[13]

University friends were surprised by the marriage; no one thought it would last.[14] It was a decision made by default by both of them and based on the thinnest evidence that such a liaison would last or be good for either of them.

Kenyon received her master of arts degree in May, and then she and Hall went off for a brief honeymoon to New York City, a place she had not previously visited. They stayed at the Plaza Hotel and took a horse and buggy through Central Park. This limited detail is provided by Hall, who adds that in these early days their relationship was "frightening," and they were "cautious" with each other.[15] Ever private, Kenyon leaves no record of what she felt or thought about these major events in her life, nor does she discuss these experiences with friends.

During the summer of 1972 they drove from Ann Arbor to the East Coast to visit Hall's grandmother Kate Wells, who at age ninety-four was now senile but still living in the ancestral family home in Wilmot. The newlyweds then drove on to Hamden to visit his mother, Lucy, who had written to Kenyon encouraging her "to take care of her Donnie."[16]

Hall took leave without pay from the university for the fall 1972 semester, and they traveled to England, supported by his second Guggenheim Fellowship. His project was to interview informants for a biography of the actor Charles Laughton, but the resistance of Laughton's wife, Elsa Lancaster, nixed the plan. He then decided, instead, to write a biography of Dock Ellis, an African American pitcher for the Pittsburgh Pirates.[17] Only Hall commented on this trip.

For the spring 1973 term, Hall and Kenyon returned to Ann Arbor to live in his old-fashioned house at 1715 South University Avenue. The place was large; it had four stories and multiple bedrooms and was next door to the home of the affable Bert Hornback, a Dickens scholar and Hall's colleague and friend. Their entertainment consisted in attending faculty cocktail parties, which they did not enjoy; reluctantly they reciprocated by giving one big party a year.

The eight months between their wedding and their return to the university had been a whirlwind of activity driven largely by Hall's schedule. Kenyon seemed like the trailing spouse, shaped by her husband's decisions and obligations, and mute about her own needs and preferences.

Although marrying Donald Hall was the most consequential decision of her life, it was only later she realized that to marry him was to marry poetry.[18] Living with Hall brought Kenyon into contact with the many male poets he brought to campus. Among the few women poets she met were Jean Valentine and Adrienne Rich, both much older than Kenyon (thirteen and eighteen years, respectively) and well-established poets. Rich, Hall's undergraduate friend and a fellow student at Oxford University, came to visit them for a week just prior to their wedding. Rich had left her husband

and was a public feminist and later a lesbian. Kenyon was impressed with Rich's toughness and strength.[19] Valentine first met Kenyon in Florida and immediately admired her; she found Kenyon to be smart, warm-hearted, and lovable.[20] Kenyon's most important female friendship from this time was with Joyce Peseroff, a Junior Fellow in the University of Michigan's Society of Fellows and a poet. Peseroff was to become an important personal and professional friend, who with another friend formed a triumvirate of women poets who met to critique their work and encourage each other.

The psychological problems of both Kenyon and Hall were not eliminated by marriage. He continued to see a psychoanalyst, and she found a university clinical psychologist whom she saw two or three times a week.[21] Although her malady was not diagnosed, Kenyon was given some cognitive methods to deal with her depression.

During the early years of their marriage, Kenyon began in earnest to write poetry. She had the leisure to do this, but she only felt free to write when Hall was away. They still related very much as student and teacher, Hall referring to her as "a talented kid poet."[22] To move beyond this hierarchical relationship, they invited others to workshop poems with them,[23] including Gregory Orr, another Junior Fellow in the society, Larry Russ and his wife, Shelly, and Peseroff. For two and a half years Orr worked with them, serving as a buffer who allowed Kenyon to express her own views. Their sessions were frank, and they had fun. Writing retrospectively, Orr claimed to have been aware even then of Kenyon's empathy and her deep longing for meaning and compassion; he called her "Our Lady of Sorrows."[24]

Two of her early poems, "Starting Therapy" and "Cages," date from this period. These poems are chilling expressions of her depression. In "Starting Therapy" she writes metaphorically of being put in a strait jacket and encountering some hovering presence.[25] In "Cages," she sees monkeys in cages that remind her of her "uncivilized" body and how "sometimes my body disgusts me."[26] Two other early poems, "The Socks" and "The Shirt," were published in 1973 in American Poetry Review. In later reflections Kenyon said she wrote poetry as "a way of making sense out of what has happened to me."[27] These poems are early examples of her self-revelation. Anger and erotic need were dominant emotions in this period of her life.

Hall was in residence at the university from spring 1973 through the following spring term. During the summer of 1974, he and Kenyon again visited his grandmother Kate, who was now cared for in the Peabody Home

FIGURE 7. Donald Hall and Jane Kenyon, early in their
marriage. Courtesy of Reuel Kenyon.

in Franklin, New Hampshire, leaving her farmhouse in Wilmot unoccupied.
This visit may have inspired them to look for a farmhouse when they returned to Ann Arbor, since they both wanted solitude and some relief from
academic life. As they searched, Hall recalled Kenyon's reminding him of
the farmhouse in Wilmot. But moving to New Hampshire seemed unrealistic, given that Hall had a tenured position at the university, with all that
guaranteed. Nonetheless, the idea remained.[28] Soon afterward, poet Robert
Graves gave a reading at the university and in conversation with Hall suggested that he consider becoming a freelance writer and give up his career
as a faculty member.[29] Even though Hall had financial obligations for his
son, Andrew, who was in college, and for Philippa, who would soon enroll,
the idea of living in New Hampshire for a year appealed to both him and
Kenyon. He had recently published *Writing Well*, a very successful textbook
for first-year college students, which yielded substantial royalties,[30] making
a move financially possible. More important, he had grown tired of faculty
infighting and administrative politics. This temporary move would offer
an escape from what he considered the claustrophobic and phony world of

academia. Since his last books of poetry had not been as well received as previous ones, he felt a change of place might be helpful. Now almost forty-seven years old, he must also have remembered his dead father's warning not to do anything except what you want to do.

Hall determined to take another leave without pay for the 1975–76 academic year and try out a new life in New Hampshire. There was nothing to lose and great pleasure to be gained by being in a place in which he had wonderful childhood memories. Since Kenyon loved solitude and profoundly disliked the university environment, she supported the move, even though it meant leaving everything and everyone she knew. This might be her adventure. She, too, had nothing to lose.

5
HOUSE OF THE ANCESTORS

Here in this house, among photographs
of your ancestors, . . .
I move from room to room,
a little dazed, like the fly. . . .
My people are not here, my mother
and father, my brother. I talk
to the cats about the weather.
—Jane Kenyon

If marrying Donald Hall was the most consequential decision of Jane Kenyon's life, moving to his ancestral home in Wilmot, New Hampshire, was the second. The house and everything in it referenced Hall's family history. It was a rambling and distinctly configured space with low ceilings. On the main floor were several rooms, including a kitchen and a sitting room, where they would spend most of their winter days. Two chairs with needlepoint cushions flanked the Glenwood stove, the principal source of heat. Hall's study was his former bedroom, the place he had first written poetry. Also on the first floor were a bedroom, a bathroom with limited facilities, a dining room, and bookshelves. The kitchen had a door to a room where tools and firewood were stored and from which a steep, creaky staircase led to the second story. There one encountered what was called "the back chamber," a storeroom crammed with antiques, memorabilia, and treasures from five previous generations. Beyond were other bedrooms, and above the kitchen was another room that came to serve as Kenyon's study. Through its dormer window she could see the barn and Mount Kearsarge in the distance.

FIGURE 8. The barn at
Eagle Pond Farmhouse.
Photo by author.

A dirt-and-gravel drive circled to the porch and led to the entrance. Route 4 divided the house from the hayfields and the nearby Eagle Pond, fed by the Blackwater River.

Kenyon's image of herself as a dazed fly roaming the Wilmot homestead completely devoid of any reference to herself or her history powerfully captures her initial encounter with the house.

Hall's sense of the place could not have been more different. It is hard to exaggerate the happiness he experienced anticipating his return to New Hampshire. Burnt into his imagination was the beauty of this ancestral 140-acre farm flanked to the south by the blue mountain, Mount Kearsarge, and the nearby granite Ragged Mountain that sloped down to the barn. Constructed of white clapboard and with green shutters, the house was surrounded by old-growth trees. Hall called it "the long white house / that holds love and work together."[1]

For Hall, the magical quality of place and landscape was enhanced by memories of his boyhood summers there. On the farm he wrote poetry and listened to stories about his ancestors and neighbors that would later

FIGURE 9. Eagle Pond Farmhouse. Courtesy of Daphne Bruemmer.

serve as the basis for much of his prose and poetry. It was the lure of place and his desire to leave the university that explained the move to Wilmot.[2]

Although Kenyon did not have the same powerful association with the place, what appealed to her was that they were leaving the city and university life for the beauty of Merrimack County and the solitude it provided. It was an Edenic world, the "restoration of a kind of paradise" she had lived as a child in rural Ann Arbor township.[3]

But Kenyon had never lived anywhere but Ann Arbor, and the world of Wilmot was Hall's. She was not sure she belonged among his people. In a later interview she said she initially felt "disembodied" and "annihilated," and she used writing to understand and control what was happening to her.[4] In a journal about losses she experienced, she said that the move initially made her depressed and gave her ulcerative-like stomach pain.[5] In the early poem, "Here," she describes her bewilderment over whether she could truly be a part of this world he so dominated:

> You always belonged here.
> You were theirs, certain as a rock.
> I'm the one who worries
> if I fit in with the furniture
> and the landscape.[6]

Hall had multiple relatives who lived nearby, and they were delighted that "Donnie was back." As Kenyon quipped, she and Hall lived surrounded by his "gene pool."[7] Kenyon was twenty-eight years old, had no job, had no professional identity, and knew no one other than her husband's relatives. Her closest friend was Joyce Peseroff, but she lived two hours away in greater Boston. Kenyon saw herself as the country mouse befriending the worldlier city mouse.

Their first winter in the house was the coldest recorded in New Hampshire history—thirty-eight degrees below zero. It remained twenty degrees below for many days. Episodically the electricity would fail; there were no storm windows, no insulation, and no central heating. They survived by hovering close to the cast-iron Glenwood stove manufactured in early 1900 that Hall fed with wood several times a day and by using electric blankets. It was a difficult introduction to New Hampshire weather.

The move in August 1975 was intended to be an experiment. Could they survive and thrive financially and psychologically in this rural environment? That was unquestionably so for Hall. The move was a "homecoming" for him. Kenyon was initially uncertain, but after a short period of time as she gained a deeper experience of the community, she came to love the house, the landscape, and the people.

On their first Sunday in Wilmot, Hall suggested they attend the South Danbury Christian Church, a white, wood-frame building constructed in the mid-nineteenth century, about four miles up the road.[8] He was a longtime member of this church, and many of his relatives were in the congregation. His grandmother Kate served as the church's organist from age fourteen until ninety-two.

In Ann Arbor they had never attended church services and expressed no interest in religion. Hall explained the cousins would expect them to attend Sunday services. Kenyon was "flabbergasted" by his suggestion, having never wavered from her youthful rejection of her grandmother's puritanical Christianity. But somehow she stilled her fears and went. She found herself among a warm and informal congregation of twenty people. When the minister, Jack Jensen, alluded to the poet Rainer Maria Rilke in his sermon, Kenyon and Hall were both won over.[9] They became faithful participants, returning week after week. Jensen and the church community would come to play an important role in Kenyon's development as a person and poet.

Within a month of arrival, they were committed to the church and embraced by the local community. On Labor Day 1975, when out-of-state summer visitors returned home, local residents showed up at the Danbury Grange Harvest Festival Parade. The charm of these neighbors and their communal events impressed Kenyon. In December they participated in the Christmas pageant, and Hall, portly and bearded, played Santa Claus there and later at the Lions Club.

The experience of life in Wilmot nourished Kenyon's psyche:

> I feel my life start up again,
> like a cutting when it grows
> the first pale and tentative
> root hair in a glass of water.[10]

At the same time she had a recurrent ambivalence: "Maybe I don't belong here. / Nothing tells me that I don't."[11] Their friend Wendell Berry suggested that Kenyon's efforts to acclimated herself to her husband's world paralleled those of the biblical Ruth to make a foreign land her home.[12]

In September Kenyon was convinced their experiment was over; she was utterly taken by her new home. Hall claimed that she threatened to "chain herself to the walls of the root cellar rather than leave New Hampshire."[13] Fate conspired to make it happen when Kate Wells died later in 1975, and the farm was put up for sale. The continuing strong success of *Writing Well* enabled Hall to make the down payment of $39,000, and he bought the property, making the farm theirs. Rooting around in his great-grandfather's papers, he found some old stationery with the address Eagle Pond Farm, named for the bald eagle that lived nearby and fished in the pond.[14] They appropriated the name for their new property. In December Hall gave notice of his resignation from the university but extended his leave for another year.

In a less-frenetic environment and daily exposure to natural beauty and the peace of rural life, Kenyon began more consistently to focus on writing poetry. Some of her initial efforts focused on her experience of her new world, particularly the signs of earlier female occupants she found every-where in the house, in a silver thimble she discovered in the woodshed, in their pictures on the walls, in the long gray hair she uncovered as she washed the floorboards. Her experience was that of

> repeating
> the motions of other women
> who have lived in this house.

And when I find a long gray hair
floating in the pail,
I feel my life added to theirs.[15]

In other early poetry Kenyon described the colors of the mountain and
the antics of birds at the feeder. She focused on the moon and her cats and
admonished herself not to moan about her new life.[16] Another poem illustrates her joy in finding that in nature, "I belong to the Queen of Heaven."[17]
She was finally at home. Her happiness grew from being like a "root hair in
a glass of water" to become more like the joy of a still-cautious lover:

Suddenly I understand that I am happy.
For months this feeling
has been coming closer, stopping
for short visits, like a timid suitor.[18]

Having decided to relocate to Eagle Pond Farm, they returned to Ann
Arbor in the summer of 1976 to pack up their belongings and say good-
bye to friends. The movers came, and Hall and Kenyon drove back to New
Hampshire with their three cats, Mio, Catto, and Arabella. In one of her
few prose poems, she records this trip and the experience of driving back
to Wilmot.[19]

While they were away, they had some improvements made to the house.
A wood-burning stove was installed in each study. A new sink and a dish-
washer were put in the kitchen. Storm windows and insulation now pro-
tected the house, and bookcases were built in all the rooms and down the
hall. After settling in, Kenyon began to paint and wallpaper the house pale
yellow, Hall's favorite color.[20]

With these enhancements complete, Kenyon tended to the yard. She
set out birdfeeders and with her *Petersen Field Guide to Birds* identified
the many winged creatures that inhabited the property. And she started a
garden, becoming an inveterate gardener, reinvigorating her youthful pleasure in working the soil. Initially, she had a vegetable garden across Route
4, but deer and rabbits made sure that was destroyed. During the fall she
prepared the planting beds for winter. In the long, dark, winter months,
she would dream about the following spring and what she might plant, and
then she would order flowering bulbs and plants from the White Flower
Farm catalog. The tentative shoots of plants found reflection in her inner
life. In "February: Thinking of Flowers," she wrote:

A single green sprouting thing
would restore me. . . .

Then think of the tall delphinium,
swaying, or the bee when it comes
to the tongue of the burgundy lily.[21]

For blooms in spring, she would later plant one hundred white daffodils near the back patio, hollyhocks on the side of the house, and iris along the barn. In summer she cleared residual brush as roses and lilies flowered. But her favorite flowers were the white peonies with crimson accents, Festiva Maxima, which she eventually planted along the front porch. She claimed the peonies were not "Protestant-work-ethic flowers": "they loll about in gorgeousness . . . they believe in excess. They are not quite decent."[22] When these were in full bloom, they would bring passersby to stop, agog at their beauty.

For Kenyon, the garden represented beauty but also the ephemerality of all things. Planting, weeding, and nurturing gave her solace and delight. She spent her afternoons cultivating her garden and her mornings in her study working on poems.[23] She believed there were similarities between her two passions, poetry and gardening. When asked by an interviewer about these similarities, she replied, "They both teach us about death and resurrection. They teach us patience, humility. . . . The love of beauty is in both. The obedience to the laws of the universe is in both, the obedience to birth and flowering and death. One must be obedient to this. One is subject to this always."[24]

Unless they were away, Kenyon and Hall adhered to a consistent daily routine. Kenyon went directly to her study after breakfast and worked for several hours. She emerged at lunch to eat in silence, usually walking around. Hall wrote all day, poetry in the morning and in the afternoon prose of various kinds. They customarily made love and had a short nap to begin the afternoon. Then she was off to do chores or work outside. They competed to see which of them would collect the mail from the mailbox on Route 4 D, where Bruce Dill, their postman and "bringer of possibilities," regularly delivered a treasure trove of letters. Letters were their lifeblood, a way of being in touch with the larger world. Hall responded promptly to each one; he claimed to write four thousand a year.[25] He loved to tell the story about Harvard paleontologist Stephen Jay Gould, who addressed a letter to him at "Ego Pond Farm."[26]

Kenyon and Hall would also compete to make the short trip to Thornley's, the all-purpose store where one could fill the gas tank and buy everything—books, pens, wrenches, eggs, milk, seeds, and newspapers. Kenyon called the store a "continuous party" where one dropped in, told stories and jokes, and gossiped.[27] They usually went to Thornley's twice a day, but if they needed information, they went to the post office, where it could be found on the bulletin board. When extensive shopping was necessary, they would drive ten miles to New London to Cricenti's supermarket or the Five-and-Dime store.[28] At home in the evening Kenyon would cook dinner, another pleasurable task, while they drank white wine as Hall read aloud. He read Henry James's *Ambassadors* several times.

Although they never reestablished the frenetic social life they had in Ann Arbor, episodically they welcomed poet friends to visit. Early on they met May Sarton, who lived in New Hampshire, and Denise Levertov, who lived first in New York City and then in Somerville, Massachusetts, and who taught at Tufts University. Hall's friends—Robert Bly, Louis Simpson, Wendell Berry, Galway Kinnell, Seamus Heaney, Wesley McNair—all visited. Many stayed the night. Their presence was intellectually and artistically stimulating, and Kenyon benefited from this interaction. But the work to enable this hospitality—preparing, cooking, cleaning up, and doing laundry—fell on her.

Hall and Kenyon put their marks on the house and yard, integrated themselves into the community, and established a work routine. For Hall this was a dream come true. In his telling they occupied the landscape of his ancestors and lived in a "house of poetry," sharing "a double solitude" and creating art.[29] This became his framing story, and he worked to make it true.

6
THE COMMUNITY OF WILMOT

I found myself
among people trying to live ordered lives, . . .
And again I am struck with love for the Republic.
—Jane Kenyon

Kenyon's encounter with the land and people of Wilmot had an unexpect-edly powerful impact on multiple levels. The rural landscape of natural beauty and solitude fed her spirit: "The beauty of this place is just so nour-ishing to me. I just can't find words for how much I love these hills and trees and rocks and stone walls and old houses and people's asparagus beds."[1] Equally powerful was her feeling of welcome from the community and Hall's family and neighbors. Her initial concern that she might not fit in was for naught: "One of the great gifts of coming here was to come into a community. I never felt a sense of community in Ann Arbor. Here I felt it immediately, and it's such a great joy to me, such a great comfort."[2]

In the mid-1970s the village of Wilmot had a population of six hundred people. Three villages—Wilmot, North Wilmot, and Wilmot Flat—made up the town, which included thirty square miles in Merrimack County. For decades, as farming and mill production declined, the area's population plummeted, but the 1970s saw the beginning of a rebound. Tourism now brought visitors, winter skiers, summer guests, and fall leafers. The town had little racial diversity but substantial economic differences. Poverty and considerable wealth coexisted.

Residents of the Granite State tended to resist restrictions on their auton-omy, as reflected in the state's motto—"Live Free or Die." This characteristic was rooted in their history as the first colony to declare independence from Great Britain. From its earliest days the state was Republican in politics, abhorrent of taxation, controlled by local institutions, and low in religious participation.

The community in which Kenyon settled was one in which her husband was to have celebrity status as a bard extolling the virtues of the people of New Hampshire. At his reading of his poetry in libraries, town halls, and church fairs, his audiences delighted in his depictions of their past and their shared myth and the way he placed his own personal history within it. While his literary achievement was broader than his adulation of rural life, this aspect of his work gave him great pleasure and made him a local and, later, national celebrity. His writing displayed a bias favoring rural sensibilities; he was loved by his hearers and readers. In a later book of essays, *Here at Eagle Pond*, praising his adopted state,[3] he rejected the larger society's stereotype of rural people, class "Rusticus," as fat in body, eccentric in personality, and redneck in culture. Hall lauded the virtues of Rusticus: hard work, preservation of the past, love of one's ancestors, stability, commitment to neighbors and relatives, and local control. He compared New Hampshire to the rural South, where the past was honored and preserved in literature and monuments. On the other hand, he ridiculed Vermonters as persons who lived for the present, were quiet, had cocktail parties, and only worked a forty-hour week in contrast to Granite Staters, who worked one hundred hours a week, were thrifty, and had church suppers of beans, franks, and Wonder Bread.

Initially, Kenyon had no similar literary celebrity. Her engagement with the community was expressed in service, particularly through work for many years as a hospice volunteer. Although she insisted she was not a "joiner," she was proud of her memberships in Habitat for Humanity and Amnesty International and her role as a solicitor for the Heart Fund. But her literary talent did not go unnoticed. Later, she was enticed by Mike Pride, editor of the *Concord Monitor*, to write for that local newspaper.

But her principal engagement was with the South Danbury Christian Church, of which she became an avid congregant. This was a radical change from her earlier life and her judgment against religious participation, memories of her grandmother's attempts to lure her into a religion of fear, and her nonparticipation, except for weddings and funerals, in church life. Hall, on the other hand, did not have a negative view of church attendance as a social experience. For him, the church had a two-thousand-year history that should be respected. Kenyon was soon elected church treasurer, a position she held for many years, despite her lack of math skills. Both she and Hall served as deacons, which in her case meant she baked bread and prepared wine for the monthly communion services. She helped organize the annual church fair and prepared food for sale,[4] sang alto in the church choir, and particularly cherished service as church custodian. Her increasing engagement with the church would deeply influence her life and art.

Kenyon and Hall both liked the church's pastor, Jack Jensen, whom they saw as an intellectual equal and who became a close friend.[5] He served two local churches and was a faculty member at what became Colby-Sawyer College. Jensen had a master of divinity degree from Yale and a PhD in philosophy from Boston University. His intellectual love was the Greek world, especially its mythology, and he wrote a long novel about the Oracle of Delphi and took student groups to Greece during the summer term. These intellectual interests were matched by an open, gregarious personality and a handsome physique. He was, above all, a pastor who was, as Kenyon related, "shepherd of his sheep, [who] . . . slipped his crook around my neck so gently that I was

FIGURE 10. Interior of South Danbury Christian Church. Photo by author.

part of the South Danbury fold before I knew what had happened."[6] Jensen also had a sense of humor and loved to garden and sing. For Kenyon, Jensen's greatest gift was that he gave her a new sense of God: "[B]efore I knew what had happened to me, I'd become a believer, which I really never was as a child. I dutifully said my prayers when I was a child, but I was afraid of that God. The God that our minister here talked about in his sermons was a God who overcomes you with love, not a God of rules and prohibitions. This was a God who, if you ask, forgives you no matter how far down in the well you are. If I didn't believe that I couldn't live."[7]

Jensen became their fast friend, although he was not beloved of everyone. On Kenyon and Hall's fifth wedding anniversary in April 1977, they renewed their marriage vows with Jensen officiating. He brought flowers and champagne to celebrate.[8] Kenyon called Jensen "the gardener of the true vine" who "radiated love." His approach to religion was first intellectual, but he pointed beyond that to a forgiving God who gave comfort and solace. Kenyon asserted that Jensen led her to discover she was starving spiritually. He sated that hunger and helped her develop a spiritual life.[9] Her experience of Jensen was reminiscent of her encounter years earlier with Robert Bly and her sense that he was in touch with some sublime power.

Both Kenyon and Hall joined Jensen's Bible study group, where members shared their religious concerns and doubts. Jensen recommended she read the Gospel of Mark and the commentaries of William Barclay to deepen her understanding of Christianity. She went on to read all four Gospels, her favorite being the mystical Gospel of John. She loved the poetry of the Psalms and the stories of the Acts of the Apostles, which describe the development of the early church. Seeing her hunger for spiritual growth, Jensen augmented his reading recommendations to include some classic Christian authors and writings—Augustine, Thomas à Kempis, Julian of Norwich, Teresa of Avila, *The Way of a Pilgrim*, and the anonymous *The Cloud of Unknowing* edited by Evelyn Underhill, an English writer and authority on Christian mysticism. Later Kenyon would also read the writings of French mystic philosopher Simone Weil and British author Karen Armstrong.

As a woman particularly aware of seasons, Kenyon became attuned to the seasons of the Christian liturgical year. She especially loved Advent, and each year during those four weeks, she re-read the four Gospels, opened the windows of the Advent calendar, and lit the candles of the Advent wreath. The rich and beautiful rituals of Christianity began to shape her daily life.[10]

Theologically, she was attracted not so much to a distant, abstract God but, rather, to the Son of God, a God of forgiveness and love with whom she shared human life. Even more significantly, however, she began to understand her life as part of a universal community of believers, the Body of Christ.[11]

Kenyon's study and reflection on Christian life prompted self-scrutiny: "Beyond the social pleasures I took from the church, I started to take comfort from the prayer of confession and the assurance of pardon. I was twenty-nine years old and by now it was clear to me that I wasn't a good person all the time. I was sometimes irritable, selfish, and slow to forgive. It eased my mind to acknowledge my failings and start over."[12]

Kenyon's spiritual deepening occurred over a period of years and went on simultaneously as she developed her poetic craft. Scriptural and religious references began to appear in her poetry,[13] and she developed a new vision. She began to write poems that illuminated how her new understanding gave access to a more expansive reality. She wanted to express "cries of the spirit,"[14] and she did so with subject matter and language that were accessible and universal. It would take years for her to fully understand what it was to be a poet, but that understanding was grounded in the community of Wilmot. As her friend the poet Charles Simic wrote, "Kenyon country is both our rural New Hampshire and her inwardness in which we all recognize ourselves."[15] Borrowing from Keats, Kenyon said, "This is the vale of soul-making. . . . This place has made us both considerably different people. The sense of community here is something I never experienced in Ann Arbor."[16] Life in the community of Wilmot had therapeutic implications: "It makes one less self-obsessed and more concerned about the needs of others. It gives you a feeling that you are part of the great stream. You're not alone."[17]

7
THE MUSES

The poet's job is to put into words those feelings we all
have that are so deep, so important, and yet so difficult
to name, to tell the truth in such a beautiful way, that
people cannot live without it.
—Jane Kenyon

Kenyon's early life in Wilmot inspired feelings that were difficult to speak about. Her life was dominated by the nearly constant effort Hall devoted to his artistic expression, work that was their sole source of income. Although she had to manage all household life, including the yard, she refused to let that define or limit her, and gradually she began to make time and space for her own poetic expression. The challenge she faced in doing so was expressed later by their friend Wendell Berry, who observed that Kenyon "had set up shop smack in the middle of another poet's subject. The other poet's claim to this subject was well established; the other poet was her husband."[1] Kenyon's decision to become a poet could have proved disastrous. It was a decision she had to continue to negotiate with Hall throughout her life.

The beauty and solitude of Wilmot gave her energy and subject matter to reflect on. In developing her craft she was often inspired by the stream of poets who visited them. Several of Hall's male poet friends would make the trip to the out-of-the-way farmhouse, and Kenyon benefited from conversation with them, but she did not have access to a culture of nurture or critique. Of course, she was married to her former poetry teacher, but with him she confronted the difficult situation of profiting from his guidance while refusing to be dominated by him. What she confronted was a difficult dance of both learning from him and remaining independent from him.

Hall was a model of the ambitious writer, and, importantly, he urged her to be ambitious,[2] a drive that had not been inculcated by her family. Kenyon developed a work routine that intersected with Hall's but was independent of it. She would invite his critique of her poems only after she had worked on them for months, and she did not always accept his criticism. Her writing habits differed from Hall's in important ways. He believed in revision and occasionally produced one hundred drafts of a poem. He worked fast; Kenyon worked slowly. Later she advised a friend about writing her first novel: "Let it grow in the dark like a mushroom. And don't pick it too soon."[3] As Hall reviewed his wife's work, he would be on the lookout for extraneous words, especially prepositions and articles, for stanzas of equal length, and for what he dubbed lifeless metaphors. He was committed to sound as fundamental to poetry, and while Kenyon respected that point of view, she came to value image as the key to lyric poetry,[4] a view she shared with Robert Bly, Hall's old friend from their Harvard days. While husband and wife were helpful to each other,[5] Kenyon was always leery of Hall overstepping his bounds. Early in their life in New Hampshire, she coined an affectionate name for him, "Perkins,"[6] a man once prominent in a Maine village. She often used it endearingly and to respond to remarks she found overbearing. "Perkins, watch your ass" could bring him to a stop when he went too far in his critique.[7]

During the first two-and-a-half years in Wilmot, Kenyon immersed herself in the work of a favorite poets, John Keats. She read and re-read all his letters, poems, and three or four of the best Keats biographies. She believed his "Ode to a Nightingale" was the most perfect poem in the English language.[8] Later, she would visit the room where he died at the Spanish Steps and his grave in the Protestant cemetery in Rome.[9] She included allusions to his work in her poems. A portrait of Keats as a young, suffering poet hung in her study, and she was delighted to share his initials, J. K.[10] Although her poetry was very different from Keats, his sensual language and emotional intensity inspired her. She absorbed his sense of the mortality of all things and the need to enter each moment with pleasure. Melancholy was a dominant theme in his verse, as it would come to be in hers. His understanding of life as "a vale of soul-making" would later inspire Kenyon to write about searching for God as her priority, surrounded by trouble and pain.[11] But she admired Keats cautiously. She did not share his sense that melancholy was to be cultivated; for Kenyon, melancholy was a "mutilator of souls."[12] Although she wrote in the tradition of Keats, she differed from him in her emphasis on place, use of ordinary language, and underlying skepticism.[13] Nonetheless, she shared with him a common longing: "It could be for beauty—/ I mean what Keats was panting after, / for which I love and honor him."[14] Her claim that the poet's job was to tell the truth in a beautiful way was rooted in her years of dedicated study of Keats's mastery of lyric poetry.

In the early years in Wilmot, Kenyon also read the female Christian mystics Julian of Norwich and Teresa of Avila. Consciously or unconsciously, she must have recognized congruity between Keats and these mystic writers. His concept of "negative capability," a willingness to pursue a vision despite uncertainty, as well as his openness and receptivity, were parallel to the mystic notion of vulnerability, a sensibility Kenyon came to naturally.

In addition to Keats, she was profoundly influenced by the writing of Anton Chekhov. His spare style, objectivity, humor, and use of physical detail were all important to her,[15] but what most impressed her were his dual qualities of detachment and compassion.[16] Chekhov's portrait hung in her study, as well, and she used an epigraph from his *The Cherry Orchard* to introduce one of her poems. During a later trip to Leningrad, she would visit his home and medical office.

Two New England female poets, Elizabeth Bishop and Emily Dickinson, were inspirational for her, as well. She was probably introduced to Bishop's poetry by Lloyd Schwartz, poet and Bishop scholar. Kenyon admired Bishop's spare, clear, and precise poems.[17] Their syntax was simple, and their language compressed, tranquil, and reserved. Kenyon resonated with Bishop's love of nature, exploration of the inner life, and trust in the world, but Kenyon never wrote critically or admiringly of Bishop's work.[18] Yet, when Kenyon attended Bishop's memorial service in 1979, she wept.[19] Although Kenyon came to Dickinson later, Kenyon's work was often compared with that of the "Belle of Amherst."[20] These two women poets shared subject matter, including the wonder of creation, the seasons, death, wrestling with God, and the struggles of the flesh. Kenyon was aware that both she and Dickinson honored beauty, pondered the mystery of existence, explored the nature of the soul and of God, and recognized the connection between depression and joy.[21] Many years later Kenyon would give a series of lectures in China on six important female American poets; Dickinson and Bishop both were included.

The Russian poet Anna Akhmatova, almost unknown at the time in the United States, also had a profound effect on Kenyon's poetry. Akhmatova's life was tumultuous. She endured illness, poverty, and a troubled family. She married three times, took many lovers, was exiled to Tashkent for years, denounced as "half-nun, half-harlot," and silenced. She was, nonetheless, a popular poet who after Stalin's death was rehabilitated.[22] Kenyon's quiet and contemplative life and her apolitical poetry contrasted strikingly with Akhmatova's, but it was Akhmatova's spirit that appealed to her.

Kenyon came to Akhmatova by a circuitous route. Three years after Kenyon and Hall moved to Wilmot, Bly came to visit. Among Hall's early poet friends, Bly took Kenyon's poetic commitment seriously, while most others saw her as Donald Hall's wife. During a conversation with her, Bly announced that it was time Kenyon selected a poet, dead or alive, and work with him as a master. Kenyon promptly rejected the idea: "I cannot choose a man for a master." Bly retorted, "Then read Akhmatova."[23] The idea appealed to her, and she began to gather up translations. Finding them unsatisfactory, she decided to make her own. Bly encouraged her to believe that whatever effort she devoted to translation would be rewarded tenfold. Hall disagreed. Although he worked in multiple genres, he never pursued translation, believing that if the original sound of the words was not there, the internal connections within the poem could not be known.[24]

Soon after receiving Bly's advice, Kenyon met Lou Teel, a student of comparative literature at Dartmouth College, who worked with her to devise a literal translation of a few of Akhmatova's poems. In 1978, when Kenyon published her first book of poetry, she included these six translations of Akhmatova's poems,[25] and between 1979 and 1984 she translated and published twenty poems by Akhmatova.[26] What Kenyon learned from her would influence all her subsequent poetry.

The poet Hayden Carruth claimed Kenyon was "our Akhmatova,"[27] but Kenyon and Akhmatova were not alike in their life circumstances; rather, Kenyon insisted she was temperamentally like the Russian poet.[28] Akhmatova wrote in rhyme and meter and was influenced by the Acmeists whose goal was "beautiful clarity"; as such, they were opposed to the Symbolists.[29] Kenyon revered Akhmatova's early prerevolutionary lyrics, and in her introduction to the translation, she commented: "As we remember

Keats for the beauty and intensity of his shorter poems, especially the odes and sonnets, so we revere Akhmatova for her early lyrics—brief, perfectly made verses of passion and feeling."[30] The preeminence of image that would be central to Kenyon's poetic craft was inspired by Akhmatova: "I came to believe in the absolute value of the image when I was working on these poems by Akhmatova."[31] The "talented kid poet" who arrived in Wilmot in 1975 was, with the help of her muses, especially Keats and Akhmatova, making her way. Slowly, her poems began to appear in some leading periodicals—*Michigan Quarterly Review*, *Harvard Magazine*, the *Paris Review*, and *Virginia Quarterly Review*, among others. But to grow and to fulfill her dream of telling the truth in a beautiful way, she would need nurture, critique, and, of course, a published book of poems. These needs were about to be fulfilled.

8

FINDING HER WAY

It's funny how everything in your life, every
experience, everything in your reading, everything
in your thinking, in your spiritual life—you bring
it all to your work when you sit down to write.

—Jane Kenyon

Kenyon's exposure to the craft of poetry was not derived only from her
reading and exposure to her husband's colleagues. It was rooted as well
in her editorship of a poetry journal that, at the beginning of her move to
Wilmot, she founded with her close friend Joyce Peseroff. The early 1970s
saw an explosion of social turmoil fueled by civil rights demands, unrest
over the Vietnam War, and women's rights. Poetry and music were vehicles
for the expression of this unrest. Women, particularly, began to employ
poetry as a means to articulate their longing and to challenge cultural restrictions.[1] Their new consciousness helped contribute to a burgeoning
popular interest in poetry readings, workshops, and university classes and
to new opportunities for publication. It also helps explain why Kenyon and
Peseroff made the risky decision in 1975 to start a new literary magazine,
one that would focus on poetry written by women. They had no start-up
funding and knew nothing of publication or production processes, so their
trepidation must have been considerable, but the adventure was irresistible.
It was a year in which both women would be leaving Ann Arbor—Peseroff
going to Massachusetts and Kenyon to New Hampshire. Their geographic
proximity would prove advantageous.

Before departing Ann Arbor the two of them visited the operations of Edward Brothers, a short-run printing company that agreed to produce five hundred copies of their magazine. They named it *Green House*, signifying the intent to nurture new poets.[2] Initially, they garnered financial contributions from family, friends, and other poets; later, they secured funding from several arts associations. The first issue appeared in spring 1976; Kenyon typed it herself on an IBM Selectric typewriter she affectionately called "Horace." The selected poems came from fifty to sixty manuscripts submitted for review.

To produce *Green House*, Peseroff and Kenyon had to learn editing, the mechanics of grant writing, production, printing, and distribution, all of which were new to them. They secured one hundred subscribers, and the remaining copies were sold to university libraries and independent bookstores. They produced a total of six issues, two each year for three years. In the process Kenyon and Peseroff became fast friends, and Kenyon gained knowledge of the minutiae of publication and exposure to the poetry community of New England. However, correspondence between them during this period confirms that it was Peseroff who was the principal driver of the project.[3]

Several of Kenyon's poems appeared in the pages of *Green House*, as did her one review, a brief critique of Kathleen Fraser's *New Shoes*, in which she tellingly wrote: "But finally the work is melancholy, full of longing for life to make sense, and of sexual longing, and grief for the lost and the dead."[4] Kenyon's work with *Green House* provided a connection to poetry that was completely independent of her husband's career and led directly from the task of editing other's poetry to the work of producing her own.

Kenyon was clearly determined to have an identity independent of her prolific husband. In what was not a common practice at the time, she kept her own name when she married, but she was not a feminist in the contemporary sense of that word. When asked directly whether she was a feminist, Kenyon responded, "I'm not an overtly political person, but I am deeply concerned with recording women's existence . . . deeply concerned that women's experience be articulated and valued."[5] Her founding of *Green House* was one way she satisfied that concern. In her own writing, poems like "Finding a Long Gray Hair," "The Thimble," and "Hanging Pictures in Nanny's Room" preserved the contribution of the women who had previously occupied the Eagle Pond farmhouse. As Peseroff observed, it was the memory of these women that helped sustain Jane Kenyon during her early days in Wilmot.[6]

Kenyon was aware of the sexist structures that shaped marriage and was thrilled when she read Dorothy Dinnerstein's *Mermaid and the Minotaur: Sexual Arrangements and the Human Malaise* (1976).[7] Using Freudian psychoanalysis, Dinnerstein argued that sexism derives from the arrangement of child-rearing as the exclusive purview of women. Women are defined as caretakers and, hence, as passive and dependent. The way to overcome this perversity, Dinnerstein claimed, was through self-awareness that would begin when men became coequals in raising children. There is little evidence about Kenyon's views on having children, but it seems that neither she nor Hall wanted them, an understandable attitude given Hall's age and the fact that he had two children. In the early poem "Falling," Kenyon alludes to her concern that she might be pregnant.[8] This proved not to be the case, but Hall in his inimitable frankness indicated that to ensure this scare did not happen again he had a vasectomy. In remarking on this situation, he writes that Kenyon supported the legality of abortion, but she would not have had one herself. She confided to him that during her high school years, she decided she did not want children.[9] Peseroff confirmed that Kenyon was grateful she did not have children, given her lifelong depression.[10]

Kenyon's marriage did not display any sensitivity to emerging feminist concerns, beyond the fact that she kept her own name. Hall opposed the Vietnam War and withheld war taxes, but his marriage reflected the traditional divisions of responsibility. He was a man many years Kenyon's senior whose expectations of women were shaped by adoring women who nurtured him during a time when traditional gender relationships were expected. It took Adrienne Rich, an avowed feminist poet, to call out his obliviousness to perceived limitations on women's creativity. In a letter to Kenyon, Rich noted Hall's lack of sensitivity in his 1978 article in *The Nation* in which he expressed no understanding of why women's poetry was almost nonexistent or why their creative contributions were negated.[11] Perhaps, it was only a feminist and longtime friend like Rich who could criticize Hall's limited understanding of feminist concerns and get away with it.

Kenyon's poetry of the early and mid-1970s was published in a variety of literary magazines. Half of these poems were composed in Ann Arbor and the others in Wilmot. She gathered them into book form and changed the book's title several times—*Under Blue Mountain, Changing Light, Cages*

FIGURE 11. Original authors of Alice James Books: Jane Kenyon (*top row, on left*); Joyce Peseroff (*top row, fourth from the right*), and Alice Mattison (*bottom row, second from the right*). Courtesy of Alice James Books.

Opening, but this was to no avail. Finding a publisher was difficult for a new and largely unknown poet. Peseroff, who had reviewed the poems and made suggestions, urged Kenyon to contact Alice James Books, which had brought out Peseroff's first book of poems, *The Hardness Scale*.

Alice James Books was a small cooperative press founded in 1973 in Cambridge, Massachusetts, and named for the novelist and diarist sister of famous brothers William James and Henry James. The aim of the press was to promote the poetry of women. All the work of the press was done by its authors working by consensus. When a manuscript was submitted, it was evaluated by co-op members whose books had come out in previous years. The individual author was then responsible for typesetting, printing, and selecting typeface, cover, and design. Authors wrote catalog copy, solicited advertisements, and ensured their work was reviewed. This was labor-intensive work that took two years. There was no formal connection between Alice James Books and *Green House*, but the poems of many women were published by both.

Kenyon's book *From Room to Room* was accepted by Alice James Books, and she worked at the cooperative for the required period, traveling from

Wilmot to Cambridge for meetings. There she met Alice Mattison, whose first book of poetry, *Animals*, was published in 1980 by the press, and who became another steadfast friend. Kenyon's engagement with this small publishing house and with *Green House* taught her much about writing poetry, cemented friendships with Mattison and Peseroff, and stoked her confidence.

From Room to Room was finally published in 1978 with a cover design by George Schneeman, a pen-and-ink drawing of four curtained windows. It was a charming cover and congruent with the book's title. Its dedication—"For My Family"—connects to the book's overall themes of being separated from family, being lost in another's home, wandering from room to room and within her own psyche, and finally being welcomed by the female ancestors, having added her life to theirs.

From Room to Room contains thirty-seven poems and opens with a section "Under Blue Mountain"—Mount Kearsarge—with poems of leaving and of arrival, most notable, "Leaving Town," "From Room to Room," "Here," "Finding a Long Gray Hair," and "Hanging Pictures in Nanny's Room." Another section, "Edges of the Map," explores her connection to her past in Ann Arbor: "My Mother," "Ironing Grandmother's Tablecloth," and "The Box of Beads." The section "Colors" offers playful poems—"The Shirt" and "The First Eight Days of the Beard." The final section, "Afternoon in the House," contains poems of nature and landscape that welcomed her. The last line of her last poem harkens back to the beginning of the book. It reiterates being again "under the blue imperturbable mountain," Mount Kearsarge, and includes the confident designation, "I belong to the Queen of Heaven."[12]

These poems were Kenyon's attempt to make sense of life in this place and community. Here are poems of happiness, contentment, resilience, anger, and depression. These last include "Starting Therapy," "Cages," "The Circle on the Grass," and "Full Moon in Winter," the latter of which speaks of anger and shouting and desire:

> Bare branches rise
> and fall overhead.
> The barn door bangs loose,
> persistent as remorse
> after anger and shouting. . . .
> my own shadow
> lies down in the cold

at my feet, lunatic,
like someone tired
of living in a body,
needy and full of desire.[13]

Also included were the translations of six poems by Akhmatova. Since the subject matter and style of the Akhmatova poems are congruent with Kenyon's, their inclusion was not a jarring addition to the book.

Sales of *From Room to Room* were not enormous, but the book elicited several reviews. Some contemporary reviewers praised it. The *Virginia Quarterly Review* saw it as a "remarkable first book" of "quiet strength and quiet violence," "an exploration of inhabiting."[14] *Ploughshares* claimed it was "transforming of home space into fine cloth" but pointed out that the language was muted and spare, sentences were declarative, syntax simple, and the mood depressive. Nonetheless, the reviewer held out hope that Kenyon might develop into a Dickinson for her generation.[15] A review in *Religion and Intellectual Life* commended Kenyon for speaking for those who experienced suffering and joy in a God-oriented existence, and Hayden Carruth wrote in *Harper's Magazine* that the poems were "poignant, ultimately joyful," and a pleasure to hear.[16] When reviewers compared *From Room to Room* to her later poetry, they were more critical.[17] Liam Rector called Kenyon's first book "unremarkable" and her poems "a description of experience rather than an experience unto themselves."[18] Paul Breslin admitted that her poetry illustrated her keen ear and eye, but the poems were "claustral," "self-limiting," "descriptive for description's sake." He said that they were "workshop poems" of a high order.[19] Wesley McNair, in a retrospective review of her poetry, claimed that the poems of *From Room to Room* ranged in quality but could be characterized as a "somewhat incoherent mixture of the happy, fanciful and the sad."[20]

From Room to Room, nonetheless, remains central to understanding Kenyon's legacy, illustrating the progress she made as a poet in a relatively short period of time. The volume reveals the complexity of her psyche, the early burdens she faced, and the themes she would continue to explore. It is true that compared to the poems of later years, those included in *From Room to Room* appear underdeveloped. It would be her sustained work for the next seven years to translate more poetry of Akhmatova that would substantially improve her writing and bolster her self-confidence as a poet.

9
A DOUBLE SOLITUDE

I sense unavoidable darkness coming near,
but come and see the Paradise where together,
blissful and innocent, we once lived.
—Anna Akhmatova

Daily life at Eagle Pond Farm involved what Hall proclaimed to be a "double solitude" lived out in the "house of poetry."[1] Like all myths, there was truth in this characterization. Kenyon relished solitude, and if Hall was away, as he was at times, she would talk to the cats or when gardening to her plants. Bird song and the rustle of wind in the trees, the occasional sound of a car on Route 4, or the slam of the mailbox being closed would break the silence. If the telephone rang, she usually did not answer. She was hyperalert to the presence of others, was easily exhausted by visitors who might drop by, and left it to the sociable Hall to entertain them. She flourished in solitude and was consoled by silence.

This solitude was helpful to her as a poet, but it meant she lived in a world seemingly untouched by the upheavals of the 1970s and 1980s. Although she sometimes was outraged by some political event, generally she was insulated from the larger world during her years in Wilmot. It was as if the resignation of Nixon, the end of the Vietnam War, the capture of hostages in Iran, the fall of the Berlin Wall, or the takeover of Tiananmen Square did not penetrate her world. She refers to none of this. This disconnection with politics was rooted in her early years in rural Ann Arbor, where her "inwardness" heightened sensitivity to emotions, and her love of the natural world and use of natural images to refer to her inner life first began to develop. She learned early on that poetry was a safe place to express her feeling.[2] This insularity would change beginning in the 1990s.

Kenyon and Hall lived by routine. In the morning he was usually ensconced in his study writing poetry, and in the afternoon he sat in his blue chair in the living room writing prose and editing. He was proud that he worked ten hours a day. If they encountered each other getting coffee or lunch, they did not speak.

It was poetry that dominated the Eagle Pond farmhouse. Hall's discipline and ambition, of which he had plenty, set an example for Kenyon, and her presence in the house made his well-being possible.[3] Each contributed positively to the other, but both were competitive, whether playing ping-pong or Monopoly. Both wanted to win, although they tried not to be competitive as poets. Even though their subject matter was often the same, their execution of poems was distinctive. Kenyon particularly loathed being compared to her husband, and she would not allow him to review or write blurbs for her books.[4] Hall was multifaceted, writing essays, reviews, poetry, and prose, but Kenyon wrote only poetry for most of her life.

They both published books of poetry in 1978. Hall's *Kicking the Leaves* sold a hundred thousand copies over the years, a success he attributed to his marriage to Kenyon and freedom from the constraints of the university. Her *From Room to Room* was clearly not competitive with his publication. It sold six hundred copies.[5]

Hall's children's book *Ox-Cart Man*, beautifully illustrated by Barbara Cooney, won the Caldecott Prize two years later. It was immensely successful, ultimately having sixty-six editions and being translated into four languages. It generated substantial royalties. He wrote fourteen children's books in all, but *Ox-Cart Man* was the most popular. It was vintage Hall, written to preserve the values of hard work and the nobility of agrarian life, which he saw rapidly disappearing. The book was based on a charming story of nineteenth-century farm life and the cyclical nature of plowing, planting, harvesting, and selling.

Its royalties plus the revenue generated by the thirty-six editions of *Writing Well* allowed him to pay taxes, the mortgage, college tuition payments for his children, and renovate the farmhouse. A new bedroom was added on the main floor, and the original bedroom became a new bathroom and laundry room. Affixed to the bathroom door was a plaque, "The Caldecott

Room," a self-deprecating acknowledgment of the success of *Ox-Cart Man*. The root cellar was enlarged, a ping-pong table was installed, and a private garden was created in the rear of the house. There Kenyon built a brick patio, laying the bricks herself, and planting peonies and daffodils up the hill behind the house.[6]

They waited ten years for their financial situation to become secure before installing central heating. They also hired cleaning help in the person of Carole Colburn. Initially, Kenyon resisted this hire in the belief that one should care for one's own living space,[7] but since neither she nor Hall was particularly tidy, this help must have been a boon. Kenyon called Colburn "a peach."[8]

Of the innumerable household chores, Kenyon loved cooking best of all. Her poetry reveals not only her pleasure in food but also its meaning as a form of sacrament and communion.[9] In a later poem, "Man Eating," she observes a man eating yogurt:

> so completely present
> to the little carton with its cool,
> sweet food, which has caused no animal
> to suffer.[10]

Preparation for dinner was a ritual shared by both. Drinking white wine, Kenyon would cook while Hall would read to her. They had a formal meal at a table set with silver candlesticks and flowers floating in a bowl. Afterwards, they might read independently or to each other—often classics by Henry James, Mark Twain, William Wordsworth, Edith Wharton, the Gospels, or seventeenth-century poetry. Although they usually ate at home, their favorite local eatery was Piero Canuto's Italian restaurant, La Meridiana, in Wilmot Flats.

In his essay "The Third Thing,"[11] Hall describes the many activities they shared, including ping-pong, swimming, and sunbathing at Eagle Pond, participating in church services and events, making love after lunch, attending free rehearsal performances of the Boston Symphony Orchestra, watching baseball games as members of the Red Sox nation, and "the third thing," poetry. Sometimes to escape the cold weather, they would travel to Florida during baseball training season or visit Key West, Barbados, or Bermuda. At other times of the year they might visit England or Italy.[12] But mostly they were at home, writing.

After the publication of *From Room to Room*, Kenyon worked on two projects simultaneously—a translation of twenty of Akhmatova's poems and the poems that would ultimately be included in Kenyon's second book. While translating the first six of Akhmatova's poems, Kenyon read Amanda Haight's 1976 biography of the poet and several translations of her poems but lamented that none of these translations got to the "soul" of Akhmatova. She translated from G. P. Struve and B. A. Filippov as a guide.

When Robert Bly read Kenyon's early translations of these poems, he was impressed, and he decided to help her get a contract with copublishers Eighties Press and Ally Press. He and Louis Simpson, Pulitzer Prize recipient and son of a Russian mother, introduced her to Vera Sandomirsky Dunham, professor of Russian at the State University of New York at Stony Brook. Although their relationship was often tense, Dunham was willing to assist Kenyon with the translations, but she did not believe their project of translating rhymed and metered Russian poetry into free verse would be successful. Kenyon remembered Dunham moaning, "This will sink us."[13] Their differences of opinion about translation reflected a larger debate within the community of translators. As Osip Mandelstam commented: "There are two different kinds of poetic translations. One kind is the rendering of verse with great skill but rather mechanically. The other is a great moment, the meeting of two poets writing in two different languages. There is sudden recognition between them, as if the poet and his translator had struck up a close friendship."[14] Clearly, Akhmatova and Kenyon were soul sisters.

In her introduction to the translations, Kenyon was forthright about how she proceeded to render Akhmatova's poetry. Because she could see no way to preserve both form and imagery, she chose the latter: "I have sacrificed form for image. Image embodies feeling, and this embodiment is perhaps the greatest treasure of lyric poetry. In translating, I mean to place the integrity of the image over all other considerations."[15] She also included a summary of Akhmatova's difficult but resilient life and explained that her translation focused on the poet's prerevolutionary, personal lyric poems, not on her later public and political ones. It was these early poems that illustrate Akhmatova's primary Acmeist principles, the use of clear language to describe the thing itself.

Kenyon saw in Akhmatova's commitment to the Acmeists a similarity with that articulated by the Imagists, especially Ezra Pound, who spoke of his "method of the 'luminous detail.'"[16] Ironically, the view that Kenyon's poetry was characterized by the "luminous particular" came from Hall's depicting it as that which "embodied powerful emotion by means of the luminous particular."[17] Neither Kenyon's writing nor her interviews used that phrase in describing her work; it was used only in Hall's later descriptions of her writing.[18]

Another similarity Kenyon found between Akhmatova's and Pound's insights was expressed by the famous dictum in his essay "A Few Don'ts by an Imagiste," which asserts, "The natural object is always the adequate symbol."[19] Kenyon adopted this wisdom almost as a mantra and often referred to the meaning contained within, namely, "that the inner world is revealed in terms of the outer world—revealed in terms of things."[20]

Twenty Poems of Anna Akhmatova, published in 1985, contained the heavily revised six poems included in *From Room to Room*, plus eleven newly translated poems and three of Akhmatova's later poems. The poems appeared in both the original Russian and in the English translation in a slim book with a portrait of Akhmatova on its cover. It was dedicated to Kenyon's mother and to the memory of her father, who had died two years earlier.

Kenyon clearly resonated with Akhmatova's life of suffering, and she learned from her poetry. Translating these poems confirmed her dedication to the personal lyric with its themes of nature, love, pain, joy, the impending "unavoidable darkness," and the paradise that was "blissful and innocent."[21] Her dedication to Akhmatova strengthened her commitment to paying attention, to the surprise twist of the last line of a poem, to clarity of language, and, most important, to the image as paramount. As she said in a later interview, "The images in a good poem came from a deep place, and this gives the poem a sense of cohesion. Almost everything else can be tinkered with, but if that is tinkered with, the whole work flies apart."[22] The impact of Akhmatova on Kenyon was especially evident in the poem "Full Moon in Winter"; it was so reminiscent of the Russian poet's work that Kenyon feared she might be guilty of plagiarism.[23]

Years later when Kenyon traveled to Moscow, she was reminded of Akhmatova, and in a poem she chronicled the poet's hard but ultimately triumphant life. Having endured revolution, loss, exile, and condemnation, Akhmatova outlived Stalin and finally received the public acclaim of the Russian people who had never forgotten her. Kenyon concludes her poem "Lines for Akhmatova" with this accolade:

In the end you outlived the genocidal
Georgian with his mustache thick as a snake.
And in triumph, an old woman, you wrote:
I can't tell if the day is ending, or the world
or if the secret of secrets is within me again.[24]

Having learned much about the craft of poetry from her Russian muse, Kenyon grew in confidence as a poet. When she finished her translations, she said:

> Then I would turn to my own poems with this tremendous
> sense of freedom, and I began to feel some power in my
> own work for the first time—I'm sure as a direct result of
> working with those translations. Now in my own work, I
> saw that there was nothing to limit me but my own imagination
> . . .
> I know that if I had not worked so hard on Akhmatova I would
> never have experienced that surge of power.[25]

Kenyon's sense of freedom and confidence would be expressed in the poems of her next volume, *The Boat of Quiet Hours*, a book of newly energized poetry.

10

STREAMING LIGHT AND DEATH

Things: simply lasting, then
failing to last . . .
into the light all things
must fall, glad at last to have fallen.
—Jane Kenyon

Most mornings Kenyon would ascend the back stairs from the kitchen to her study. In winter the wood stove would have heated the room already. The sloping ceiling and bookshelves against the yellow walls made the small room feel cozy. Photographs of her family, Hall, Adrienne Rich, Jane's various muses, and an icon of Christ kept her company. On her desk were her typewriter and her vinyl Oxford pocket dictionary. Sometimes she would play her music tapes, her favorites being the compositions of Mahler, Schumann, Tchaikovsky, Mozart, and Beethoven. From the gabled window she could see Mount Kearsarge, although in winter the vista was often obscured by New Hampshire's gray clouds. The lack of light in the room was compensated for later by a light machine that helped her deal with seasonal affective disorder. Here was her silent space. It was here she translated Akhmatova and wrote the poems that would be gathered into her next book. She would wait expectantly for the arrival of the mailman, hoping to find a poem had been accepted in some magazine.[1] In winter when out-of-doors activities were limited, and she was unable to garden, she enrolled in a local exercise class to keep fit. There she met neighbors and fellow church members. In other seasons she walked and hiked, and occasionally she made the challenging climb up Mount Washington.

By 1980 her work was beginning to bring wider recognition as a significant poet. In January she accompanied Hall to a poetry gathering for sixty poets in Washington, DC, sponsored by the National Endowment for the Arts and hosted by President Jimmy Carter. In April she gave a workshop, "The Language of Art—Poetry," at the Museum of Fine Arts in Boston.[2] That summer they attended the Centrum Arts Festival in Port Townsend, Washington, where she met Tree Swenson and her first husband, Sam Hamill, founders of Copper Canyon Press, an important publisher of poetry. Swenson was a book designer who would come to play a significant role in Kenyon's professional and personal life. Their friendship was sealed when Kenyon gave her a signed copy of *From Room to Room*.

While she was becoming more peripatetic because of her career, Kenyon was by this time also finding herself more deeply rooted in Wilmot. She and Hall purchased burial plots in the Proctor Cemetery in Andover, four miles north of the farmhouse. Hall suggested this purchase signified their "marriage to a place."[3] Neither anticipated that she would be the first to use it.

Kenyon continued to be engaged in the life of the church—serving as deacon, treasurer, and custodian. Even though she was disturbed by the sexism of the institution and its language, she stayed because she needed the Lord's Prayer and Communion.[4] Increasingly, she was interested in the Trinity, especially the Third Person she called the Holy Ghost. She conceived of this Third Person as the feminine aspect of God's unity. Her interest in this doctrine may have been fueled by her reading Richard of Saint Victor, the twelfth-century prior of the Abbey of Saint Victor and influential theologian of the Trinity.[5]

Her regular church participation and mystical and theological reading began to produce a transformative experience of her world that reached a crescendo in Lent 1980 during Hall's absence. Kenyon wrote, "In 1980 I had an experience that changed my understanding completely, changed my way of being in the world."[6] She described the experience as being in the light: "I really had a vision of [light] once. It was like a waking dream. My eyes were open, and I saw these rooms, this house but in my mind's eye. . . . I also saw a great ribbon of light and every human life was suspended. There was only this buoyant shimmering, undulating stream of light. I took my place in this stream and after that my life changed fundamentally. I relaxed into existence in a way that I never had before."[7]

When Hall returned home, he remembered finding her in a "quiet, exalted, shining mood."[8] She said she felt a presence in the room that stayed with her, and she experienced it as the Holy Ghost. She would repeatedly refer to the power of this experience. Hall identified it as the incident that prompted her to write the poems "Briefly It Enters and Briefly Speaks" and "Who," both of which appear in her subsequent volume of poems.[9]

"Briefly It Enters" is a visionary poem describing the presence of the great I Am, who expresses itself in multiple ordinary ways. In litany form and without using religious language, Kenyon brings the reader to the final stanza: "I am the one whose love / overcomes you, already with you /when you think to call my name." This is a stunning poem born of an extraordinary experience and affirming the reality of Divine love permeating the most ordinary aspects of life, an invitation to timelessness and to going beyond. When Joyce Peseroff read the poem, she commented, "This is wonderful. I don't know anyone else who could write such a thing."[10] But former negative religious experiences meant that the validity of the experience could not go unexamined. In the poem "Who," written about the same time, Kenyon questions her inspiration:

> Who is it who asks me to find
> language for the sound
> a sheep's hoof makes when it strikes
> a stone? And who speaks
> the words which are my food?[11]

Kenyon also saw she needed to go beyond traditional religious characterizations of divinity. Rather than portraying the Holy Spirit in traditional terms, she reconceptualized it as a bat breaking into her room. In her poem, "The Bat" the season is winter, and the speaker is reading about rationalism when suddenly a bat enters the room, evading all attempts at capture. Kenyon analogizes this invading creature to the Third Person in the Trinity:

> The cats and I chased the bat
> in circles—living room, kitchen,
> pantry, kitchen, living room. . . .
> At every turn it evaded us
>
> like the identity of the third person
> in the Trinity: the one
> who spoke through the prophets,
> the one who astounded Mary
> by suddenly coming near.[12]

This sense of a Divine reality breaking into her consciousness would continue to be a feature in her writings. A later article, "Gabriel's Truth," describes how Mary's consciousness taught her to live in hope, respond in love, and be faithful in the worst circumstances.[13] Kenyon saw Mary's experience as applicable to everyone, because the spirit or inspiration is always breaking in.

The 1980 Lenten experience was followed by many more. She claimed she "had many mystical experiences, and these have been the most joyous moments of my life, the most illuminating, the most peacemaking moments of my life." Initially, she was embarrassed to speak of them: "There are some things that go on in your spiritual life that must go on in secret. They cannot be talked about. They must not be talked about. They're between you and God only." But gradually this fear of disclosure not merely abated but disclosure began to be a part of her craft. Later she said, "My spiritual life is so much a part of my intellectual life and my feeling life that it's really become impossible for me to keep it out of my work."[14]

It also changed her behavior. She began to engage in community service; this was something entirely new for her. The suggestion to do this was planted by Jack Jensen, but it might have been confirmed by her visionary experience and her reading of Julian of Norwich, from whom she absorbed the idea of God as both a suffering God and a God of love. And she felt a sense of indebtedness: "I'd like to give back some small part of what I owe."[15] In January 1981 she began training as a volunteer with the Hospice of Kearsarge Valley, even though her friends questioned whether this was the best kind of work for someone who had bouts of depression.[16]

Preparation for hospice work included attending classes, reading assigned books on dying, and learning about the dying rituals of various denominations.[17] It also required responding to questions related to her own death and negative life experiences. She admitted there had been times in her life when she wanted to die and that she was afraid of both physical and psychological suffering. When asked to describe her desires for her own death, she indicated she wanted to be holding someone's hand, hear the music of Mozart or Beethoven, be surrounded by flowers from her garden, and to receive Communion.[18] As for losses in her life, she mentioned among others her disastrous experience teaching a course at New England College in Henniker in 1980.[19] She blamed herself for being temperamentally unsuited for teaching and felt it resulted in a loss of self-esteem, but she also thought the experience strengthened her resolve to give herself fully to writing poetry.[20] She was adamant: she would rather bag groceries than teach.[21]

She wrote several poems related to her teaching experience. In one she held the students accountable for her teaching phobia.[22] In another she admitted her sarcasm wounded a student, and she had been cruel.[23]

Kenyon served as a hospice volunteer for eleven years. She could not have imagined that her first hospice patient would be her own father. Reuel Kenyon's health had been fragile since childhood, afflicted as he was with bronchitis, pneumonia, and pleurisy and then cancer of both the colon and the thyroid. Despite this fragility, he was a joyful man and full of gratitude.[24] In April 1981, after learning Reuel Sr. had inoperable lung cancer, Kenyon and Hall left for Ann Arbor to help Polly care for him.[25] They remained there for six months until October when he died. He spent his last days in the hospital, confused and inconsolable, receiving oxygen and narcotics. A year later his ashes were scattered in the two places he loved: Ann Arbor and Eagle Pond Farm. Kenyon was devastated by his death, a loss exacerbated by the deaths two years later of her Grandmother Dora and Aunt Geraldine.

The long, hard dying of her father prompted Kenyon to write several poems. In a letter to her friend Alice Mattison, she admitted these poems were "terribly costly for me."[26] The poems, "Reading Late of the Death of Keats," "Inpatient," and "Campers Leaving, Summer 1981," appeared in her next book, as did "Yard Sale," which she called "a ten-cent poem," describing her efforts to assist her mother in selling the debris of her father's life. In "Travel: after a Death," she chronicles the trip she and Hall made through Dorset and Devonshire the following year; the poem concludes with a line about her constant preoccupation: "Oh, when am I going to own my mind again."[27]

The most poignant death poems, however, were written years later. In "Reading Aloud to My Father," she describes a man who ceased eating or drinking and was incapable of hearing music or reading the written word. In this poem she challenges Vladimir Nabokov's belief that life is "a brief crack of light / between two eternities of darkness."[28] She argues rather that life itself is the abyss; "that's why babies howl at birth, / and why the dying so often reach / for something only they can apprehend."[29] In another poem, "We Let the Boat Drift," written on the fifth anniversary of her father's death, she is unable to accept how the cancer annihilated "the whole man sense by sense, thought / by thought, hope by hope."[30] She recalls his weeping when he realized his life was less than perfect. The most tender of these later poems is "The Stroller," in which Kenyon imagines her view of the world from her stroller at age two and at age four untying her father's shoes when he returned from work.[31] The final recollection is of her father's rendering of the stroller, which reminded her of his benign, caring, and curious eyes. His drawing of the stroller recalled for her what she had lost with his death.

Kenyon was not "going to own [her] own mind" anytime soon. By April 1982 she was profoundly depressed. Hall records that she began a torrent of crying, and for three days she remained in a fetal position and was inconsolable. She would not allow him to touch her and would not let anyone see her. Initially, she was seen by her internist and gynecologist, Donald W. Clark, who prescribed medications.[32] It was only beginning in 1989 that Charles Solow, head of psychiatry at the Dartmouth-Hitchcock Hospital, began to dispense the myriad drugs she used for the rest of her life.[33] It was Solow who finally diagnosed her with bipolar II disorder.[34] She was mostly depressed and seldom manic.[35]

The death of her father prompted Kenyon's first major psychological break, but there would be others. Hall recalls incidents of her banging her head against bathroom pipes, her suicidal impulses to hang herself with a horse's harness, her temptation to drive into a stone wall, and her self-hating response to receiving too many Christmas gifts.[36]

When Kenyon was deeply depressed, she was unable to write, unable to initiate anything; she could hardly move. When moderately sad or after sex, which always seemed to rejuvenate her, she could revive and sometimes write poetry, but these poems increasingly had depression as a theme.

The year 1982 was a time of great sadness, but encouraging events bolstered her. She was awarded a Creative Writing Fellowship from the National Endowment for the Arts, which brought with it $12,500. She often joked that she was supported by a perpetual "Hall" Fellowship,[37] but now she began to bring in limited earnings herself. She gave poetry readings at Frost Place, Robert Frost's former home in Franconia, New Hampshire; at a New England Coalition on Nuclear Pollution meeting; and at the New Hampton School. These readings and awards boosted her confidence. But most important for her development as a poet was the beginning of a new long-term relationship with her friends Joyce Peseroff and Alice Mattison.

During the Thanksgiving holiday, Kenyon and Hall visited his mother in Hamden. While there, Kenyon invited Mattison, who lived nearby in New Haven, for tea and a chat. Remembering how helpful it had been to have Gregory Orr participate in poetry workshops with her and Hall and having shared her poems with Peseroff for several years, Kenyon now proposed to Mattison that the two of them join with Peseroff to discuss their poetry. Her friends would prove to be a godsend to Kenyon both personally and as an artist.

This community of three would freely critique each other's work and discuss their successes and disappointments.[38] Although Hall would continue to serve as the first reader of Kenyon's poems, she would never send out a poem that had not been critiqued by these women, who referred to themselves as "the workshop" and humorously as "the Mrs. Bomblatt's Society."[39] Hall occasionally referred to the three of them as "the committee." They met three or four times a year, rotating their gathering's locations in Lexington, Massachusetts, halfway between Wilmot and New Haven; less frequently at Mattison's home or at Eagle Pond Farm; and a few times at the Lord Jeffrey Inn in Amherst, Massachusetts. Usually, they met for two-day sessions beginning with lunch, working in the afternoon, going out to a restaurant for dinner, and resuming discussion the following morning. Each would bring a clutch of poems to read aloud and discuss in detail.[40] At their first meeting in January 1983, Kenyon brought "Trouble with Math in a One-Room Country School House." For the next eleven years, they met in person, corresponded by letter, and spoke by phone. Mattison wrote Kenyon every Monday morning, sometimes with the salutation Janio or Janiekins. Kenyon responded sometimes with Dear Chum or Dear Pal. They shared not only their work but the details of their lives, their publishing victories and rejections, their joys and sorrows, recipes and garden tips. During this time Peseroff had a child, and Mattison raised three boys. They each worked hard to maintain an artistic life, inspiring each other as they made their way.

These workshop sessions and the friendship they produced gave Kenyon intimate women friends and greater confidence as a poet. She enjoyed this comradery immensely, and after a particularly lively meeting, she would exclaim, "I have such clever friends." In a later interview she said, "My women friends in particular give me the courage I need to just be who I am."[41] At this point her intimate circle included Mattison and Peseroff, but other women poet friends, too, Maxine Kumin, Marie Howe, Jean Valentine, and Carolyn Finkelstein, came to be part of her circle, cheering her on.

Kenyon relished these friendships, even though they seemed to negatively impact Hall. Although he did not oppose these women personally, Kenyon's absence from the house sometimes made him listless and unproductive. He claimed to be at peace and able to work energetically only when she was home.[42] He loved the comfort of her presence and increasingly became possessive of her. When she was away workshopping and giving readings, he would call many times for reassurance. For her part, Kenyon was touchy about Hall using his influence to secure speaking engagements for her or arranging to have her poems published. Early on in their marriage, she went on tours with him, but she soon gave up the practice after feeling she was treated as "the wife." She wanted recognition for her own work, not as Hall's appendage. If she received negative comments on her work, she might respond with the sarcastic one-liner, "It simply kills me that not every human being on earth loves every word I have ever written."[43]

The early years of the 1980s were difficult for Kenyon. Her visionary experience helped her see the suffering brought on by the loss of her father and the debilitating bouts of depression as suffused within the visionary image of light. That image was at the core of her poem "Things," which closes her second book of poetry. It announced what she had learned during these challenging years: "into the light all things / must fall, into glad at last to have fallen."

11
THE BOAT OF QUIET HOURS

And, as the year
Grows lush in juicy stalks, I'll smoothly steer
My little boat, for many quiet hours,
With streams that deepen freshly into bowers.
—John Keats

John Keats appears prominently in Kenyon's *Boat of Quiet Hours*. He is there in its title, in its opening quotation from "Endymion," in its lush, sensual language, in the sense of the mortality of all things, and in what he called "negative capability,"[1] that is, when a person is capable of being in uncertainty and does not rely on fact or reason.

Themes from Kenyon's first book are carried over into this second volume, but the two books are remarkably distinct.[2] *The Boat of Quiet Hours* includes Kenyon's visionary experience described in "Briefly It Enters and Briefly Speaks" as well as several poems about death. But new themes are also introduced: depression, spiritual insight, and a longing she could not name. These themes stemmed from the influence of Akhmatova and the death of Jane's father.[3] The former fueled her longing, the latter her depression. She describes her longing in "Ice Storm":

> The most painful longing comes over me.
> A longing not of the body. . . .
>
> It could be for beauty
> I mean what Keats was panting after,

for which I love and honor him;
it could be for the promises of God;
or for oblivion, *nada*; or some condition even more
extreme, which I intuit, but can't quite name.[4]

In poems of death and depression she speaks of anger and remorse, the dust of the universe, and suffering: "sometimes what looks like disaster / is disaster."[5]

By January 1983 the sixty-two new poems that would become *The Boat of Quiet Hours* were gathered and readied to be shared with a publisher. The poems were initially reviewed by Hall, but then she continued to tinker with them as they were critiqued by Peseroff and Louis Simpson. After a brief trip to Barbados in February,[6] she returned home ready to offer the manuscript to a publisher. Thanks to Bly, her Akhmatova translation would soon be released, and many of her poems had already appeared in major literary magazines. As she waited for a publisher's response, there was great rejoicing when the *New Yorker* for the first time accepted one of her poems, "Thinking of Madame Bovary." Kenyon believed publication in the *New Yorker* was "the height of ambition,"[7] and over the years many of her poems appeared there. That same year Henry Lyman interviewed her for his radio program, *Poems to a Listener*. During the program she read several of her latest poems and described one of her principal goals in writing them: "It's a way of making sense out of what has happened to me." She added that "in paying attention to the physical world we enter something wonderful."[8] The parallel efforts to understand life and herself and to express the wonder of nature would continue to powerfully influence her poetry.

Kenyon had reason to believe that *The Boat of Quiet Hours* would easily find a home. But this was not to be. She first sent the manuscript to Graywolf Press, but publisher Scott Walker reluctantly turned it down, based on the firm's fiscal constraints. The intervening years of waiting for its publication would prove very discouraging, and if there were ever a time when she might have given up her poetic vocation, it was then. But she never abandoned the quest for publication. She sent her work to Alice Quinn at Knopf, who kept the submission for over a year. Kenyon changed the title to "The Little Boat," then to "The Pond at Dusk," and contacted Wesleyan and Princeton University Presses; W. W. Norton; Farrar, Straus, and Giroux; and Holt, Rinehart, and Winston. She held out hope that Knopf might come through in the end with an offer, but Hall actively discouraged that hope, which left her furious. In a letter to Mattison in fall 1985, Kenyon wrote that Hall

> overheard me telling my mother on the phone that I am very hopeful about Knopf, and he has just come here to discourage me, I *swear*. He came to straighten out my thinking. I am shaking with anger. It is not just the desire to protect one from disappointment. His male dominant juices are flowing. I asked him to *believe* that it can happen. You have to believe it *can* or it *won't*. He is just like his mother in this. Devil take it![9]

Finally, with the support of Tess Gallagher, a Graywolf author, the press reconsidered its prior decision and agreed to publish *The Boat of Quiet Hours*; it would be Kenyon's longest book of poems. Perhaps because of her previous work with *Green House*, she was very particular about layout and typeface, insisting that the book be printed in Bembo typeface. Determining the cover was simple because Graywolf's graphic designer, Tree Swenson, and Kenyon both liked the painting of Claude Monet's *La Barque*, which each of them had seen at the Musée Marmottan Monet in Paris.[10] The book carried a dedication, "For Perkins," and acknowledged the help of Joyce Peseroff and Alice Mattison. Maxine Kumin and Jean Valentine wrote blurbs for the back cover, as did Annie Dillard, who commended Kenyon as "one of the most powerful poets writing today." Adrienne Rich privately congratulated Kenyon for her work and calling her "a born poet."[11]

The sections of the book are structured around the four seasons: "Walking Alone in Late Winter," followed by spring's "Mud Season," summer's "The Boat of Quiet Hours," and fall's "Things." In each season there are poems of inspiration and suffering. She writes of her childhood, death and sorrow, human affection, domestic life, the beauty of place, and interior struggles. The volume opens with "Evening at a Country Inn," in which sadness and beauty are juxtaposed. The comfort of an evening in an inn is contrasted with a father's preoccupation with a son's car accident.[12] To ease worry, the speaker calls the father's attention to a truckload of hay: "I wish you would look at the hay—/ the beautiful sane and solid bales of hay."[13] Here beauty is offered as a remedy for anxiety and despair. "Rain in January" speaks of weather that makes one feel "pale, / useless, and strange," and in "Bright Sun after Heavy Snow," the melted snow reveals everything to be flawed.[14] In "Depression in Winter" Kenyon writes that although one is "greedy for unhappiness," by accident one can find light and heat that bring calm.[15]

Anger is a theme in both "Walking Alone in Late Winter" and "Portrait of a Figure near Water."[16] In this latter poem, the speaker retreats and burns alone in anger, then water enters soundlessly, a balm for the fire in the brain, a kind of unexpected grace. "Back from the City" is an explicitly religious poem. The speaker describes her three days of feasting in New York City and the piety she felt viewing a replica of the sculpture the Pietà in The Met's Cloisters. On leaving the museum she encounters a man "down on his luck" who asks for money. She turns away but hears the words of Christ: "Do you love me? . . . Then feed my sheep."[17] This failure to meet the needs of another is connected to "Apple Dropping into Deep Early Snow." When she sees a shriveled apple falling into a snow drift, she wonders if she is numbered with the damned, those who cry, "outraged," "Lord when did we see you?"[18]

In "Mud Season," spring is analogized to purgatory; it is a place of waiting for life to emerge. Here, from what seems dead, the first shoots of asparagus emerge like the rising "fingers of Lazarus." Only later will the purple crocus present an "exultation."[19] In the five-line poem "Depression," Kenyon analogizes the anger of exclusion, of being overlooked, of being of no import, being dust.

> . . . a mote. A little world. Dusty. Dusty.
> The universe is dust. Who can bear it?
> Christ comes. The women feed him, bathe his feet
> with tears, bring spices, find the empty tomb,
> burst out to tell the men, are not believed.[20]

Summer includes the poems "Thinking of Madame Bovary," in which the poet lauds "love's tense joys and red delights," but she also uses a twig to thwart an ant's effort to fulfill its desire by blocking its way.[21] In "April Walk," she encounters a huge, prehistoric grandfather turtle that serves as a reminder to not be agitated by change.[22] When writing of high summer, she speaks of bees that "rummage through the lilies, methodical / as thieves in a chest of drawers."[23] In "Philosophy in Warm Weather," life "reconvenes," a poppy "shouts," and the crow pulls up corn.[24] The warm weather brings her outside, collecting money for the Heart Fund, and in "Wash," she captures a small pleasure of ordinary life, a laundered blanket drying in the fragrant wind.[25]

The final section of The Boat of Quiet Hours contains some of Kenyon's finest, most luminous poems. This section opens with a testament to joy.

"Song" affirms natural, human happiness, "but even this / is not the joy that trembles / under every leaf and tongue."[26] "Things" is the concluding poem, announcing that things last, then fail to last, and fall into light.[27] In between these two memorable poems are verses about her father's death, recollections of her travels to "siren Italy,"[28] and her visionary poems, "Briefly It Enters and Briefly Speaks" and "Twilight: After Haying," in which she masters the use of imagery. In "Briefly" she says:

> I am the blossom pressed in a book,
> found again after two hundred years. . . .
>
> I am the maker, the lover, and the keeper. . . .
>
> When the young girl who starves
> sits down to a table
> she will sit beside me. . . .
>
> I am food on the prisoner's plate. . . .
>
> I am water rushing to the wellhead,
> filling the pitcher until it spills. . . .
>
> I am the patient gardener
> of the dry and weedy garden. . . .
>
> I am the stone step,
> the latch, and the working hinge. . . .
>
> I am the heart contracted by joy . . .
> the longest hair, white
> before the rest. . . .
>
> I am there in the basket of fruit
> presented to the widow. . . .
>
> I am the musk rose opening
> unattended, the fern on the boggy summit. . . .
>
> I am the one whose love
> overcomes you, already with you
> when you think to call my name. . . . [29]

In "Twilight: After Haying":

> Yes, the long shadows go out
> from the bales; and yes, the soul
> must part from the body:

what else could it do? . . .
These things happen . . . the soul's bliss
and suffering are bound together
like the grasses. . . . [30]

This twining of joy and bliss with suffering and sorrow is central to Kenyon's understanding of reality. It is also the basis of her intense sense of pleasure in the ordinary, pleasure to be seized in the moment. In "Coming Home at Twilight in Late Summer," her preoccupation with all there is to be done is displaced by the seduction of the lush pears growing in the meadow. She seizes the moment and eats a pear and is grateful.[31]

Reviews of *The Boat of Quiet Hours* were positive and established Kenyon as an up-and-coming poet. Greg Kuzma, in the *Iowa Review*, calls her work "remarkable," a revelation of how one can live a life of beauty in the face of fear, sadness, and anger. He notes that although each poem is informed by pain, the poet, nonetheless, seeks to understand that pain; the result is powerful poetry.[32] Marianne Boruch suggests these collected poems are like a daybook, recording ordinary things and showing reverence for routine.[33] New Hampshire poet Maxine Kumin sees a connection between Kenyon's translation of Akhmatova and these poems. In both there is an "exquisitely exact lyricism," and Kumin calls Kenyon's poems "intelligent, perfectly honed," combining gravity and wit.[34] Linda Gregerson, reviewing for *Poetry Review*, calls *The Boat of Quiet Hours* a "contemplative" book that is never self-indulgent and whose chief quality is the "beauty of repose."[35] Richard Katrovas hears in these poems the voice of mourning and praising, a voice witnessing to bliss and suffering, and Carol Muske comments in the *New York Times Book Review*, "These poems surprise beauty at every turn and capture truth at its familiar New England slant. Here, in Keats's terms, is a capable poet."[36] In a later review, Roberta White concludes that in this volume Kenyon "fully shapes her artistic self" and reveals "a pilgrim soul" caught between "bliss and despair."[37]

Waiting for the publication of *The Boat of Quiet Hours* was taxing, but once achieved, it established Kenyon as a master of her craft and a woman of spiritual depth. She was a young poet to be watched. She would not disappoint.

12
WAITING

Life is odd. . . .
I too am waiting, though if you asked
what for, I wouldn't know what to say.
—Jane Kenyon

While awaiting publication of *The Boat of Quiet Hours*, Kenyon felt she was waiting for an elusive something. Her daily routine gave no hint of what it might be. Her quiet life went on punctuated by occasional invitations to read her poetry and successes in placing her poems in magazines. She continued as a hospice volunteer and was active in the church. As a principal worker at the annual church fair, she oversaw the bake sale, dressed in her yellow apron, which she wore like a vestment.[1] She continued to sing in the church choir, and she composed a hymn that was performed. "As Bread Must First Be Broken" was written to the musical score of "Groeswen" by J. A. Lloyd, and her lyrics evoked the suffering of Jesus memorialized in bread and wine.[2]

There were familial joys, as she and Hall celebrated their wedding anniversary with an evening at the Mount Washington Hotel and attended the wedding of Hall's daughter, Philippa.[3] Every month Kenyon and Hall would drive to Connecticut to visit Lucy Hall, and many summers Reuel and Dawn Kenyon and their daughter, Bree, would visit from Ann Arbor, as would Alice Mattison and her family from New Haven, Connecticut. There were professional successes as well: In 1986 Kenyon was awarded a New Hampshire State Council on the Arts Fellowship, which brought with it an award of $2,000.[4]

FIGURE 12. (*Left to right*) Bree, Jane, and Polly Kenyon. Courtesy of Reuel Kenyon.

But the midlife restlessness, the waiting for an unknowable something, worsened into several bouts of profound depression and ensuing hospitalization. Their family internist, Donald W. Clark, admitted her to the New London Hospital and oversaw her various medications: first, lithium, which suppressed creativity, and then Nardil, which kept her from depression but made her combative. At times she needed stronger and stronger doses. Hall said, "Depression was a third party in our marriage."[5] Kenyon was alternatively listless, self-loathing, and impulsive and unable to sleep. When at home and depressed, she was reclusive and refused visitors. Previously arranged dinner engagements sometimes had to be canceled.[6] Gradually, she began to understand the biological roots of her depression. A few years later she told Mattison: "All my life I've thought my illness was my fault, but I am really beginning to see that the blame belongs with my neurotransmitters."[7]

Hall wrote extensively about her episodes of mania and their depressive effect on him. He was particularly perplexed by his wife's uncharacteristic impulsiveness, bossiness, and dogmatism. He was further alarmed and confused by the "erotic hunger" that consumed her. On her thirty-seventh birthday in May, she was overcome with sexual desire, and he recorded that it seemed as if they made love all day.[8] He described his response to her mania: "Then I understood, with shame, that for years I had used her depression to think well of myself: I was the rock, unchanging in all weathers; I was the protector. Now her manic elation and her certainty cast me down. After this first episode of her mania and my response, I put away my complacent self-congratulation."[9]

It is unfortunate that Kenyon's only description of these difficult episodes was in the poem "Sun and Moon." This was dedicated to Clark, who day and night, like sun and moon, appeared at her bedside in the hospital and about whom she always spoke admiringly. "Sun and Moon" was rejected by several publications, but ultimately it was included in *The Boat of Quiet Hours*.[10] In the poem she spoke honestly about her illness, her need for medication, and her mental fragility; she claimed writing it was "the riskiest thing I have ever done."[11]

Mattison related that Kenyon was reluctant to write about difficult issues in her personal life: "You write very honest poems about serious problems in your own life, like 'Sun and Moon,' but you wouldn't allow yourself to write that openly about situations that involved Don or your mother or other people."[12] Kenyon was a private person who shared little of herself except in her poetry, and even there her revelation was limited. That left it to Hall to tell her story for her.

While continuing to experiment with various depression drugs, she had a cancer scare in 1986 that increased her anxiety.[13] She found a nodule on her neck, which proved to be a mucoepidermoid carcinoma, but the tumor was encapsulated. After its surgical removal, no metastasis was evident, and she needed neither chemotherapy nor radiation. However, the possibility of cancer took an emotional toll. Although Clark was not her surgeon, she continued to see him regularly. Her daily planners between May 1985 and December 1986 show at least twenty appointments with him. He continued to prescribe medications for depression, and so they must have discussed her psychiatric problems.

Hall, too, had health problems. In the late 1970s when he was fifty years old, he was diagnosed with adult-onset diabetes. He delayed surgery, and thanks to Kenyon's learning to adapt their diet to the needs of a diabetic, he changed his diet and lost fifty pounds. But the disease affected his ability to perform sexually, and this was accompanied by diminishment of his poetic creativity. He later graphically described his sexual impotence, its resolution through penile surgery, and the happiness both he and Kenyon experienced after many years of suffering. Hall said that during this time his wife was kind, "but she was not content with our curtailment—a monogamous woman in her thirties for whom lovemaking was primary."[14] Kenyon leaves no comment on this personal matter.

As a gift for Hall's birthday in September, she had an ancestral bed restored, painted, and inscribed with the phrase, "Sleep, Balmy Sleep," a phrase taken from a poem by colonial woman poet Annis Stockton. Later, Hall published "The Painted Bed," a poem of mourning and sensuality.

But for Kenyon a major emotional uplift of the mid-1980s came from the acquisition of a dog. Both Peseroff and Mattison were dog owners, and Kenyon was especially enamored of Peseroff's little Westie, Duncan, for whom Kenyon volunteered to serve as godmother. Kenyon had been a cat person, and when she and Hall married, they had several cats, and they brought several with them when they moved from Ann Arbor. Over the years, they acquired new ones. When one died, it would be buried near the barn. In the poem "The Blue Bowl," a cat burial is memorialized. It tells of a cat being buried with its blue bowl, as in the burial rituals of primitive people.[15] But it was the arrival of a dog and the affection he engendered that would be most important for Kenyon.

Augustus, that is, Gus, Gussie, Gusto, was a mutt, half golden retriever, half sheepdog. Kenyon claimed to be "head over heels for this boy." The excuse she used to acquire Gus was to get "Perkins off his ass,"[16] but this did not work. Gus was Kenyon's dog, and it was she who walked him every morning up the New Canada Road.

Gus was a reject who was beaten by his previous owners, and when Kenyon adopted him, he became devoted to her.[17] She referred to him as "dear mongrel," her "spiritual leader," who was entirely forgiving, silly, earnest, hardworking, never discouraged, and incapable of bitterness or cynicism. He was her "Zen master" who lived in the present.[18] Gus became the subject of several of her poems, including "Biscuit," "After an Illness, Walking the Dog," and "With the Dog at Sunrise," as well as a later article, "The Physics of Long Sticks."[19] Soon after Gus was acquired, Ada arrived. She was dubbed "wicked cat" and "the little dickens," who, ironically, adored Gus but only tolerated her masters. Both animals became important members of the family.

The publication of *The Boat of Quiet Hours* would increase Kenyon's visibility, build her independent reputation, and begin to remove her from

Hall's shadow. It was not that he was unconscious of the problem Kenyon endured as a poet who was also his wife: "When we were first married, and for about ten years thereafter, we sometimes had a problem when others would treat me as the poet and her as the little wife who wrote poetry, and isn't that adorable? Nobody said those words, but that was the tone."[20] There was also a tone of condescension when men asked if she had published or felt dwarfed.[21]

That tone decreased as she began to give more public presentations. Locally, she gave readings at the Peterborough Town Library, the Unitarian Church in New London, and with Maxine Kumin at the Concord Public Library. Further afield she read her poems at the University of Toledo, for which she proudly earned $500. In 1987 she was invited to read at Plymouth State College, which later would present her with the Granite State Award for outstanding contributions to New Hampshire.

At her readings, Kenyon was strikingly impressive, a woman who became more beautiful with age. She now often used contact lenes instead of glasses, and her long hair had a shock of gray. She wore earrings and enjoyed wearing scarves, which brought color to her face. But it was her voice that was most memorable. Its pitch was low, carrying great authority. She spoke slowly, with a sensitivity and deliberateness arising from some interior depth where joy and sorrow were intertwined. What she said and how she said it drew many to her.[22]

She continued to be deeply affected by Hall's negative regard of her work. She confided in Alice Mattison that she was bored with her writing and that Hall had extensively criticized her poem "No Steps." Mattison consoled her: "Somehow I feel as if Don's esthetics these days aren't yours, or aren't yours entirely, that he is coming at poems with a lot of requirements that exist before the poem is written, like requirements about line length or stanza length, and that you are a much more organic poet who does not rule out anything in advance but chooses technical devices to suit the particular message or subject of the poem. . . . But it must be so hard and disappointing that he doesn't like them, whatever the reason."[23]

But the end of Kenyon's boredom came from another quarter, when an invitation arrived from the US Information Service requesting Hall to give lectures on American poetry in China and Japan in March 1986. To his credit he lobbied hard to have Kenyon accompany him and give presentations. They were to spend a month in China and two weeks in Japan lecturing to university faculty, students, and societies of writers.[24] They were hosted at banquets in freezing buildings, attended an Easter service in a Methodist church in Beijing, climbed the Great Wall, ate dumplings, and saw armies of blue-coated peasants. These images were captured in Kenyon's poem "Cultural Exchange."[25] They traveled to Beijing, Xi'an, Chengdu, Guangzhou, Shanghai (their favorite city), and to the alien and exotic Shenyang in Mongolia. In her lectures, Kenyon focused on women poets and included poems by Mattison, Peseroff, and herself.

Uncharacteristically, she recorded an experience she had in China when she queried a Chinese peasant about whether there had been any positive aspect of the Cultural Revolution. He responded that carrying stones made him strong but that he was given bread by his grandmother and that was a sign and hope of a better world to come. He said he learned that God is not only near us but inside us. This prompted Kenyon to recall a recent incident from her hospice work when for fear of embarrassment, she had not said to a dying patient that the "kingdom of God is within you."[26]

In Japan they visited Buddhist temples and the capitals—modern and ancient—Tokyo, Kyoto, and Nara, as well as Hiroshima. They had prepared lectures on contemporary American poets but had to improvise when audiences inquired about T. S. Eliot and Robert Frost.

Kenyon was less comfortable in Japan than she had been in China. At this point she was homesick, a feeling expressed in the eponymous poem "Homesick," which reflects on the smells and strange foods of foreign places.[27] The sexism she encountered in both China and Japan remained a potent memory. Their hosts spoke only to Hall; she was clearly his subordinate. She wrote to Peseroff that there are a "lot of sexist, 'second-fiddle' problems here. Painful."[28]

Up until this trip, Kenyon had not traveled extensively in the non-Western world. Her worldview was narrow, restricted in many ways to the domestic scene. The trip broadened her perspective and confirmed what she knew in its more subtle form, namely, that women were undervalued as poets. This realization built on an experience she had prior to their departure for Asia. In January, Bert Hornback invited Hall, Galway Kinnell, Seamus Heaney, and Wendell Berry to give readings at the University of Michigan. Kenyon went along with Hall. After a splendid evening, the group reconvened informally the following day. At one point Kenyon was asked to read one of her poems; she pulled out "Twilight: After Haying."

Berry, who was well-acquainted with Hall and Kenyon, confessed that he had not read her poetry, but on hearing it he was astounded at its beauty. He remembered her gifts of "quietness, gentleness, compassion, elegance, clarity and her awareness of mystery." He saw her as "authentically a poet of inspiration,"[29] not merely as the wife of Donald Hall.

This same astounding realization that Jane Kenyon was a gifted poet was illustrated again in a letter of apology from Philip Levine, poet and friend of Hall, to Kenyon a few years later. Levine said that he did not realize Kenyon wrote such wonderful poetry until he stumbled on a copy of *The Boat of Quiet Hours* in the library. He acknowledged her as a "master poet," whose poems "must be some of the most gorgeous domestic poems *ever* written." This experience confirmed for him again that some of the best poets are quietly among us.[30] Disregard of Kenyon's separate identity as a significant poet was not limited to audiences in China and Japan. In a letter to Mattison, Kenyon related an indignity that recalled those of her foreign travels: "A high school in Peterborough, N.H., wrote to me, asking me to participate next spring in their Young Authors Program. The letter begins, 'Dear Mrs. Hall . . .'" Kenyon asked Mattison, "Shall I kill them or just say I'm busy?"[31]

Hall was cognizant of this problem, and he shared his wife's concern. He told Mike Pride, "There would be people who would say how nice it was that I was all full of big ideas and that she was so sweet and simple. She'd want to break their jaws. She did affect simplicity, but she wasn't simple. Her style was a glass of water—a hundred-proof glass of water."[32] Hall wanted Kenyon's success, but as it came, it challenged their relationship. *The Boat of Quiet Hours* established Jane Kenyon as a serious and important poet. It seemed to portend some new beginning in her life as poet and wife.

13
A MOMENT IN MIDDLE AGE

There is a moment in middle age
when you grow bored, angered
by your middling mind,
afraid. . . .
That day the sun
burns hot and bright,
making you more desolate.
It happens subtly, as when a pear
spoils from the inside out
and you may not be aware
until things have gone too far.
—Jane Kenyon

The year 1987 was no exception to the intertwined joys and sorrows that marked Kenyon's life. It began wonderfully but then inaugurated two years of deep depression,[1] in which "the soul's bliss / and suffering [were] bound together / like the grasses."[2]

Once *The Boat of Quiet Hours* was accepted by Graywolf Press, Kenyon continued sending new poems to magazines for publication. Two poems appeared in *Ploughshares*, and Joyce Peseroff, editor, selected three others to be included in the 1987 *Ploughshares Poetry Reader*.[3] Kenyon's poetry readings gave her broader visibility. She read at the Woodberry Poetry Room at Harvard University with Frank Bidart, Carolyn Chute, and Justin Kaplan and gave a reading on the *New Letters on Air* radio program.[4] But it was the two-day poetry event sponsored by the National Endowment for the Arts, held at the Library of Congress in March, that gave her national prominence. On the first day, thirty former poetry consultants of the Library of Congress (now called poet laureates) read from their work, and the following day, fifteen new-generation American poets read from theirs. Kenyon was paired with Judith Moffett and read "Twilight: After Haying" as well as other poems. For her participation she received a check for $1,500.[5]

In May, to celebrate her fortieth birthday and to attend the second marriage of Geoffrey Hill, she and Hall traveled to England. Hill, an acclaimed poet, was an old friend of Hall from Oxford University days and, as Hall had, was marrying a much-younger woman, Alice Goodman, an American poet, librettist, and later Anglican priest. While in England, Hall took Kenyon to Oxford to show her his old haunts, including his college, Christ Church, and the village of Thaxted in Essex, where he lived for two and a half years at the end of the 1950s.

After their return home, an exciting opportunity emerged for Kenyon. The South Danbury Church received an invitation to participate in an international exchange organized by Bridges for Peace, a Christian organization sponsoring reconciliation events with the Soviet Union. A year earlier, Soviet president Mikhail Gorbachev introduced glasnost, a policy for openness and reforming transparency. This gave hope for heightened communication with the West during the Cold War. Since she was a great lover of Russian literature, especially Anton Chekhov, Ivan Turgenev, and Anna Akhmatova, Kenyon was a likely participant in this exchange. The intent of the project was to send a team of Christians from New England to the USSR for two weeks to meet with counterparts and then to have New England communities host a Soviet team. The trip was planned for fall 1988. Kenyon looked forward to this adventure as her first solo travel experience.[6] But Hall did not want her to go. The poem "While We Were Arguing," with its allusions to tears shed, may refer to their disagreement over this trip.[7]

While the beginning of the year was joyful, by July Kenyon plunged again into deep depression, which she claimed was "out of control." Her hospitalization for a few days began two years of episodic periods when she could barely function. Her poem "Now Where?" speaks of her confusion and depression, which she personifies.[8] Depression wakes and walks with her, robbing her of sleep and mocking her belief in God. She is like a widow who is borne along by day and night.

Difficulties in her relationship with Hall were becoming evident. There were unresolved issues between them and a certain weariness. Hall's publishing successes continued to build. *Seasons at Eagle Pond* was published and proved to be very popular, and *The Happy Man* won the Lenore Marshall Poetry Prize awarded by the Academy of American Poets for the most outstanding book of poetry published the previous year. The $25,000 prize made him a "happy" man. But it did not resolve his midlife anxiety, which was reflected in his book-length poem *The One Day*, which won both the National Book Critics Circle Award and the Los Angeles Times Book Prize in poetry. Kenyon's worries were expressed in "The Pear," in which she alludes to things having gone too far. The feeling of depression was reinforced by the dejection she felt after the failure of her applications for a Guggenheim Fellowship and a National Endowment for the Arts grant.

Her bottled-up anger was increasingly troubling. Kenyon and Hall fought infrequently, but when they did, it was "catastrophic."[9] There was tension between them over her financial dependence on Hall and over his desire to have her spend more time with him. She admitted her depression made her irritable, and she did not know how to deal with her anger. She tended to withdraw and then explode. She was very sensitive to any slight. When she and Hall did a benefit reading for Habitat for Humanity in New London, she was miffed that in advertising the event the local paper printed a much-larger photograph of him than of her. She quipped to Alice Mattison that this confirmed the Freudian dictum, "Anatomy is destiny."[10] She was "touched," however, that her doctor, Donald Clark, attended the event.[11]

Despite her emotional turmoil, Kenyon was able to write poems that focused on the challenges others faced. In the poem "At the IGA: Franklin, New Hampshire," she chronicled the life of a mother of three children with little means who reflects on her past actions that shaped her difficult life.[12] A few years later she and Hall traveled to Charleston, South Carolina, where she visited a Civil War museum and was prompted to write "At the Public Market Museum, Charleston, South Carolina," one of the best poems of this difficult period.

> Who would choose this for himself?
> And yet the terrible machinery
> waited in place. With psalters
> in their breast pockets, and gloves

knitted by their sister and sweethearts,
the men in gray hurled themselves
out of the trenches, and rushed against
blue. It was what both sides
agreed to do.[13]

Her trip with Bridges for Peace in October 1988 was central to the broad-
ening of her worldview. The US team spent one week in Russia and another
in Tallin, Estonia, visiting collective farms, schools, factories, and churches
and meeting with peace committees.[14] In Moscow, she toured Chekhov's
house and medical office, and in Leningrad, she was thrilled to see places
associated with Akhmatova, which she wrote about in her poem "Lines
for Akhmatova."[15] Perhaps rather than have her feelings injured by the
absence of recognition for herself as poet, as had happened in China and
Japan, Kenyon introduced herself to her Russian and Estonian hosts not
as a poet but as custodian of the South Danbury Church! On returning
home, she presented the church with a memento from the trip, a lace doily,
which continues to grace the church's altar even today. Kenyon's reciprocal
obligation was to speak about the trip to civic associations and to host a
Soviet team the following year, in 1989.

Because Kenyon would be gone to the Soviet Union for two weeks, Hall
decided to visit England while she was away. As it turned out, he was miserable and depressed on the trip. No one in Oxford remembered him, and he
was lonely and bored.[16] When Kenyon's return plane was delayed, he was
frantic. After her return, the unresolved anger and sadness between them
came to a head. She wrote to Mattison, "Perkins has settled down but he
was *very bad* to me over this trip. I don't want to think about it."[17] Mattison
responded that Hall is "reassured by dependency and alarmed by independence."[18] For his part, Hall explained that when he heard his wife's stories
from the Russian trip, he burst into tears, hurt she had gone without him.
He admitted she was less needy that he was.[19] Perhaps to ease the tension
between them, as well as to escape the cold, they traveled to Key West in
December.

Kenyon's midlife boredom, irritability, and depression continued in 1989.
She observed, "I have been low. I've been quite low."[20] Some of it was due
to Hall's possessiveness; he wanted her home with him, and he was moody
and grumpy when she was not.[21] If visitors arrived to see her, he insisted

her time with them be limited. Understandably, she was happy to be alone while he was away. As she confided to Mattison, "Can't live with him. Can't live without him."[22]

Her mother, who continued to be depressed and was getting on in years, was subtly suggesting she wanted to leave Ann Arbor and move to New Hampshire. Mother and daughter were very different personalities. Polly was pragmatic and constantly busy. She focused on her daughter's domestic life and sent her recipes, made clothes for her daughter and Hall, and kept her up to date on events in Ann Arbor and in the family. Kenyon was convinced that her writing would be impeded if her mother was nearby and was not ready to take on this responsibility.[23] Later she wrote Mattison, "My family makes me sad. Being with them makes me sad and being away from them makes me sad."[24] Her contacts with Hall's former wife were also difficult. In April Kenyon attended the baptism of and reception for Philippa's baby, Allison. But this joyful celebration was marred for her because she felt Kirby Hall treated her icily.[25] The emotional stress left her disoriented, and in cleaning the church afterwards in her role as custodian, she drank the blessed baptismal water because she felt she knew of no other way to dispose of it properly.

All her stress was compounded by her "broken-heartedness" over the church's pastor, Jack Jensen, who had been diagnosed with stomach cancer and afflicted with considerable chest pain and trouble breathing, which so debilitated him that he was forced to give his sermons sitting on a high stool during church services.

Under the circumstances, it is unsurprising that Kenyon felt afflicted by a lack of poetic creativity. She was not pleased with her poem "Three Songs at the End of Summer," which was reprinted in *The Best American Poetry, 1989*, and told Mattison that the poem "is personal and painful and it is the kind of poetry I'd like to turn away from. There's very little invention in it. It is memory and reportage."[26]

Through this difficult period, Kenyon kept on with public readings. Marie Howe, a faculty member of Tufts University, invited her to read there in February 1989. Their friendship was cemented earlier when Kenyon wrote Howe at the death of her brother from HIV.

According to Mattison, Kenyon thought Howe was unearthly,[27] and Howe believed Kenyon was a poet who combined gravity, spirituality, and erotic energy. She loved Kenyon's poetry because of its abiding love of the world and its "compassion, humor, honesty and clarity."[28] Kenyon did not want Hall in the audience at her Tuft's reading, and she made sure he did not accompany her. Later in the summer, Mattison arranged to have Kenyon and Hall read at Yale. Kenyon petitioned her friend: "I know you won't let it degenerate into DONALD HALL!!! oh, and his wife who is also a poet."[29] Mattison responded, "I don't think you should worry much about the DONALD HALL!!! phenomenon. You have a following in this town as you'll discover."[30]

Kenyon now began to give a few readings with Hall. She appeared with him, Maxine Kumin, and Charles Simic on New Hampshire Public Radio, where she read, among other poems, "Ice Out."[31] Rain, snow, fog, storm, wind, and sun were mentioned in many of her poems. "Ice Out" was no exception.[32] Mattison commented that Kenyon always began her poems with a "weather report."[33]

During most of 1989, Kenyon wrote of her depression, inability to sleep, nausea, withdrawal, irritability, and resulting dreams of suicide. It was one of the worst depressions of her life. She told Mattison in mid-June: "You are one of the few people, I think, who realizes that my life is hard. It seems hard to me. Even though I am exceptionally fortunate. Living with Don has given me much, but it also exacts much. Now he's watching me closely to see if the Prozac is going to make me manic."[34]

A few days later Mattison commiserated: "You are right that your life is hard. Being married to another writer is hard for a writer no matter who it is. I think it would be worse if your career were going badly or if you were the same age. But even so it has to be hard. . . . Also, Don is competitive. Boy is he competitive. . . . He is one of my favorite human beings, absolutely, but he's *hard*."[35]

Kenyon was now under the care of Charles Solow, head of psychiatry at the Dartmouth-Hitchcock Hospital, who managed her medications and did talk therapy. Solow diagnosed her in 1989 as having a form of hypomania followed by depressive episodes. She was forty-two years old.

During this middle-age moment, Kenyon was offered two opportunities for growth. The first was to organize the one-week visit of two Estonians sent by Bridges for Peace. In mid-May Ravio Jarvi, an illustrator of children's books, and Toivo Pelli, a Baptist minister, arrived from Estonia. Before they landed Kenyon picked up trash along Route 4, something she did twice a year. She wanted the area to look presentable.[36] With her friend Mary Lyn

Ray, she showed the visitors around the community and brought them to visit a school, hospital, factory, the nearby Shaker village, and a five-and-ten store. The Estonians were celebrated at a tea and attended a potluck supper at the South Danbury Church. It was a joyful weeklong visit.[37]

The second opportunity was an invitation by Mike Pride, editor of the *Concord (NH) Monitor*, to write articles for and about the local community. Initially, she was reluctant to take on this responsibility, but she finally agreed.[38] It turned out that writing prose gave her new energy, that it was "shaking something loose" in her because it was less meditative and more outward and communal than poetry.[39] She was grateful to Pride for this invitation.

Her first article was on the recently deceased Edna Powers, whom Kenyon called "an endangered species," a lifelong Democrat in a Republican area and a beloved member of the community.[40] Because Kenyon earned $35 per column, she wrote not for the money but to honor the community she had come to love; she considered this writing a form of civic engagement.[41] She covered a wide variety of subjects: gardens, the seasons, the town dump, the church fair, her dog, her grandmother, her minister. Her first article came out in 1989, and she continued with the paper for the next five years.

In the late 1980s Kenyon was beloved in the community and increasingly an acclaimed poet. Her constant depression was treated with a cocktail of drugs, some successful, others not. The drugs kept her functioning, but she had many unresolved issues in her life. The one remedy that unfailingly relieved her, at least temporarily, was sex.[42] She had a great psychic need for sex and was attracted to men who gave off an erotic energy. She was also increasingly irritated with Hall and railed then and later against what she considered his bullying, his assertion of opinion as absolute law, and his sarcasm.[43] She looked elsewhere for affirmation.

It is no surprise then that at this time—from mid-1987 through mid-1989—Kenyon had an intimate affair with a man about Hall's age whom they both knew. Kenyon was deeply depressed, and it seemed that only drugs and frequent sex gave relief. She told no one of this affair until a few years later when visiting Mattison she confided in her. "I don't regret for a moment our conversation. It was a relief to tell you. I think it is a sign that I am beginning to heal that I could tell you about it."[44] Her paramour was unmarried at the time, but he ended the affair with Kenyon because he was about to marry. Who initiated the affair is unknown. Since Hall was frequently away, they probably carried on their trysts during that time. For Kenyon love, gratitude, revenge, or a desired cure for depression may have all contributed. She may have loved her paramour, but even with her complaints about Hall's possessiveness and bullying, she also loved him and needed him. What is clear from Kenyon's letters to Mattison is that she enjoyed this illicit relationship, was furious when it ended, and would have continued it if this lover had encouraged her.[45]

Kenyon asked Mattison not to tell Hall or anyone else about this episode.[46] She said that if Hall knew, "it would kill him."[47] Whether Hall did know at the time or later is unknown. However, Hall had a great capacity for not knowing. As Kenyon had indicated, he was "the Charles Atlas of Denial."[48] What is clear is that Kenyon continued to ponder her relationship with this lover and to harbor ill will toward him for ending it. She told Mattison, "God, I hope that man skis into a tree. This is a major failing in my spiritual life, my abiding ill-feeling toward this man."[49] A few days later she said: "I have not forgiven myself, and that he simply wasn't adequate to the situation. He couldn't help it. It still hurts. This anger is perhaps a way in which I continue to punish myself, and it is also the only tie to him I still have. Perhaps that is why I *cherish* the anger so much. . . . I need so much to just put his burden down."[50]

For long after this relationship was over, she still pondered the affair. In a letter to Mattison she confessed, "You know, I can't really bear to think about the good times with my ex, because the truth is that if he made a single conciliatory move I would be right back in his armpit. Unbelievable as that may sound. . . . I think I feel so savage in his presence because I still love him with his quirky mind and his very interesting ways in bed."[51]

Whatever Kenyon's ongoing amorous desires, she received another emotional blow in the fall of 1989 when she was confronted with another reality of great import: Donald Hall was diagnosed with colon cancer. The prognosis was not good.

14
THE COMING EVENING

Let it come, as it will, and don't
be afraid.
—Jane Kenyon

Accepting what the future portended would have been no small task as Kenyon entered the last decade of the century. Her husband was gravely ill, and her beloved Jack Jensen was facing death.

Hall and Kenyon were speechless in fall 1989 when they received the diagnosis of Hall's colon cancer. Surgery removed the cancer, but the outlook was not hopeful. The possibility loomed that, given their age disparity, Kenyon might, indeed, be a widow for many years. As Hall recuperated, Kenyon wrote "Chrysanthemums," chronicling his hospital stay and how she pushed the morphine pump every eight minutes as he lay semi-conscious. There in the hospital the senses of smell and sight dominated, particularly the scent of mums mixed with hospital smells. On the return home from the hospital, Hall and Kenyon wept in gratitude for being alive.[1]

By February 1990 Hall was strong enough to make another trip to Rome, where they revisited Keats's room, saw a lock of his hair and the ring he gave Fanny, and went to the Protestant Cemetery, where he is buried.[2] They also visited religious sites, including the Mamertine Prison, where St. Paul is reputed to have been imprisoned, and the Abbey of the Three Fountains, where he is supposedly buried.[3]

When Hall and Kenyon returned to Wilmot, they learned of Jensen's rapid decline. Jensen had become Kenyon's companion in spirit, a man who brought together a love of religion, philosophy, and history in a way that fed her soul; he assured her of forgiveness and deepened her spiritual life.[4] In his final hours on March 17, 1990, she and Mary Lyn Ray, a friend and church member, stayed with him through the night, repeating the litany "Lord have mercy, Christ have mercy, Lord have mercy."[5] He was fifty-seven. Kenyon described his death as "beautiful" and said that he became more radiant as the end neared. She often thought about what he had given her: "Over the years my poetry changed to reflect my awakening. Life changed profoundly. I began to be grateful for things that I had always taken for granted."[6] Soon afterward she published "A Gardener of the True Vine" in the *Concord (NH) Monitor*, a eulogy for this man who meant so much to her.

She also wrote two poems in his memory. In "In Memory of Jack" she describes herself like a deer who bolted to him in his suffering and death.[7] And in a later poem, "Moving the Frame,"[8] she speaks of shifting his photograph on her desk hoping that his eyes might meet hers. Two years after his death she organized a memorial service for a small group at Colby-Sawyer College, where he had taught for thirty years. Friends gathered, read Scripture, prayed, and dedicated a marble bench in his memory. Kenyon took possession of the high stool he sat on as he preached as a relic; it remains in the kitchen of the farmhouse to this day.

Jensen's death had little impact on the productivity of the occupants of Eagle Pond Farm. Despite both his continuing cancer treatment and the trauma of Jensen's death, Hall kept up his prodigious output. He was working on five new books. He also kept up a busy schedule of readings all around the country, and he received more accolades: the 1990 Los Angeles Times Book Prize and the Frost Medal. He was always proud of his productivity. Kenyon felt he had the energy of three people and said that he would make a "very bad Buddhist" because he was always thinking of the next thing and never was where he was. But she fully understood that her productivity depended on his, because if he did not work so hard, she would not have the luxury of writing what she wanted to write.[9]

Kenyon's public appearances increased, too. In 1990 she read in Ann Arbor, Pittsburgh, and Oneonta, New York, and in bookstores in Washington, DC, and Concord, and she appeared again on *Poems to a Listener*, hosted by Henry Lyman. But the event of the year was the publication of *Let Evening Come* with its fifty-seven poems, the most popular of which was its title poem.

Let Evening Come was dedicated to her mother, who had mentioned the phrase "let evening come" when Kenyon visited her in Ann Arbor and who now was ill.[10] Kenyon had no anxiety over finding a publisher; Graywolf Press was happy to have her submission, and she would again have Tree Swenson as her graphic designer. It was Swenson who helped her select Edward Hopper's painting *New York, New Haven, and Hartford* for the cover with its railroad tracks in the foreground and the dusk of evening descending over the distant houses. Kenyon selected the *New Yorker* editor William Maxwell's statement, "So strange life is. Why people do not go around in a continual state of surprise is beyond me," as the epigraph that opened the volume.

Although the poems of this book are mostly dark, some are joyful, reflecting again the two aspects of Kenyon's psyche. Some came from her deepened religious sensibility; she later claimed the poem "Let Evening Come" was given her by "the muse, the Holy Ghost." When the collection was finished, she realize it needed something redeeming; "'Let Evening Come' just fell out. I really didn't have to struggle with it."[11]

> Let the light of the late afternoon
> shine through chinks in the barn, moving
> up the bales as the sun moves down.
>
> Let the cricket take up chafing
> as a woman takes up her needles
> and her yarn. Let evening come.
>
> Let dew collect on the hoe abandoned
> in long grass. Let the stars appear
> and the moon disclose her silver horn.
>
> Let the fox go back to its sandy den.
> Let the wind die down. Let the shed
> go black inside. Let evening come.
>
> To the bottle in the ditch, to the scoop
> in the oats, to air in the lung
> let evening come.
>
> Let it come, as it will, and don't
> be afraid. God does not leave us
> comfortless, so let evening come.[12]

She acknowledged that "the writing of 'Let Evening Come' was a mystical experience. I felt calm, energetic, and lucid, and these words came to me." Drawing on Keats's insight of "negative capability," she insisted, "I knew in some way more than I know."[13] She said she intended the poem to illustrate a passage from the Gospel of John, "The light shines in the darkness, and the darkness has not overcome it."[14]

It may be true that relative to other poems, "Let Evening Come" came easily but not without considerable reworking. Twelve revisions of the poem are extant,[15] and she conferred with both Hall and Mattison about stanza breaks and the last lines. She substantially modified the final lines, which originally read:

> Let it come
> as it will, and don't be afraid.
> Have a little faith, and let evening come.[16]

This was changed to the more explicitly religious:

> Let it come, as it will, and don't
> be afraid. God does not leave us
> comfortless, so let evening come.

When Peseroff read the poem, she saw a connection between it and Kenyon's earlier "Briefly It Enters, and Briefly Speaks" and suggested that the title of this new book might be "Let Evening Come."[17]

Let Evening Come is called a "sunset" collection because most of the poems are melancholic.[18] "The Pear," "Let the Boat Drift," "Waiting," "Now Where?" and "The Letter" all reflect the darkness of her mature poetry. Included is a clutch of poems about her early life, indicating a renewed interest in the shaping influences of her youth. These include "Catching Frogs," "In the Grove: The Poet at Ten," "Staying at Grandma's," "A Boy Goes into the World," and "Learning in the First Grade." Another group of poems chronicles her spiritual search. The four-line "Looking at Stars" is a rejection of a "dry," "abstracted" "God of curved space" who will not help us. Rather, she turns to the son whose blood was splattered on his mother's robe. It is he who understands the tragic nature of existence.[19] In "Last Days" Kenyon writes of her ambiguity toward death,[20] and the volume's final poem, "With the Dog at Sunrise," is a reflection on death and the lifelong search for God accompanied by pain and difficulty. She wrote "Searching for God is the first thing and the last, / but in between such trouble, and such pain."[21]

By far the most moving and well-known poem of the book is "Let Evening Come."[22] Each stanza begins with the gentle plea for acquiescence to the inevitable. The incantation of the word "let" forms a kind of litany, reminiscent of prayer.[23] The repetition produces a stillness and calm as the reader is directed to the natural rhythms of the light, to a cricket, the stars, a fox, and the wind. It is these that admonish the reader to not be afraid, all is cared for by God. Although this poem is widely read at funerals, its implications are more universal; it urges readers to look to the natural world as a guide to how humans might live and deal with sorrow.

Most critics were kind in their reviews, but poetry editor David Baker quarreled with the quality of Kenyon's work. He noted that although the book has a few good poems, most are journalistic, private, and confessional. He found the subject matter too limited and the poems terse and redundant of her earlier poetry.[24] Stronger praise came from *Publishers Weekly*, which commended the "subtle tension" underlying these poems and her "unadorned prosaic speech," but the reviewer added that her language sometimes "falls flat," marring her poems.[25] In the estimate of poet and essayist Judith Kitchen, most of the poems are melancholic, but they are filled with empathy and compassion. *Let Evening Come* was a "book of middle age" in which everything is held in abeyance, in a state of waiting.[26] Kenyon's friend Marie Howe wrote an appreciative review in which she characterized the poems as "quiet," "fierce," and "lyrical." Written as they were out of deep necessity, they are poems that both "trouble and nourish."[27]

Other journals carried positive reviews as well. *Harvard Book Review* credited the poems with being honest, intelligent, sensual, and informed by a shrewd lyricism. It was a book in which the poet married passion with understatement,[28] and Louis McKee in a brief review commented that Kenyon "stands tall among this new generation. Few writers see so well and speak so well of what they see."[29] In her essay "Vision, Voice, and Soul-Making in *Let Evening Come*," Judith Harris suggested that Kenyon captures the essence of Keats's soul-making and that her poems focus on the last things.[30] Mike Pride praised Kenyon's poetry,[31] but she was irritated he mentioned her work in relationship to Hall's. She complained to Mattison: "The *Monitor* piece came out. It talks a lot about me in relation to Don, something I think is unfortunate. It is also clear that the author respects Don's poems more because they are harder to understand."[32]

Given the extensive critical acclaim of *Let Evening Come*, Kenyon might have been jubilant, but she was at a turning point as she attempted to establish a poetic distance between herself and Hall.[33] Later, in reflecting on this time, Hall acknowledged their competition, and as Kenyon became more successful, his poetry deteriorated. The pupil had exceeded the teacher.[34]

Because Hall was a successful prose writer as well as poet, he may have felt challenged by Kenyon's successful essays in the *Concord Monitor*. Kenyon related to Mattison: "I showed Perk my piece about the septic tank ['The Honey Wagon']. He was awful to me about it. 'Not everyone thinks shit is as exciting as you do.' 'What did you write this for? Because you wanted money?' 'What does this mean?' . . . He was merciless. I'll do as I please with that piece, make no mistake. . . . He thinks he *owns prose*."[35] Kenyon rejected Hall's dismissive claim that she wrote prose to make money and countered that she wrote prose "so I feel like an adult."[36]

Alice Mattison was sympathetic with her friend's need for distancing. She urged her to get to work and to face the fact that she lived with someone who insisted on the right to do his own work. She needed to do the same. She admonished Kenyon: "You have to set aside a time to sit at your desk, and you have to be fierce about it. You have to say, 'I am sorry, but I cannot accompany you to your swearing-in as Lord of All the Poets in the Palace of Ice and Diamonds, because I feel the edge of a corner of a hint of a scrap of a poem coming, and I must stay home and wait for it.'"[37]

Facing continued cancer chemotherapy, Hall was even more eager for his wife not to travel without him, and he groused to Mattison once again in fall 1990 about Kenyon's visiting her mother and doing a reading in Ann Arbor.[38]

Kenyon reached a point where she was able to affirm her own voice.[39] In a 1990 interview with Pride, she said Hall was a statesman of poetry who had a lot of answers: "He knows things nobody else knows. But I also know things nobody else knows."[40] She claimed that her strength came from increasing success and visibility as a poet and from a developing spiritual life. She told Pride:

> I've become more overt about my spiritual life. My spiritual life is so much
> a part of my intellectual life and my feeling life that it's really become im-

possible for me to keep it out of my work. . . . My spiritual life has become something that I cannot suppress. It's so much a part of me. The danger, of course, is that one might brag spiritually. . . . and yet I take chances. I also open myself to ridicule by thoroughly secular intellectuals.[41]

A disorienting attack on Kenyon's spiritual life would come not from "secular intellectuals" but from an experience the following year in a far-off land, India.

15
WIDENING VISION

Everyone needs art, but not everyone knows it. . . .
People must have it, or they sicken. It is soul food.
—Jane Kenyon

In the fall of 1990 Kenyon experienced one of her worst bouts of depression. Her poem "Back" tells of coming out of this experience with the help of drugs: "Suddenly / I fall into my life again. . . . I can find my way back."[1] Even though she came "back," she felt powerfully that something important was missing from her life. She told Mike Pride, "I need to be working on a kind of frontier where I don't know myself what's going to happen next."[2] In her poem "August Rain, after Haying," she expressed this need as a thirst, using the language of Psalm 63:

> The grass resolves to grow again,
> receiving the rain to that end,
> but my disordered soul thirsts
> after something it cannot name.[3]

In the psalm, the soul thirsts for God, yet Kenyon expresses no certainty what her disordered soul sought.

Depression had one positive result: it increased her empathy for others. When she was younger, she wrote that it was better to do something useful like "pin the clean / sheets on the line" than to moan about your life.[4] But her empathy for the suffering of others grew as her depression increased. In her poem "Back from the City," her compassion for others combined with a personal responsibility to "feed my sheep." Mattison, who worked at a local soup kitchen every Monday, remembered a time Kenyon accompanied her to feed the hungry. Viewing the situation, Kenyon burst into tears.[5] Mattison and Peseroff jokingly accused Kenyon of discovering pain everywhere. Kenyon's poem "Coats" is illustrative of their differences. It describes a man emerging from a hospital, tears staining his face, with his wife's coat over his arm, with the implication that his wife had died. Mattison mischievously suggested that the man might be bringing the coat to the dry cleaners while his wife had a facelift![6] As Kenyon's depression became more pervasive, everything contributed to it. She told Mattison, "To give you an idea how my mind works when I'm down: When the paper toweling runs low on the roll it makes me sad! Everything makes me sad. Birdsong makes me sad. Late summer flowers make me sad."[7]

Meanwhile, her life proceeded according to routine. She continued to meet with Peseroff and Mattison, which gave her encouragement, help, and pleasure. Although, as always, she had minor physical maladies, generally she was fit. She and her dog, Gus, walked up Ragged Mountain every day, she worked in her garden for much of the year, and occasionally, in her purple boots, she hiked Mount Kearsarge and Mount Cardigan. Three times she undertook the six-hour trek to the summit of Mount Washington, the "great-grandmother mountain," grateful for the cog railroad to bring her down on the return trip.[8]

She continued to give workshops, readings, and lectures. In the summer she gave a talk on poetry and read her poems at Frost Place and at a literary conference in Enfield, New Hampshire. She did a reading at the University of Massachusetts Creative Writing Program, served on a subcommittee of the New Hampshire State Council of the Arts, received the Sara Teasdale Award in Poetry from Wellesley College, and was honored by the St. Botolph Club, a private social club for artists in Boston. In the fall she attended a reunion of Hopwood Award winners at the University of Michigan, where she and Hall gave separate readings. In the question period she was asked more questions than he was. She had come into her own, right there among old friends. Her life was full, and her poetry was gaining prestige. But her depression was always there.

She and Hall continued to attend the South Danbury Church, but she began to bring a political consciousness to the experience. During one Sunday service in July, Kenyon recited a prayer she had written asking God to give a true understanding of his infinite love, which overcomes sin, brutality, and acts of injustice. She asked for help to remember that God's love is closer to us than we are to ourselves and added a lament about the recent appointment of Clarence Thomas to the Supreme Court. The prayer closed with a plea for help to bring goodness from the ashes of Thomas's recent confirmation after US Senate hearings.[9]

A new presence affected her routine, the arrival of Polly, who had decided to sell her house in Ann Arbor and move to Wilmot. Kenyon returned to her childhood home to help her mother sort through the detritus accumulated over many decades. "Spring Changes" describes their sorting, and "The Stroller" evokes remembrances of her past.[10] In this long poem Kenyon describes how encountering her father's drawing of her childhood stroller prompted reflection on her early life, her love for her father, and her family's socioeconomic status compared with her mother's wealthier and more-sophisticated customers. From all available mementos of her family's past, Kenyon selected for herself her father's drawing of the stroller and a yellow pottery vase.

Initially, Polly stayed at the farmhouse with her daughter and son-in-law, but eventually she moved nearby. Although Kenyon feared having her mother in Wilmot would disrupt her writing, she was touched by the new realization that her mother really loved her.[11] What the presence of her mother did mean was that Kenyon would need to attend to her. It also meant less attention to Hall, who became more possessive.

The presence of her mother provoked Kenyon's deeper reflection on her childhood. In "The Argument" she describes the smell of woodsmoke, reminding her of the fire and sulfur of her grandmother's God "who disapproves of . . . dancing, strong waters, and adultery." Kenyon asks: might she be like Judas, the foolish virgins, or the rich young man who would burn in these fires?[12] Mattison recalls Kenyon expressing concern that the poem might make people suspect her adulterous affair.[13] Other childhood memories were included in an unfinished prose article, "Childhood, When You are In It . . . ," in which, among other themes, she chronicled her spiritual development from her grandmother's influence through that of Jack Jensen.[14]

Kenyon and Hall were both excited by the possibility that arrived next. An invitation from the US Information Agency offered them the opportunity to lecture in India for the month of November 1991. This experience was to have dramatic consequences for her, widening her horizons and challenging her religious belief and self-identity. She and Hall traveled to Bombay, New Delhi, and Madras, and Kenyon went alone to Bangalore and Allahabad. They gave lectures and interviews, attended banquets, and met with faculty, students, and government officials.[15] A boat trip on the sacred Ganges River was a startling experience for Kenyon, who recorded the trip in her journal. After returning to Wilmot, she wrote fifteen drafts of "Woman, Why Are You Weeping?"[16] in which she explained how their Brahmin guide, Rajiv, introduced them to rituals of death carried out in the Ganges, the cremation of bodies of the dead, the scattering of ashes and marigold flowers. He explained how in Hinduism suffering was cyclical and followed from one's karma. When Kenyon saw a dead baby floating in the river, she was horrified and wept. Rajiv calmly explained that if poverty precluded cremation, a dead body might, nonetheless, be immersed in the sacred river.[17]

The impact of this experience on Kenyon was profound, confusing, and heart-wrenching. The poem's title derived from the encounter of the weeping Mary Magdalene at Jesus's empty tomb. When the Magdalene was asked why she was weeping, she responded, "Because they have taken away my Lord." This was Kenyon's experience: India had taken away her Lord, the one whose life was within her, whose anguish she knew, to whom she had spoken. She was offered instead Brahman, Shiva, and Vishnu, whom she did not know. The "many-headed and many-armed" Indian gods did not care for her; suddenly she questioned the meaning of her life, and she was frightened by the realization of the absurdity of all religious forms. In India suffering was calmly accepted. When she asked what was to be done about the dead baby, there was no answer, only wind, water, and the sound of the boatmen. The God she had known was leaving her.

This poem expresses the destructive nature of the experience for Kenyon's sensibilities and self-conception. She believed she was made in the image of God, but now her God had vanished, and her world was destroyed. She feared that her inner life was a "delusion," "a lapse of rationality," that she had made up a "cozy Christ" for her own comfort. She returned home enamored of Indian food, textiles, art, literature, and the kindness of the Indian people but with a mind and heart assaulted. When she returned to church, she no longer experienced the old comfort; she felt only "apathy and bafflement."[18]

Peseroff and Mattison, both secular Jews, were nonplussed by Kenyon's response, and Mattison argued that Kenyon's experience of the truth of Hinduism should not challenge the veracity of her personal experience of Christianity. Mattison could not abide Kenyon's self-denigration. India had come between these dear friends. Mattison and Kenyon continued their disagreement in their workshop and in letters.[19] Kenyon maintained that Mattison had been harsh and unkind and had no right to criticize her inner life.[20] Ultimately, their disagreement abated, and although the poem was intended for publication, Kenyon "yanked" it from the manuscript. It was Peseroff who convinced her to withdraw it. Kenyon accepted that "everyone" had misgivings about the poem's logic. Something was clearly wrong with it, and she did not know how to fix it.[21] "Woman, Why Are You Weeping?" was not published in Kenyon's lifetime.[22]

These travels to India, China, Japan, Russia, and Estonia clearly opened up Kenyon to a world beyond her domestic life in Wilmot. The experiences combined with a deeper understanding of Bly's claim that poetry could be a public moral force meant that Kenyon began to write poems that were more expansive in content and more self-revelatory.[23] These would appear in her next volume, *Constance,* which included "Sleepers in Jaipur," "Gettysburg: July 1, 1863," "Three Small Oranges," and "Potato," all manifesting a much-wider communal and moral vision. "Sleepers" concerns the plight of the Indian poor who suffer from the heat in their stick huts but who, nonetheless, engage in lovemaking, which produces new life, "a gift from God."[24] "Gettysburg: July 1, 1863" deals with Union and Confederate soldiers waging war.[25] She found her experience of the Gettysburg battlefield "terribly moving,"[26] and she produced an extraordinary antiwar poem told through the life and death of a young Union soldier who was shot and died while hearing his own groaning. The poem's sentiments about war paralleled those she felt about the Gulf War, which she criticized in a scathing article for the *Concord (NH) Monitor,* condemning the bombing of Baghdad and the war.[27] In another war poem, "Three Small Oranges," she again focused on a single individual whose simple life was lived out against the backdrop of torture and bombing.[28] When asked about the differences between Hall's and her war poems, she said his were declarative, loud, and outward, and hers were personal; she was a miniaturist, and he was "painting Diego Rivera murals."[29] Another poem, "Potato," details the act of disposing of a partially spoiled potato in the compost.[30] There it "reviles" her over the fact that she could have made a shepherd's pie to feed a hamlet. The poem is an expression of her legendary sense of guilt and empathy for the needs of the poor and hungry. These poems express a broader recognition of human suffering and accompanied a continuing flow of poems reflecting her own personal suffering from melancholy. She was finally achieving an important goal: to make sense of and understand what was happening to her and to write for the sake of others who suffered.

16

THE POET LAUREATE OF DEPRESSION

And from that day on
everything under the sun and moon
made me sad.
—Jane Kenyon

The defining event of 1992 was Kenyon's public and painful revelation of her lifelong depression and her reliance on drugs to keep functioning. Although she had written several poems about depression, "Having It Out with Melancholy," her longest poem, was unmatched in its power.[1] The poem was originally submitted to the *New Yorker* but only "Back," its final stanza, was published. This necessitated writing another concluding stanza, "Wood Thrush."

"Having It Out with Melancholy" is a nine-part, personal lyric, the story of Kenyon's lifelong affliction that she names melancholy, the older designation that is particularly associated with artists.[2] Unlike her mentor Keats, she believed that melancholy was not to be cultivated but held at bay. The poem's opening epigraph is taken from another mentor and medical doctor, Anton Chekhov: "If many remedies are prescribed for an illness, you may be certain that the illness has no cure." This quotation alerts the reader to Kenyon's conclusion: Her illness is chronic; it will come again.

The first section of the poem, "From the Nursery," sets out the theme. Here, melancholy is named the "bile of desolation," harkening back to the medieval cause of depression, black bile. She personifies it as "the anti-urge" and "the mutilator of souls."[3] This demon ruined her from birth,[4] teaching her to wait for death and to live without gratitude. In the section "Bottles," she lists her weapons, eleven different drugs.[5] What follows is "Suggestion from a Friend," a two-line admonition of the popular belief: "You wouldn't be so depressed / if you really believed in God." The next section, "Often," suggests that her only retreat from "massive pain" is sleep, but what follows, "Once There Was Light," breaks with the previous sections as she recalls her experience of 1980 when she encountered herself as a speck in a river of light, floating with the whole human family—the living, the dead, the unborn.[6] But the demon crow pulls her out of that calm reverie. Although she is given temporary comfort by her dog, she is tired of being "stouthearted," tired of trying. She experiences self-alienation, describing herself as "a piece of burnt meat." Although her drugs bring her back to life, her "credo" is to believe only in the moment, knowing that "the Unholy Ghost" will come again. In the poem's final section, "High on Nardil and June light," she waits for the wild song of the wood thrush and a return to ordinary contentment.

This autobiographical poem is a gift to fellow sufferers, assuring them that while their affliction is chronic, ordinary contentment would temporarily return with the help of medication and the beauty of nature. "Having It Out with Melancholy" distinguishes Kenyon from the "confessional poets"—Sylvia Plath, Anne Sexton, John Berryman—whose depression ended in suicide. Gregory Orr argues that unlike these confessional poets, "postconfessional poets" bring their survival skills to bear in autobiographical poetry and thereby reconcile self and the world. Although Orr does not specifically name Kenyon as a "postconfessional poet," in this instance she clearly illustrates his claim.[7]

The new iteration of the poem was published in *Poetry* and was first read at Frost Place to an attentive audience of seventy people.[8] During the reading, she paused for a few minutes to hold back tears. Afterwards, many attendees surrounded her to share how meaningful her words were to them personally.[9] She related, "When I've read any of these poems that really dwell on depression, people come up to me afterward and hug me."[10] This major poem would appear in her 1993 volume, *Constance*, along with many of her other poems of depression.

As the psychiatrist Peter Kramer remarks, the poem bears "witness to a scourge, as survivors bear witness to political and moral outrages. The poem is both art and a public act on behalf of fellow sufferers." Unlike the

Romantic understanding of depression as a profound perspective on the human condition, Kramer argues that Kenyon reflects a new perspective on this malady; it is a biologically induced, insistent condition that requires drugs to control this "pure hell."[11]

Kenyon's motivation in creating the poem was the desire to increase people's understanding of this disease and ease sufferers' burdens.[12] Paul Breslin, a psycho-political poet, suggests that Kenyon offers poetry as a "counterforce" to depression, and Gregory Orr, a poet and friend from Michigan days, claims that in "Having It Out with Melancholy," she confronts disorder and survives it by use of imagination. He insists, however, she is not simply a poet of survival but also of transformation.[13] Commenting on Kenyon's poems of depression, Adrienne Rich wrote to commend Kenyon's efforts "in refusing to play out the scenario of madness that is so encouraged for women poets. . . . At a certain point, having looked at the lives and deaths of my women contemporaries I decided that society was mad—with stifling of women."[14]

As Kenyon revised the poem, tragedy continued to haunt her and challenge any temporary contentment she might experience. She expressed her growing sense of the fragility of life in the poem "Otherwise."[15] Unknowingly, it was a portent of things to come. Like "Let Evening Come," "Otherwise" was incantational, containing the chant-like repetition of the words "it could have been otherwise" as a kind of clarion call.

The poem forcefully utilizes Kenyon's technique of phrase repetition, but she did not restrict its use to her poetry. At times in the poetry workshop, she would say, "I have such clever friends. I have such clever friends," and Gregory Orr notes that in earlier workshop sessions, she would repeat, "What fun we're having. What fun we're having."[16] Mattison recounts that when Hall made boring jokes, Kenyon would say, "Put the cover over his cage." And she would repeat it again.[17] So it is perhaps unsurprising that the practice came to be incorporated in "Otherwise."

"Otherwise" is important not only for this quality of incantation but also for highlighting ordinary pleasures.

> I got out of bed
> on two strong legs.
> It might have been
> otherwise. I ate

cereal, sweet
milk, ripe, flawless
peach. It might
have been otherwise.
I took the dog uphill
to the birch wood.
All morning I did
The work I love.

At noon I lay down
With my mate. It might
have been otherwise.
We ate dinner together
at a table with silver
candlesticks. It might
have been otherwise.
I slept in a bed
in a room with paintings
on the walls, and
planned another day
just like this day.
But one day, I know,
it will be otherwise.

The poem captures the reality that all these ordinary pleasures are fleet-
ing. One day it all will be otherwise. The poem is quintessential Kenyon:
moments of matchless joy are so often accompanied by a sense of impending
loss. Take pleasure in that moment, it will not last. "Otherwise" expresses her
underlying anxiety that her husband's presence "could be otherwise," but as
the months went on, it was evident that he would survive. That powerfully
renewed her awareness of the need to have faith in life despite the suffering
that inevitably accompanies it. In mid-April 1992, she wrote "Have Faith and
the Mud Will Dry," an optimistic article published in the *Concord (NH) Monitor*, in which she found hope in mud season, comparing it to purgatory. It
was a time of waiting, when only muddy ruts are evident, and a fresh wind is
needed to restore everything. In the article she quotes Isaac Bashevis Singer,
who said, "Faith will come afterward." She writes of how as a dutiful gardener
she carries on in mud season, burning bamboo, the "cockroach" of plants,
and cutting back brush. She urges, "Act as though you had faith."[18]

She would need that faith to carry on not only in her garden but in her life. Cancer would prove to be the "cockroach" of Hall's anatomy. Having seemed after two-and-a-half years to be cancer free, a routine scan revealed he had metastatic liver cancer. He was sixty-three years old. Such metastasis is often a death sentence. The diagnosis prompted unbelief and "howling" in their house.[19] Two-thirds of his liver was removed, and the prognosis was poor; he had only one in three chances of surviving five years. Both husband and wife prepared for the worst.

Ten days after his surgery and before he began chemotherapy, his mother had a heart attack. He and Kenyon rushed to New Haven, Connecticut, to care for her for several days.[20] On returning home Kenyon draped a string of tiny Christmas lights around the headboard of the painted bed and began daily massages of her husband's body. Hall's chemotherapy treatments lasted into the fall, during which time Kenyon read the poetry of Elizabeth Bishop for her own consolation.

Kenyon chronicled these calamities in "Joys amid the Shadows of Sadness," which appeared in the *Concord Monitor*. In it she quotes the psalmist who says we are as the grass, but she suggests we are also like the peonies that flower and fade; we either accept suffering in faith or in resignation. She wrote that in the face of sadness both were trying to "simplify, appreciate, stay close, be kind, tell the truth, work as we are able, rest." They were getting an education in what it meant to be human, "in love despite fear, in the amazing resilience of the human body and living abundantly with more joy."[21] This was said with a "stiff upper lip." They both believed Hall would die soon,[22] as did everyone else.

During Hall's hospitalization, Kenyon composed "Pharaoh," in which she observes that "things are off." Nothing is right, not food, nor touch, nor the kindness of friends. Waking in the night she saw her much-diminished husband lying like an Egyptian king, with his feet elevating the blankets. This was the image of a man hovering between life and death.

> I woke in the night to see your
> diminished bulk lying beside me—
> you on your back, like a sarcophagus
> as your feet held up the covers. . . .
> The things you might need in the next
> life surrounded you—your comb and glasses,
> water, a book and a pen.[23]

In the liminal space between seemingly terminal illness and the hope for survival, Kenyon wrote "Notes from the Other Side," a poem unique in her repertoire.[24] Much of her poetry is autobiographical and points to the real experienced in the moment. In this poem she imagines afterlife almost entirely in negative terms. On the other side of life there is no despair or fear or illness or poverty; no plastic, bad books, or contrition; no gnashing of teeth. What one encounters on the other side is "mercy clothed in light." The theme of light that threads through much of her poetry is realized in its fullness in this poem.

Even though she suffered extremely high anxiety during the summer, she decided to "go naked" in order to determine if she really needed her psychiatric medications.[25] Her psychiatrist, whom she called her "mixologist," had prescribed a variety of drugs for the last eleven years, and she was weary of their side effects, the constant changing of medications, and the waste of money. She gradually tapered off, and by June she was drug free; unsurprisingly, in August she crashed and was unable to write poetry for the next seven months. Solow searched for the appropriate drugs to stabilize her.[26] Ultimately, she concurred that she needed medication. When asked what else most helped her during this difficult time, she used religious language seemingly unaffected by the change of consciousness she experienced in India: "My belief in God, such as it is, especially the idea that a believer is part of the body of Christ, has kept me from harming myself. When I really didn't want to be conscious, didn't want to be aware, was in so much pain that I didn't want to be awake or aware. . . . I've thought to myself, 'If you injure yourself, you're injuring the body of Christ, and Christ has been injured enough.'"[27]

She also insisted she was learning from her own experience: "When you get to be my age and you've lived with depression for a number of years, you begin to have a context for believing that you will feel better at some point. You have been through it enough times so that you know, sooner or later, if you can just stick it out, it's going to lift. It's going to be better."[28]

Hall's illness and the fragile condition of his mother were followed by other misfortunes. Lucy continued to have emergency hospitalizations, and Polly fell in the bathtub and cracked her ribs. Kenyon herself had a freak accident with a lawn mower that resulted in a bloody leg wound.[29]

These stresses, her ongoing depression, and her growing sense of self-confidence as a poet created more friction between her and Hall. This was not spoken of publicly, but she shared with friends her husband's increasing possessiveness and controlling behavior. She told Mattison: "We had a big fight last night about whether I will go to Washington, DC. Perkins always puts things in global terms—I care more for the dog than I do for him, etc. He uses his cancer to win arguments these days."[30] She lamented his manipulative behavior and expressed her pleasure in being able to do what she wanted to do when he was away.[31] She complained that he considered himself the prose writer in the family and is highly critical of her efforts in that genre: "He is so damn hard on my prose. Sarcastic. When we're talking about poetry, I know I'm on firmer ground, but with prose he can reduce me to a pulp. That's why I need you, [Alice] and Joyce, who had a good idea about the structure in the beginning [of the children's book she is writing], and Mary Lyn, who knows what she's doing in these matters, to balance the sledgehammer treatment I get from P[erkins]."[32] Despite the conflict, Hall dedicated his next book, *The Museum of Clear Ideas*, to Kenyon. These poems were very different from his previous poetry. The book was organized around the nine innings of baseball but included a discussion of art, love, sex and death. Kenyon did not like the poems and gently told him so. They both wept. It was only after Kenyon's death that Hall believed his poems again gained vitality.[33]

The year 1992 was very difficult for Kenyon, an "annus horribilis," yet it was as well an "annus mirabilis," as her reputation as a promising poet grew exponentially.

17
POETRY MATTERS

> [Poetry] matters because it's beautiful . . .
> because it tells the truth, the human truth about
> the complexity of life . . . about what it is to
> be alive, about the way of the world, about life
> and death. [It] embodies that complexity and
> makes it more understandable, less frightening,
> less bewildering. It matters because it is
> consolation in times of trouble. . . . Poetry has an
> unearthly ability to turn suffering into beauty.
> —Jane Kenyon

Jane Kenyon's forty-fifth year was one of myriad difficulties and peril but also a year of public acclaim. Her confidence increased as awards and opportunities accumulated. Early in February 1992 she read her poetry at the prestigious Folger Shakespeare Library in Washington, DC,[1] and the following year Henry Lyman invited her to read again for *Poems to a Listener*, where she principally read poems from *Let Evening Come*. During the intermittent discussion, Lyman asked her, "What's the really interesting reality?" and she responded, "It's the *inwardness* of things. That's where the news is."[2]

Her most treasured accolade came shortly after her appearance at the Folger. She was offered a Guggenheim Fellowship for 1992–93. Her friend Hayden Carruth had been one of her referees. She was "immensely heartened" by this victory and posted the letter of announcement on the refrigerator. The award brought with it $30,000, far more than she had ever received from her publications. While this was a financial boon, she thought of it principally as affirmation of herself as a poet. It helped sustain her during the difficulties of the year.[3]

Another honor was an invitation to be a featured poet along with Hall sponsored by the Geraldine R. Dodge Foundation Poetry Festival in Waterloo, New Jersey, in September. While there, Kenyon participated in several presentations. She appeared twice with Hall, speaking about how they worked as poets living together, then once by herself with Sharon Olds and Luci Tapahonso and on a panel with Tess Gallagher, Lucille Clifton, W. S. Merwin, and Galway Kinnell.[4] Appreciation of her talent was confirmed in mid-December when journalist Bill Moyers came to Wilmot to do preparatory interviews with both her and Hall for a documentary, "A Life Together."

It was against the backdrop of these considerable achievements that she began to publicly reflect on poetry and the role of the poet, something she had not done previously. Although she never considered herself a theoretician, her small but significant contribution to poetics forms an important part of her legacy. In a series of statements and interviews, including the previously noted one with Lyman, she defines poetry and its importance and meaning for the individual and society.[5] Her ruminations are more like prompts for reflection rather than a systematic exploration. In one, she rejects British American poet W. H. Auden's warning, "Poetry makes nothing happen," as erroneous.[6] She insists that poetry does make things happen.[7] She defends poetry in two statements made to New Hampshire artists and writers during her three-year term as an advisory councilor for the New Hampshire State Council on the Arts.[8] In them she offers testimonials analogizing art to food for the soul, needed by everyone lest they become ill. She calls artists "keepers of the flame," and she urges them to offer their talents to the community despite the decline in national funding for the arts.[9]

In "Thoughts on the Gifts of the Arts" she reflects on the difference between the media and the arts. The former reported on outer life, the latter on inner life. But she saw the inner strengthening the outer, because the arts encourages a longing for the well-being of the planet, promotes awe in the face of life and death, and deepens an understanding of the soul. She warns that if society neglects the inner life, it would become violent and no longer value existence.[10]

Finally, in the lecture "Everything I Know about Writing Poetry," delivered at a literary conference, she urges poets to observe and love the world and so make readers more alive. The poet does this by embodying feeling within an image and by expressing the image in fresh, specific language. In doing so something new and universal is made. She invokes the metaphor as "the engine of poetry" and conceives of the poem as how the inner world is revealed the outer world. Kenyon encouraged artists of all types to tell the whole truth, to not be afraid, take risks, be tough, protect their time, feed their inner life, avoid noise, be themselves, go for walks, and take the phone off the hook.[11] On her own phone she pasted a sticker: "Just say no."

Kenyon's statements reveal an understanding of poetry as a public good and do so precisely at a time when she herself began writing poems that engage larger societal issues. In contrast to her youthful political noninvolvement, she insists artists had an obligation to take political stands, especially when politics influenced the creation of art. Any thinking person, she asserts, must be an informed participant in a democracy. She knew of no poet who was not political, either by demonstrating or signing petitions, and urged that one must be involved in the common life; the alternative is despair.[12]

In these public declarations and in a series of interviews, Kenyon spoke intimately about the craft of poetry and her vocation as a poet. For her, one function of poetry is to keep the memory of people, places, things, and events alive,[13] an aspiration she shared with Hall. Poetry, she said, tells us what is valuable and who we are.[14] Art itself comes out of life and gives back to life by healing, consoling, and holding grief, diluting it through companionship and the creation of a communal sensibility. The work of the poet is to tell the whole truth in a beautiful way and to put into words feelings all humans have.[15] She told Moyers in "A Life Together," "There really is consolation from sad poems. And it's hard to know how that happens. There's the pleasure of the thing itself, the pleasure of the poem, and it works against the sadness somehow."[16]

In a conversation with Mike Pride, Kenyon asserts poets have rich and sometimes overwhelming lives and feel things more deeply than nonpoets.[17] Their vocation is to mirror the soul of both the individual and the nation and to report on that inner life to others.[18] By telling the truth with beautiful language, poetry has a "spiritual" dimension and poets a "priestly" function. They push back against disorder and grief, offering healing, intercession, and confession.[19]

As critics have noted, the uniqueness of much of Kenyon's poetry derives from its ability to bridge hope and doubt, and its power flows from speaking honestly about both.[20] Her poems accept reality and the human condition and do not attempt to transcend it. Rather, she is joyful in the pleasure of the moment, which will pass.

Although Kenyon expressed discomfort about discussing the spiritual aspect of her poetry, she could not suppress it.[21] She believed in what she called the "great goodness" that made suffering endurable and that was the source of life and poetry. The "great goodness" pervaded everything.[22]

18

THE BUSIEST YEAR

I am working at one thing—the short
lyric. It is all I want, at this point: to write
short, intense, musical cries of the spirit.
—Jane Kenyon

The year 1993 was one of the busiest for both Kenyon and Hall. Kenyon, who had just received a Guggenheim Fellowship, published her fourth book of poems, *Constance*, which received the Frederick Bock Prize from *Poetry*, and its poem "Having It Out with Melancholy" was included in *The Best American Poetry 1993*.[1] Hall received an honorary degree from the University of Michigan and published two books, *The Museum of Clear Ideas* and *Life Work*, which was nominated for a National Book Award. During the year Bill Moyers and his New York film crews recorded them at various locations. His episode "A Life Together: Poets Donald Hall and Jane Kenyon" premiered later in 1993 on PBS's *Bill Moyers Journal*. It was seen by millions, awarded an Emmy, and placed Kenyon and Hall in the very select pantheon of nationally recognized poet celebrities. Kenyon was portrayed as a rising star who had finally come into her own. In a *Boston Globe* article, Hall and Kenyon were headlined as "poets at their peak" and dubbed "the Brownings of America."[2] As usual, the newspaper article focused principally on Hall, who was described as a "rapid fire raconteur" and a "showoff," and less on Kenyon, who was depicted as "mellow" and "self-deprecating." Together, the journalist Patti Hartigan claimed, they exuded a certain "harmony."[3]

Their "busyness" was played out against a backdrop of physical exhaustion and anxiety. They were the walking wounded. Although Hall's cancer was in remission, and he had seemingly beaten the survival odds, anxiety about his future health was always under the surface. Their personal responsibilities for their aging mothers, who had both moved nearby, increased as well. Much of these women's supplemental care fell to Kenyon. Overwhelmed, she wrote, "I've said it before and I'll say it again, I need a wife."[4] Alice Mattison agreed: "That man you are married to is so dear and needy and unconscious. . . . He loves you so dramatically and spectacularly, but I wish he'd help in the garden a bit or maybe dust the furniture."[5]

To make matters worse, episodes of acute sadness continued to afflict Kenyon. She confessed she was "paralyzed by depression,"[6] and constant experimentation with various drugs was debilitating, as were their side effects. Jack Jensen's death deprived her of anyone with whom to discuss her religious quandaries, and her spiritual life was growing thin. It was evident to others that she was worn out. A description of her by an attendee at one of her readings at the 1993 Miami International Book Fair is telling. Although her manner was honest, straightforward, dignified, and "utterly self-aware," her visage was "warm but strained."[7]

Neither Hall's nor his wife's illness nor the demands of parental care impacted his prodigious output. He claimed to "adore the routine of work."[8] It was his way of defying death and distracting himself from fear. But it seriously impacted Kenyon. Depression, exacerbated by her feeling of being trapped, made her irritable and testy with him. Their public comments about their relationship were always judicious, but private correspondence allowed Kenyon to vent. She told Mattison, "Our conversation on the phone just about saved my life. I have so much inside of me that I must not let show. If I couldn't let it show a little to you, and to Dr. S.[olow], I think I would simply explode."[9] Regular contact with Mattison and Peseroff provided critical release. She commented that their workshop "means everything to me. . . . It has helped me to stop regarding Don's opinion as absolute law, it has given me balance and support when I needed it. I can't conceive of working without it."[10] A month later she said she did not want to be "bullied" by him anymore. She also confessed that they had a screaming fight over how family members had treated her. She was so furious with him she ran away, planning to spend the night at the nearby Ramada Inn, but he tracked her down and brought her home. Their fighting continued, and she

admitted that when fighting, they said awful things to each other. She was
sure Hall did not understand her, and she felt adrift in the universe.[11] When
publicly asked these same questions, she dissembled. In their interview with
Marion Blue given one month after she wrote to Mattison, Kenyon said: "I
think Don understands me when work is very absorbing," and later in the
interview, "There really is very little discord between us."[12]

Her unresolved feeling about her love affair continued to weigh on her,
and she sought frequent counsel from Mattison, to whom she expressed
deep gratitude for her understanding and insight, particularly hearing her
out about her paramour. Kenyon confessed in this letter, and in one written
a week later, that although she read Mattison's recent letters many times,
she burned any that made reference to her affair, "just to be careful."[13] This
was the marital context of the "busiest" year. It is no wonder she wrote of
a "disordered soul."

When January arrived, Bill Moyers and company descended on Wilmot
to film a reading by Hall and Kenyon in the Wilmot town center. The community turned out in full force to hear them. Kenyon read several of her
poems,[14] but the centerpiece of her presentation was "Having It Out with
Melancholy." Although she had read this previously at Frost Place in Fran-
conia, here she was reading to intimates—family and friends. Her friend
Mike Pride, on hearing her read and observing the audience's reaction, inquired whether she would write an article on depression for the newspaper.
She agreed to consider his request but never complied.[15] She wrote her last
article for the *Concord Monitor* in December of that year.

Perhaps stimulated by this community event at the town center, Kenyon
and Hall composed the poem "Words for a Warrant" celebrating civic life
in the town of Wilmot. It was published in the town's 1993 annual report
and serves as a companion to Kenyon's "American Triptych," written when
she first arrived in Wilmot. Like it, "Words for a Warrant" reflects their
commitment to town government, New England–style:

> When the stream by the Town Hall rushes
> with meltwater, and early sap drips
> into buckets until dusk; when the dirt back
> roads thaw by noon and freeze again at night.
> Bob looks for his gavel, and townswomen
> tuck the town warrant into knitting baskets.
> At seven o'clock on the first Tuesday in March

we enter the warm room, with its loved
and extremely uncomfortable benches, and
to the business of governing ourselves. Once a year,
for a couple of hours, we are civil and deliberate.
Then we stand stretching, happy
to go home, and step out into the clear,
cold night, under the legislature of stars.[16]

Moyers's "A Life Together" aired on television at the end of 1993.[17] It
was a compilation of interviews with both Hall and Kenyon, clips of them
reading in Wilmot and in New Jersey at the Geraldine R. Dodge Poetry
Festival, and shots of them in the farmhouse, in church, and walking in
the surrounding countryside. Thirty-five hours of film were reduced to a
fifty-six-minute show in which Hall received twice the coverage given to
Kenyon. The program revealed their very distinctive personalities. Hall, a
performer by nature, was engaging and charming. Kenyon, with her long,
curly mane of hair, her feminine gestures, and her pauses, came across as
sensitive, thoughtful, and calm, a woman who spoke with extraordinary
honesty about her depression and inhabiting the "land of the living dead."
"A Life Together" projected a unique and exceptional marriage of poets living and working together in a relationship dominated by Hall in a mostly
mythical harmony. Even Hall realized that this constructed story had its
flaws. As he later related: "After twenty-one years of marriage I gradually
came to realize that the myth—Jane passive, me aggressive—was no longer
entirely true. Maybe Jane in her twenties took cover in my shadow, but at
forty-six she cast her own lively shadow."[18]

A number of trips contributed to their busyness. Early in the year they
were both invited by Bert Hornback, their friend and former colleague at
the University of Michigan, to read at Bellarmine College [now University],
a Catholic institution, in Louisville, Kentucky. While there they visited
longtime friends Wendell and Tanya Berry at their nearby farm. Springtime
brought another lovely occasion. Old friends Tree Swenson and Liam Rector, who had recently moved to Boston, decided to hold their wedding on
the back patio of the farmhouse. Tree carried a bouquet Kenyon created
from garden flowers, and the seven participants read excerpts from Eliot's
"Four Quartets." Kenyon claimed to see a sign of good luck when it began
to sprinkle.[19] The proximity of Swenson, who like Kenyon appreciated the

visual arts, meant that they would make frequent forays to the Isabella Stuart Gardener Museum and the Boston Museum of Fine Arts to admire the paintings of Claude Monet and seventeenth-century Dutch artists.

In what was a new experience for Kenyon, she starred with Hall in A. B. Gurney's *Love Letters* at the Papermill Theatre in Lincoln, New Hampshire. Friends and family attended to cheer them on. This was a special delight for the extroverted Hall, who had always wanted to be an actor. In the summer they spent an afternoon at MacDowell, a community of artists in Peterborough, New Hampshire. Kenyon would subsequently write "Afternoon at MacDowell" about being there with Hall, who was still thin and wan from his second bout with cancer.[20] Lines from the final stanza of this poem would become permanently associated with their lives together: "What . . . will keep you safe beside me."

Having achieved a new measure of acclaim, Kenyon was the subject of four important and revealing interviews in 1993. These give insight into her mature reflections on her life, her vocation, and the nature of poetry. Interviews with Moyers and with David Bradt, a friend and professor at New Hampshire College, were of Kenyon alone. Two others, with independent journalist Marian Blue and with Terry Gross, interviewer for National Public Radio's *Fresh Air*, were done in conjunction with Hall. In these last two, as usually happened when they were together, Hall dominated the conversation.

The Moyers interview lasted two hours and was the longest of the four. Some of its material had appeared in "A Life Together," and some was unique to this interview. Responding to Moyers's wide-ranging questions, Kenyon spoke of how poetry offered her a way to control the events in her life. It was a "refuge" both in her early life and in her first years in New Hampshire when she felt "disembodied." She remarked on how her expansive gardens grounded her in her new home. In discussing the craft of poetry, she acknowledged that writing poetry was a hard, exhausting, and intense experience, but it was made possible because she had a simple life. Asked why she wrote about depression, she explained she did it to foster understanding of the disease and to "ease people's burdens." As for her own depression, she said it was a genetic malady. Drugs helped, but in her case so did her belief in God, especially the notion of being part of the Body of Christ. This belief kept her from harming herself and from feeling a sense of worthlessness.

She shared with Moyers the story of her initial rejection of religion, becoming a believer with the help of Jack Jensen, and her experience of seeing a ribbon of light in which everyone had a place. It was this latter experience that changed her fundamentally. She claimed she was a believer in a God who forgives, and if she did not believe that, she could not live. Finally, she confessed that the past year had been full of upheavals that made it difficult to concentrate. Her closing comment to Moyers was that although there were experiences in life that were almost unbearable, she believed there was also a "great goodness." "Why," she asked, "when there could have been nothing, is there something? This is a great mystery. How, when there could have been nothing, does it happen that there is love, kindness, and beauty?" The interview ended with these questions unanswered.[21]

Like the Moyers interview, the one with Bradt was recorded at the farmhouse in 1993 but was not published until three years later. In it Kenyon comments on the importance of poetry and art in general, calling it the "mirror of the soul." She was flattered when Bradt compared her poems to those of Emily Dickinson and agreed that like Dickinson she thought about her soul and was searching for God. For Kenyon the work of the poet was to express deep feeling and to tell the truth in such a beautiful way that people cannot live without it. Poetry, even sad poetry, gives consolation. She quoted Akhmatova, her Russian muse, that poetry "is joy and it is pain."

She said her devotion to poetry began in childhood, when she found solitude in nature; this turned her inward. It was the move to Wilmot that made her a different person. Here she was given a subject to write about and a supportive community, something she lacked in Ann Arbor. Place had made her a poet, and she admitted poetry was the only thing she was fit to do, except maybe landscape gardening. Bradt asked about her favorite poets, and in naming them she recalled how she came to do a translation of Akhmatova and why she emphasized image over form. She acknowledged the absolute value of the image, which comes from a deep place that "gives the poem a sense of cohesion."[22]

Blue conducted her interview with Hall and Kenyon in April at the annual meeting of the Association of Writers and Writing Programs at Old Dominion University in Norfolk, Virginia. Part of the annual meeting in Norfolk included a panel on the work of Hall, with presentations by his friends Robert Bly, Galway Kinnell, and Louis Simpson. Given that there was ongoing concern over Hall's health, the panel was a kind of oral Festschrift organized by Liam Rector in appreciation of Hall's wide-ranging contributions to both poetry and prose.

The principal theme of Blue's interview was the relationship of two poets living and working together. Kenyon stuck to her public dissembling about tensions in the relationship, asserting there was little discord between them and that she thought Hall understood her even when she was not very present. Hall remarked that initially they did not fight but, rather, got very polite when they differed. But Hall, who could not restrain his characteristic frankness, later modified his remarks to say that when they did fight, it was terrible. When queried about Hall's influence on her as a poet, Kenyon responded that although her poetry was very dissimilar from his, Hall and his friends, nonetheless, had a great influence on her. Without hesitation she claimed that Hall taught her to be ambitious and to accept criticism and praise with equanimity. As well, she acknowledged the importance of workshopping her poetry with Joyce Peseroff and Alice Mattison.

Continuing her interview, Blue, who was aware the public would lump husband and wife together, asked about competition between them. Hall suggested that being from different generations helped minimize their rivalry, and as they developed, people saw them more in their own right. Both Hall and Kenyon worried that it would be assumed that Hall promoted her work, but Hall indicated that since Kenyon now was successful, he could more freely argue on her behalf. Kenyon added that their visions were very distinctive.[23]

The final interview of the four, with Gross, was recorded in September, directly before Hall and Kenyon left for India for the second time. Again, a major theme was their marriage and their work, a subject that fascinated the public. The interview began with a question about Hall's health. Kenyon said she and Hall were extremely close, they lived together twenty-four hours a day, and she would be devasted to lose her "pal." When Gross asked if there was friction between them, Kenyon replied, "Sometimes," while Hall answered, "No." Both admitted to being depressed and said that somehow when one was ill, the other rose to the occasion, to help the weak one. When Gross queried them about differences in their poetry, Kenyon offered the example of their war poems. She called hers a woman's poem, personal, inward, and grief-stricken, and his a man's poem, public and political. Hall graciously credited her with writing the better poem and opined that his poem was noisy, sarcastic, ironic, and bombastic. Gross asked in closing whether they knew if their work was good. Both admitted to uncertainty about it and that the conviction that one is doing good work comes and goes. Kenyon insisted that despite those feelings, both of them shared an ever-present drive: "But the thing that does not come and go, the thing that remains constant for both of us is the desire to really make art, and to embody the truth and to make something beautiful, and to make something that really makes people's lives better and gives them deeper understanding of their own existence and great joy because of beauty. That desire never goes no matter how depressed I am about what I've been writing lately or not writing. I still have that desire and I know in Don too it is very strong."[24] Kenyon and Hall shared "the third thing," a commitment to poetry.

19

DECIDING TO LIVE

> We asked ourselves, "Should we not go to
> India because something might happen?
> I might get sick again, or he might get sick
> again, or his mother might die." And,
> you know, I guess we just decided to live.
> —Jane Kenyon

A return to India must have raised concerns. It was only a little more than
a year since Hall's second surgery. Could they endure the rigors of a three-
week schedule of lectures, seminars, readings, interviews, official lun-
cheons, and meetings with faculty, students, and others every day? Could
they withstand flying from one city to another, being hosted by different
guides in every place? The deteriorating health of Lucy Hall also weighed
against going. But they rejected having lives dominated by these fears and
decided to seize the opportunity to visit India again. They began to prepare
lectures and select readings.

Directly after the NPR interview with Terry Gross, Hall and Kenyon left
for the airport and were on their way to the subcontinent. Polly agreed to
live in the farmhouse for the three weeks they were away to care for the dog
and cat, Gus and Ada. Their schedule in India was punishing, as expected,
and it required them to visit many major cities, including Bombay, New
Delhi, Madras, Pondicherry, Gujarat, Ahmedabad, and Trivandrum, the
capital of Kerala. In her 1993 India journal, Kenyon records that they visited
Gandhi's ashram in Ahmedabad, and they also included the ashram of the

poet-philosopher Sri Aurobindo in Pondicherry.[1] While in Pondicherry, Kenyon purchased a white salwar kameez, the typical attire of the Punjab, and at some point, she also bought a large bronze statue of Ganesh, the elephant-headed Hindu god and patron of authors. In their travel they reconnected with Indian nationals whom they had met during their previous trip, one would suspect including some of the Indian women who were working with Kenyon to produce an anthology of their writing.[2] Events in Kenyon's life would soon make this effort impossible, and the volume never materialized.

Apparently, some of their seminars were repeats of those given during their first trip, but Kenyon specifically mentions a new one she gave to academics and journalists on spirituality in contemporary American poetry.[3] She claimed it was a difficult presentation, and she was glad when it was over.[4] There is no indication that this second trip to India helped her to resolve any of the questions raised in her poem "Woman, Why Are You Weeping?" such as her personal belief and the role of institutional religion.

In the fall both *Constance*, which was dedicated to Hall, and *The Museum of Clear Ideas*, which was dedicated to Kenyon, were released.[5] The dedication of her book reads, "Perkins, ever for Perkins," but she also mentioned perpetual thanks to Alice Mattison and Joyce Peseroff.[6] *Constance* was Kenyon's shortest volume, containing a mere twenty-eight poems, all written after the publication of *Let Evening Come* in 1990. This had been a period of great suffering when depression substantially impaired her productivity. But the poems in *Constance* were some of her most important, the centerpiece of which was "Having It Out with Melancholy," which had been written earlier but now published in this volume. In *The Boat of Quiet Hours* and *Let Evening Come*, Kenyon had tried to "write around" her depression, but it was an enormous presence in her life, and she was "tired of lying."[7] Consequently, in *Constance* she confronted her depression directly and frankly. She did so because she hoped to help others who suffered. She quipped, "At least it's good for something besides just washing my dirty laundry in public."[8] She believed that if her efforts were merely personal, she would be wasting her time.[9]

The cover of *Constance* features a reproduction of the 1896 painting by the American artist Albert Pinkham Ryder, *Constance*, which Kenyon had seen in the Museum of Fine Arts in Boston. The painting depicts a stormy sea, an ominous sky, and a small boat with figures of a mother and child.

This threatening scene set the tone for what critics would call Kenyon's "dark" poems. Although in this volume she deals with her father's death, her own depression, and fear for the life of her husband, to call *Constance* a book of "dark" poems is too simplistic. It is best described as containing poems of both trust and doubt. The reader is immediately alerted to this complexity by the opening epigraph, a fragment from Psalm 139. In part it reads:

> O Lord, thou hast searched me.
> Whither shall I go from thy spirit?
> or whither shall I flee from thy presence?
> If I ascend up into heaven, thou art there:
> if I make my bed in hell, behold, thou art there. . . .
> Yea, darkness hideth not from thee;
> but the night shineth as the day. . . .
> the darkness and the light are both alike to thee.

In an interview, Kenyon acknowledges that the poems of *Constance* are dark, but she nuances this with a distinctly religious explanation of the meaning of the book's poetry as framed by the psalm: "The psalmist says, darkness and light, it's all the same. It's all from God. It's all in God, through God, with God. There is no place I can go where Your love does not pursue me. The poems in this book are very dark, and many of them I can't read without weeping."[10]

The opening psalm is followed by "August Rain, after Haying," a poem in which Kenyon confesses she "thirsts" for she knows not what. The emotional complexity of these poems is part of her genius. What she offers is not the consolation of belief but, rather, a response of trust in the givenness of life and the gift of the present moment.[11] Poetry, beautiful in image and language, is a priestly offering that mediates between hope and despair. Her poems of depression are universalized so that they could be entered into by others; some readers will be helped to understand depression, and others will feel companionship as they suffer. The poems are not an expression of self-pity but, rather, a gift to readers. In *Constance* Kenyon was in her métier as a poet.

Even in their darkness, these poems announce a regenerative force. This does not mean that suffering is escaped. Suffering is ubiquitous, causing one to doubt, but then ordinary life becomes a refuge. "Having It Out with

Melancholy" affirms this final gift. The poem opens as a battle between depression and the drugs that control but do not permanently defeat desolation. The "Unholy Ghost" will come again, but relief is given when Kenyon hears the "wild, complex song" of the wood thrush, and she is "overcome / by ordinary contentment." The unspoken teaching of Kenyon's poetry is that the joy in the given moment must be grasped. One must choose to live.

Constance contains poems of memory. "The Stroller" recalls her young life with her father, and "The Argument" shows how the smell of smoke triggers memories of her grandmother's vengeful god and the condemnation she might receive. She recalls in "In Memory of Jack" and "Moving the Frame" how she rushed to her beloved pastor as he lay dying and how she kept his memory alive. In "Litter" she reveals memories of her mother-in-law, Lucy, as Kenyon uncovers the detritus of her sick room, and in "Chrysanthemums" she recalls how she administers her husband's morphine while the smells of the flowers mix with hospital odors.

In the section "Peonies at Dusk" are poems of depression in which Kenyon remembers confronting days and nights of endless desolation in "Insomnia at the Solstice," and in "Back" she reveals how with the help of new drugs, she returns to life. Some of the poems in Constance focus on a new, less-autobiographical subject matter and are written in the third person. Two are antiwar poems; "Three Small Oranges" is about the first Gulf War, and "Gettysburg: July 1, 1863" addresses the Civil War. "Sleepers in Jaipur" treats poverty in India, and "Potato" contends with hunger and the inequity of food availability.

Finally, there are poems that speak to Kenyon's craft. "A Portion of History" illustrates how smells and sounds are the stimulus for poetic creation, and "Peonies at Dusk" demonstrates how scent and light prompt the poet to respond to the luxuriance of these flowers. But Kenyon's talent is revealed most prominently in her acclaimed "Having It Out with Melancholy" and in the volume's last three poems, "Pharaoh," "Otherwise," and "Notes from the Other Side," each written quickly and immediately prior to submitting her manuscript. These poems form a meditative triptych introduced with a stanza from a Shaker hymn. Although Kenyon was familiar with the several Shaker communities in New Hampshire, the selected stanza was probably chosen because it relates both to Psalm 139, in which an all-knowing God guides and holds the sufferer, and to The Boat of Quiet Hours, where the "little boat" guides "beyond this vale of sorrow." The Shaker stanza reads:

Watch ye, watch ye
and be ready to meet me,
for lo, I come at noonday.
Fear ye not, fear ye not
for with my hand I will lead you on,
and safely I'll guide your little boat
beyond this vale of sorrow.[12]

This borrowed stanza introduces "Pharaoh" and "Otherwise," poems of loss and acknowledgment of death, and the more hopeful "Notes from the Other Side." It is noteworthy that *Constance*, which begins with the consolation of Psalm 139, ends with "Notes from the Other Side," a poem where the "vale of soul-making" ceases, and mercy and light prevail.

Poets and literary critics have agreed that *Constance* contains some of Kenyon's best poetry. Poet and editor David Barber praised these poems as immediate, solemn, economic, and direct but was critical of how their calm veneer covers over thorny, unresolved questions. He argues that "Pharaoh" is the single most memorable of these poems and that Kenyon's honesty and clarity are not merely virtues but powers.[13] Kenyon's friend and poet Marie Howe comments that these poems are about ordinary "messy," "tragic," and "sweet" life and that Kenyon's "soul" is in constant relationship with the "soul" of the world. She acknowledges that Kenyon focuses on the "minute particular" and has an abiding love of the world and the creatures in it. She sees Kenyon as a "spiritual poet with a Christian heart," but she is also faith's antithesis, a poet of despair. Howe contends that the poems of *Constance* are free of self-pity, yet they are the most painful of Kenyon's corpus.[14] Todd Davis and Kenneth Womack, critiquing *Constance* and several other of her volumes, point out that while faith played an important stimulus in Kenyon's approach to living, hers is a complex and difficult faith. God's presence is not obvious in the world, hence, her searching. The power of her poetry derives from her honesty, which acknowledges that joy and pain are intertwined. In *Constance* she expresses doubt and fear that the words of Psalm 139 cannot eliminate. These seeming contradictions are not overcome by abstract theology but by the experience of everyday life that gives relief from pain.[15]

Once Kenyon and Hall returned from India in mid-September, they were regularly busy promoting their new books. They gave readings and did book signings in Kansas, Chicago, Minneapolis, Des Moines, Iowa City, Miami, and in venues in New Hampshire. Hall relished this whirlwind of activity, but Kenyon complained they were too busy. Of course, they took pleasure in being with friends. Prior to Christmas they visited Wendell and Tanya Berry, with whom they had begun the year. Wes and Diane McNair; Liam Rector and Tree Swenson; Joyce Peseroff and her husband, Jeff White; Joy Harjo; Phil Levine; Dan and Pat Ellsberg; and Andrew and Philippa and their families all came to visit. Kenyon and Hall saw Polly and Lucy regularly and attended cultural and church events. By Christmas Kenyon was exhausted.[16]

Because they had a major commitment in mid-January for which they had to prepare, there was no time to rest. They had been invited to participate in the first residency program of the Bennington Writing Seminars in Vermont, founded by Rector. Part of the requirement for the program was a ten-day on-campus residence for students. Both Kenyon and Hall were committed to be there for five days during which time they each would give lectures, mingle with students, and attend student readings. Kenyon was nervous about the lectures, but she wrote to Alice Mattison that this opportunity would "turn me back to all my dears—Keats, Bishop and Akhmatova."[17]

FIGURE 13. Jane Kenyon and Victoria Clausi at Bennington College, 1994 Courtesy of Cynthia Locklin.

At the residency Kenyon would sit by the fireplace in the afternoon and read her poems aloud for any students who gathered. In a large classroom with elevated seating, she gave her lectures; Hall was excluded, and the lectures were not taped. Her commitment was to give three lectures on her muses. She said she considered Keats a proponent of the "fuck and die school of poetry," of which she counted herself a member.[18] Her presentations on Keats and Elizabeth Bishop were not lectures per se but readings of their poetry with her commentary. The presentation on Akhmatova was more formal, including a discussion of translation and the importance of image. What came across was Kenyon's spiritual depth and her accessibility. Her demeanor was calm and her manner generous and unpretentious. She authentically listened when others spoke.[19] Rector claimed she could make silence speak; he called her a "walking Quaker meeting."[20]

As the busiest year ended, Kenyon and Hall looked forward to 1994. They had decided to live, and that decision had rewarded them. But the decision would be open to her for only a few more years.

20
ANNUS HORRIBILIS

But there is something in me that will not
be snuffed out even by this awful disease.
—Jane Kenyon

Their participation in the Bennington Writing Seminars residency was a great success, but Hall and Kenyon were delighted to return home after the previous busy months. Kenyon developed some flu-like symptoms on their return, but she soon recovered. She had no inkling that the "awful disease," her depression, would be replaced by something more lethal.

At the end of January 1994, Hall was off to do a reading and lecture in Charleston, South Carolina, when he learned that Kenyon had a severe nosebleed and was admitted to the Dartmouth-Hitchcock Hospital. She remained there for a month while Hall stayed in a nearby motel, and Polly again moved into the farmhouse to care for the animals. After many tests, transfusions, and chemotherapy administered from an IV pole Kenyon called "Igor," she was diagnosed with acute lymphoblastic leukemia. Initially, chemotherapy brought the leukemia into remission, but it soon returned. Her disease involved a fusion of chromosomes into so-called Philadelphia chromosomes, which had a particularly poor prognosis, and chemotherapy could not guarantee against a relapse. The only course of action that had any realistic hope was a bone-marrow transplant (a technology still in its infancy in 1994) to replace the bone marrow that was producing the deformed cells. Reuel was tested, but his bone marrow was not a match, and so the search began for a donor through the National Marrow Donor Program. During this period, Kenyon was precluded from taking her depression medications.

When friends learned of the diagnosis, they were horrified. Alice Mattison called Joyce Peseroff to tell her; Peseroff said it was "like hitting her with a board."[1] Other friends were riddled with concern, too. Liam Rector and Tree Swenson came to visit, as did Wendell and Tanya Berry and Galway Kinnell. Mattison and Peseroff were in frequent contact and visited as they could. Kenyon's minister, Alice Ling, came several times and brought Communion. Kenyon gave Ling a quotation from Thomas Merton's *Thoughts in Solitude*. Like Psalm 139, Merton's words reflect the deeply religious sensibility Kenyon was bringing to her suffering:

> My Lord God, I have no idea where I am going.
> I do not see the road ahead of me. I cannot know
> for certain where it will end. Nor do I really know
> myself, and the fact that I think I am following
> your will does not mean that I am actually doing so.
> But I believe that the desire to please you does in
> fact please you. And I hope I have that desire in all
> that I am doing. I hope that I will never do anything
> apart from that desire. And I know that if I do this
> you will lead me by the right road though I may know
> nothing about it. Therefore I will trust you always
> though I may seem to be lost and in the shadow
> of death. I will not fear, for you are ever with me,
> and you will never leave me to face my perils alone.[2]

If Kenyon's diagnosis was not a sufficient assault on Hall's and Kenyon's well-being, Lucy Hall, now age ninety and living in a nursing home, died in March. They received a call at four a.m., and Hall raced off to be with his dying mother; he did not reach her in time. This death had an impact beyond the expected death of a failing mother; it was a huge loss for Hall. Lucy, a widow of many years, played an outsized role in her son's psyche and, hence, in their lives. Confronting her death, he distracted himself by planning her memorial service in Wilmot and a June burial in Connecticut and by calling a realtor. Kenyon wrote four poems about her mother-in-law's death. In "The Call" she details Hall's racing to be at his mother's bedside, and in "How Like the Sound" she describes his weeping big, hot tears. "In

the Nursing Home" creates an image of Lucy as a grazing racehorse awaiting a return to the security of the stables and ends with the plea, "Master,
come with your light / halter. Come and bring her in." "Eating the Cookies"
was a poem of grieving in which Kenyon recounts emptying Lucy's room
of debris and ritually eating a cookie after each stage in the process.[3] What
was most revealing, however, was Hall's poem, "Song for Lucy,"[4] in which
he depicts his mother's adulation of him as her only child. When his father
died at age forty-two, Hall became the center of his mother's attention and
admiration. As a Freudian, he resonated with the claim that a man would
thrive if in childhood he received his mother's complete devotion. Hall
concludes his paean with the words, "Love was her enterprise." "Song for
Lucy" goes a long way in explaining both Hall's emotional neediness and
his relationship with Kenyon. As he craved his mother's entire affection,
he also needed his wife's. He created the myth of their mutual devotion,
and Kenyon did not publicly challenge it.

While convalescing from her chemotherapy treatment, Kenyon con-
tracted pneumonia, and one of her medications, Prednisone, made her
body and face puffy, and chemotherapy rendered her bald. She recoiled from
what she encountered in the mirror. With greatly diminished energy, she
could only devote a minimal amount of time to writing. Hall had to take
up house chores, which exhausted him.

As soon as *Constance* had gone to press, Kenyon began working on new
poems. Six of these were published in magazines, but fourteen others were
unpublished and stashed in her study; Hall had not seen them. They are
wide-ranging, but except for "Spring Evening" there were no nature themes
among them. Two of her best poems of this period were "Happiness" and
"Mosaic of the Nativity: Serbia, Winter 1993."[5] Happiness, like the prodi-
gal son, turns up unexplained, but happiness is available to everyone and
everything. Kenyon uses the repetition of a litany:

> It comes to the monk in his cell.
> It comes to the woman sweeping the street. . . .
> to the child
> whose mother has passed out from drink.
> It comes to the lover. . . . and to the clerk stacking cans of carrots
> in the night.

It comes even to the boulder, the rain, and the wine glass. Happiness is
being what a thing is. The poem is provocative, arresting, and optimistic.

But as always Kenyon recognizes the dark side of the human condition. "Mosaic of the Nativity," about the brutal Bosnian war, depicts a God who made everything for his joy, but the descendants of Cain are free to do evil by bombing the infirmary and the communal well. Ultimately, God shares that suffering in creating Mary, who births the Christ, who then suffers with humans.

Remarkably, in the midst of her own suffering, she wrote one of her most beautiful and pleasure-intoxicated poems, "Dutch Interiors."[6] It is dedicated to Caroline Finkelstein, who shared a love of the visual arts and with whom Kenyon often visited the Boston Museum of Fine Arts. The poem opens with a reflection on how in the art of "the cold reaches of northern Europe," "Christ has been done to death" "a thousand, thousand times," but of the domestic scenes in Dutch paintings, of cheese, the spaniel, the yellow dressing gown, she asks,

> Now tell me that the Holy Ghost
> does not reside in the play of light
> on cutlery!

For Kenyon, the realm of the ordinary is not only pleasurable but sacramental. Commenting on this poem, Finkelstein calls Kenyon a "beacon" who illuminated every painting and showed her things she never would have seen herself.[7]

The trilogy of poems "Man Eating," "Man Waking," and "Man Sleeping" focuses on paying complete attention, desiring darkness, and recognizing the evil of homelessness, respectively. "Surprise" is a poem of betrayal, and "No" a poem of fear of death, probably about the burial of Lucy Hall. A particularly revelatory poem, "Reading Aloud to My Father,"[8] was written years after her father's death and serves as testimony of his role in his daughter's psyche. It contains her quarrel with poet Vladimir Nabokov about her belief that life itself is the abyss.[9] Another kind of darkness is captured in "The Way Things Are in Franklin," in which Kenyon describes the decline of the town of Franklin, New Hampshire, as businesses and social life depart, leaving a dreary world behind.[10]

Finally, "Afternoon at MacDowell" harkens back to Hall and Kenyon's visit to this artist colony soon after his second surgery. In the poem Kenyon attests to art's power but fears it cannot save Hall from death.[11] As they waited for a bone-marrow match for Kenyon, they tried to live a normal, albeit slower, life. She received a new leukemia medication, Cytarabine, which gave her additional energy, and in April they celebrated their twenty-second wedding anniversary. Hall gave her a ring of pink tourmaline surrounded by nine small diamonds. She named it, "Please don't die."

Amid all these medical issues Kenyon must have been heartened by the proposal from the new editor of Graywolf Press, Fiona McCrae, encouraging her to publish a new and selected book of poems. But the happiest moment may have been when she learned in May that she had been awarded the biennial PEN/Voelcker Award for Poetry given to "one for whom the exceptional promise seen in earlier work has been fulfilled and who continues to mature with each successive volume of poetry." This award, given by PEN International, brought with it a prize of $5,000. It was Mattison who nominated her for the award, and members of the award committee, Robert Creeley, Amy Clampitt, Philip Levine, Lucille Clifton, and Anthony Hecht, affirmed the nomination. Because Kenyon did not have the energy to travel to accept this honor, she asked her friend Jean Valentine to do so in her stead.

Mattison was particularly ravaged by grief over Kenyon's condition and in her phone calls kept repeating, "You are going to live." Kenyon asked her to put these words in a cross-stitch, which she subsequently hung over the painted bed.[12] Her old friend and poet Hayden Carruth, a fellow depressive, began writing a series of fifty letters to cheer her. In these tender and loving missives, Carruth wrote about ordinary life, the weather, flora, and fauna, avoiding direct discussion of her illness. He reminded her that previously her will and desire brought her through difficult times, and they would do so again.[13]

Hall was beside himself with worry. Motivated by a desire to protect his wife's limited energy and probably also to possess her more for himself, he greatly restricted access to her. This was particularly aggravating to Mattison, who complained that six trips to visit her friend had been postponed. She told Hall he was "hogging" his wife. He laughed.[14] Mattison continued to call and write, expressing how much she loved Kenyon, wanted to be with her, and dreamed about her. Peseroff and Finkelstein called and wrote frequently, as well.

As they waited for a bone marrow match to be found, Hall began a new poem, "Her Long Illness."[15] It was written in the third person to objectify the situation and in the present tense, later to be changed to the past. The absence of punctuation was meant to convey how one day faded into the next. After seven months of waiting, a female marrow donor was found, and Hall and Kenyon prepared to leave for the Fred C. Hutchinson Cancer Research Center in Seattle, Washington, a premier hospital for the new bone-marrow-transplant therapy. This hopeful development was immediately dimmed when Polly was diagnosed with lung cancer, as her husband had been years before. Because it was a wrenching decision to leave her behind, they planned to bring her to Seattle for treatment once they were settled. Meanwhile, their friend Mary Lyn Ray would be Polly's caretaker. Hall writes of their departure at 5:30 a.m. on a Sunday in late October. They hugged, wept, said good-bye to the ailing Polly, and left, hoping against hope for "continuing life."[16]

Kenyon would endure one hundred days of sequestration, first in isolation in the hospital and then as an out-patient in their apartment on Spring Street, a block and a half from the hospital. She remained hopeful that leukemia, this "awful disease," would not "snuff her out."

21
"PLEASE DON'T DIE"

Our job is to love, and work, and to cause no harm.
—Jane Kenyon

"To love and work and to cause no harm" was Kenyon's credo, but it was swallowed up by one in which her total effort was now directed toward surviving this new menace of leukemia. Lamentably, it is difficult to know her own reflection on how she responded psychologically to this life-threatening period. With few exceptions, there are no poems, letters, interviews, or journal entries by her for these last months of her life. The principal details of her stay in Seattle both in the hospital and as an outpatient in the apartment on Spring Street are provided by Hall.[1] He wrote and spoke extensively about this time both in print and in interviews after her death. Unsurprisingly, it was a miserable time for both of them. Hope was thin and fear dominant. Her work was to fight for her life. She did not want to die, and Hall feared that his cancer might recur, and he would be unable to care for her.

They flew to Seattle at the end of October 1994, and Kenyon entered the hospital known as the "Hutch." Hall set up life in their nearby apartment. Kenyon was apprehensive about the transplant procedure, which involved chemotherapy delivered through a catheter, the destruction of her bone marrow, and the infusion of the marrow of the donor. When Hall visited her in the hospital, he was required to be garbed in gown, mask, booties, and gloves. Her treatment caused immune-system weakness, and to ensure she remained free of infection, he could not touch her. As she waited for infusion day, she received calls and letters from friends, including her pastor Alice Ling. Ling would call, read her prayers she had written, and then send them on to her by mail. One of Ling's prayers survived; it must have given Kenyon comfort in her plastic, tube-riddled world:

> As all else is stripped away, you come close. Never one
> to be told where you cannot go, Ever-Present God, you
> cross the line, coming close and holding me tight. You
> sing your songs to me and rock me in the warmth of
> your embrace. You reach through the plastic and join our
> hands as you long ago intertwined our hearts. As the
> bone marrow drips into my bones, you seep into my soul.
> O God, the Source of all Healing, take my hand and hold my
> heart and walk with me through all the days that lie ahead.
> Be my hope and lead me out of sterility and back into Life.
> In the name of Jesus, who showed us the depths of your
> love and the endlessness of your life. Amen.[2]

After the bone marrow transfer on November 18, Kenyon's pain was severe, and she was given a morphine drip. Her mouth sores precluded her from eating much, and she frequently vomited what she did consume. After a few weeks and supported by a walker, she could walk in the hospital halls, but she was very weak and tired easily. Hall would visit every day, bring her clean clothes, eat in the hospital cafeteria, and attend classes to learn how to care for her as an outpatient to their apartment. As always, he continued to write. In this case he worked on two poems, "Without" and "Her Long Illness."

Kenyon's depression intensified when she learned that her mother's cancer had spread to her other lung. Polly's chemotherapy and radiation treatments would end, and this meant that their plan to bring her to Seattle to continue treatment was no longer possible. Her mother was dying.

Weak and depressed, Kenyon was discharged from the hospital to their apartment on December 20, right before the Christmas holiday. To bring some cheer to their lives, Hall purchased a plastic Christmas tree, and she strung it with tiny lights and decorated it with paper ornaments Philippa's children made. He read the Christmas story from Scripture, and on Christmas morning they exchanged gifts. Liam Rector and Tree Swenson visited, but their time together was marred by Kenyon's constant vomiting. Her sumptuous Christmas dinner consisted of applesauce, Ensure, and a bit of bread with jelly.

This tiny glimmer of Christmas joy ended and was replaced by both routine and calamity. They lived leukemia night and day for months. There was the daily schedule of pills, temperature taking, and tube cleaning. Hall managed her regimen of twenty medications. Hospital personnel visited every day to draw blood, monitor vital signs, and help with showering. The frequent visits to the hospital involved arduous preparation and effort.

The side effects she experienced were typical. She lost weight, was weak, became bald from the chemotherapy, and had bone pain and constant nausea. She got shingles and had a temporary bout of diabetes that required insulin. She slept for hours and when awake would stare into space. Her ability to think and remember diminished. When asked the name of the president or where she was, she was unable to recall. Neuropathy affected her hands and feet, and her mouth sores and difficulty swallowing made eating complicated. At times she was incontinent and lost control of her bowels. According to Hall, she questioned why she had put herself through this agony and whether these therapies would help her live. All this colored Hall's life, and he had nightmares and trouble sleeping. As they could, friends kept in touch by phone and letter. Mattison, Peseroff, and Finkelstein were particularly faithful, calling once a week, and Mary Lyn Ray kept them appraised of Polly's condition. Hall answered the phone and opened and read her letters, ensuring Kenyon had little direct contact with friends, although occasionally she would write a postcard or respond to a brief phone call. When asked how she was doing, she would answer, "I'm doing."[3]

Her anxiety about her mother deepened. Although she was three thousand miles away and unable to help her, she must have been comforted by the fact that Polly was well cared for. Kenyon called her mother twice a day. In late January news came that Polly had died. Kenyon said she wanted to die, too, so she could be with her mother. Hall immediately made arrangement for Polly's cremation. Later, her ashes were scattered in Eagle Pond as her husband's had been years earlier.

Good news arrived at year's beginning. Governor Stephen Merrill named Kenyon to a five-year term as poet laureate of New Hampshire.[4] But even this honor did not cheer her. Hall convinced her not to decline the position, even though she lacked the capacity to fill the role. He took over in her stead. He knew what the position entailed, having previously served as the state's poet laureate himself.

Kenyon's treatment inflicted psychological as well as physical maladies. Some of her myriad drugs made her fearful. At one point she believed Hall, who had frequent episodes of vertigo, was having a heart attack. She called the hospital, and medics rushed in. After checking his heart and blood pressure, they convinced her he was fine and was going to live. Her fears also led to a psychotic break and admission to the psychiatric ward of the hospital. She was convinced that she did not have leukemia and that the insurance company would discover this and expropriate Eagle Pond Farm. She insisted she was a "wicked" person. Ultimately, she was released from the psychiatric ward and was without any memory of the episode.

By late February she was discharged to return home; they had spent 124 days in Seattle. Medical opinion was that if a patient survived with no relapse during a 100-day period, chances of survival were good. She was to continue to be monitored locally in New Hampshire. Her doctors and nurses in Seattle, especially her hematologist, Kris Doney, had grown fond of Kenyon, and she and other hospital workers all bid her good-bye and God-speed. The apartment was packed up, and Hall and Kenyon readied for their departure on February 24. Jubilant family and friends awaited them with placards at New Hampshire's Manchester Airport. Wearily, they returned to the farmhouse, where the ever-enthusiastic Gus greeted them. As they unpacked, they encountered the possessions of the newly deceased Polly. Two days later they attended church, where congregants cheered them. In the afternoon Philippa and her family came to visit. In her profoundly weakened condition, Kenyon was hoping to live.

22
FALLING INTO LIGHT

I believe in the miracles of art, but what
prodigy will keep you safe beside me.
—Jane Kenyon

Returning home provided a sense of normalcy. The hope was that within
a year or two Kenyon would be able to drive, to work in the garden, and
to write for long stretches of time. Her intent now was to stay well, gain
weight, get physically strong, and enjoy what she could. But at this point
she was weak and needed a bevy of assistants to help life go on. A nursing
assistant gave daily baths, physical and occupational therapists worked to
restore her health, and a cleaning woman brought order to the house. Hall
shopped, cooked, walked Gus, and fed the birds, but because he was not a
gardener, preparation for spring planting did not happen. He was not much
interested in gardening.[1]

By early March, although thin and bald, she was able to go for short
walks and to visit with a few friends. But an attack of severe abdominal
pain brought her back to the hospital, where it was discovered she had gall-
stones, a side effect of her leukemia treatment. To reduce the possibility of
infection, laparoscopy surgery was done. Weakness, fatigue, and isolation
continued. As she observed the world around her, she conceived her last
poem, "The Sick Wife."[2] Because her deformed fingers made her incapable of
writing, this poem was dictated to a neighbor who cared for her while Hall
was away for a day. Written in the third person, the poem captures a sense

of dependence and isolation as it describes the quick movements, energy, and freedom of those who were not infirm. While the poem is neither bitter nor angry, it is unremittingly sad and loveless, illustrating the emotional emptiness of an ill woman's condition.

Kenyon's condition was monitored by her biweekly blood tests at the Dartmouth-Hitchcock Hospital, where her hematologist, Letha Mills, and the hospital nurses welcomed her. Up through early April the tests gave her hope that her leukemia was in permanent remission, but then the April 11 test proved otherwise. Mills brought Kenyon and Hall into her office to announce that the leukemia had returned. She surmised Kenyon had perhaps a month to live. They were devastated; Hall wept, but Jane asked only if she could die at home. When they returned to the farmhouse, they gathered all her medications and disposed of them. Nothing more could be done.

The following day Hall began to inform family and friends of Jane's situation. They were grief-stricken and made plans to visit, although Hall again restricted visits to twenty minutes. Philippa and Andrew; Mattison and her husband, Edward; Peseroff and her husband, Jeff White; Rector and Swenson; Mary Lyn Ray; Reuel Kenyon; Caroline Finkelstein; and Drs. Mills and Solow came to say good-bye. Kirby Hall sent a letter thanking Kenyon for her kindness to her children, Andrew and Philippa.[3] Many wept. Friends sent flowers, but Jane did not want them near her. Still others brought food, which helped sustain Hall. When Alice Ling was with them, they experienced grace. Otherwise, grace seemed absent from their lives.

They filled their days with reminiscing about their travels, swimming in the pond, playing ping pong, walking Gus, reading aloud, discussing poetry, and lovemaking. April 17 was their twenty-third wedding anniversary, which they knew would be their last. Hall recorded her saying, "Dying is simple. . . . What's worse is . . . the *separation*."[4]

For long hours she would lie in the painted bed with its tiny Christmas lights draped over the headboard and the cross-stitch plaque, "You Are Going to Live," on the wall above. Her only medication now was a morphine drip to ease pain. Sometimes she could rally strength to address an end-of-life concern. They worked on her obituary, which she wanted to include mention of her Guggenheim Award. They discussed the funeral program and the hymns and poems to be read. They addressed the distribution of her small estate among Reuel, Philippa, Andrew, and Hall, and her request that her papers be deposited at the University of New Hampshire, where Hall's archive was housed. Hall would ultimately curate her papers, deciding what would be retained and what discarded. Her burial place would be near a small stand of birch trees at the nearby Proctor Cemetery, where they had purchased a double plot years before, a sign that they had "married this place." Hall suggested that when dear Gus died, his remains might be scattered on her grave; Jane replied that it would be good for any bulbs planted there. The following year Geoffrey Hill and Alice Goodman, to honor their friendship with Jane, planted bulbs at her grave, and when Gus died in 2000, Hall kept his word. Gus joined his beloved Jane, and Ada joined them a few years later.

Kenyon insisted that she wanted to work on the final collection of new and selected poems Graywolf proposed; Hall suggested it be called *Otherwise*.[5] They created a collection that would include twenty new poems and 154 poems from her earlier books. Mattison and Peseroff, her intimate friends who helped make her the poet she had become, were asked to approve the selections. Doing this work gave Kenyon a moment of joy; she exclaimed, "Wasn't that fun?" and repeated it again. She asked that the new poems that had not yet appeared in print be sent to the *New Yorker*, *Atlantic*, *Poetry*, and *Harvard Magazine*. A remaining issue was whether "The Sick Wife" should be included. Finally, Kenyon agreed that it be included as an "unfinished" poem. The inclusion of "Woman, Why Are You Weeping?" was not discussed, and it was not included. After her death Hall, Mattison, Peseroff, and Gregory Orr unanimously agreed to include it in a posthumous publication; making it available would not be able to hurt her.[6]

During Swenson's final visit, she helped Kenyon select a painting for the cover of *Otherwise*, a kitchen-garden scene, *Le mur du jardin potager, Yerres*, by Gustave Caillebotte.[7] Using this painting Swenson designed the cover and again used Kenyon's preferred Bembo typeface. Because it was put together quickly, *Otherwise* did not have the unity of her previous volumes, and it also had no dedication.

Gradually Jane became weaker; she was unable to speak, and her breathing became labored. She had told Hall earlier that in dying she did not fear punishment, but she did not speak of paradise or life on the other side, either. Hall thought that she received no consolation from her continuing belief in God.[8] Her work now was to finally let go, she "must fall, glad at last to have fallen."[9] Writing had been Hall's way of staving off despair, and as he stayed beside her, he wrote primarily about what was happening inside himself.[10] As she requested, he held her hand as she died on the morning of Saturday, April 22, 1995. Reuel had flown in from Ann Arbor, and at the time of her death he was out walking Gus. He said he heard her call his name.[11]

The following day the *Concord Monitor* carried her obituary, and by Monday it was printed in the *Boston Globe, New York Times, Washington Post, Philadelphia Inquirer,* and newspapers in Texas and California. Governor Stephen Merrill designated April 25 a day to remember Jane Kenyon's life and achievement in New Hampshire.

The open-casket viewing was set for Tuesday at Chadwick's Funeral Home in New London, New Hampshire. Lucy Hall's viewing had been held there the previous year, and Hall's grandmother Kate had been laid out at Chadwick's in 1975. Jane was clothed in the white salwar kameez she had purchased in Pondicherry, and an Indian scarf was draped over her shoulder. She had decided not to wear her wig. Her pink tourmaline ring, the "Please Don't Die" ring, was removed before burial and given to Philippa.

The funeral service was scheduled for Wednesday, April 26, at the South Danbury Church.[12] As it turned out it was a beautiful day, breezy and bright. Although the church could comfortably hold only about ninety people, by 2 p.m., it was packed with two hundred friends, neighbors, and fellow writers. A hundred others listened to the service over the loudspeaker in the churchyard. Among the writers attending were Robert Bly, Louis Simpson, Frank Bidart, Geoffrey Hill, Caroline Finkelstein, Wesley McNair, Charles Simic, Gregory Orr, Ellen Bryan Voight, Sharon Olds, Galway Kinnell, Robert Pinsky, Liam Rector, and, of course, Alice Mattison and Joyce Peseroff, who served with others as pallbearers. Mike Pride, Tree Swenson, and Mary Lyn Ray were also in attendance. Kenyon's doctors, Letha Mills and Kris Doney, who flew in from Seattle, also were there.

Alice Ling presided and offered reflections and prayers. It was a tender service. Rector read "Let Evening Come" and "Otherwise." Psalm 139 was read, and those gathered sang three heart-rending hymns: "Love Divine All Love Excelling," "Come Thou Fount of Every Blessing," and "Abide with Me." Holding back tears, Ling sang "Amazing Grace" a cappella. On the cover of the program was a photograph of Kenyon taken by William Abramowicz at the Dodge Poetry Festival a few years earlier. After the service, about two hundred people repaired to the Proctor Cemetery, lining two miles of the road with cars. Ling offered prayers as the coffin was placed in the earth. Kenyon's *Amor Mundi* had ended. The ever-spontaneous Bly began to sing "Amazing Grace," and others joined in. Ultimately, a black granite gravestone would be placed there with the inscription she wrote when Hall was ill, but now there was no prodigy to keep him safe. At Hall's death, his name would be added.

After the interment, everyone was invited to Eagle Pond Farmhouse for coffee and cake provided by neighbors and church friends. People spilled out of the house onto the lawn. It was April, and hundreds of daffodils planted by Jane long ago were in full bloom. Finally, after three hours of gathering, mourning, and reminiscing, the last guests departed. Hall was left alone to deal with the unimaginable, the absence of Jane. Before retiring, he and Gus drove the four miles back to the cemetery, and in the moonlight, he said a final good-night to his wife of twenty-three years.

THE AFTERMATH

Our marriage was close, and dread of
separation only brought us closer until it
seemed that we made a single soul.
—Donald Hall

The weeks after Kenyon's death yielded further evidence of the impact of her poetry. Fifteen hundred letters of condolence poured in. They came from friends and acquaintances, people who had heard Kenyon read, and those who loved her poetry. Hall answered all those with return addresses. To sustain a sense of her presence, he immediately gathered up photographs of her and lined the walls of his study with them, and he and Gus would visit her grave several times a day.

After her death he wrote "Weeds and Peonies," a poem centering on the changes in her garden where peonies burst out amid the unattended weeds. It speaks of his desire for her return and of how, like her peonies, she toppled.[1] The poems "Weeds and Peonies," "Her Long Illness," "Without," and "Last Days" and several letters addressed to his late wife were included in his book, *Without,* published in 1998. In these letters he speaks to her as if she were alive about cleaning out her Saab, his daily routine, his difficulty in discarding her clothes, finding the tokens of tribute on her grave, memories of Advents and Christmases past, their time in Seattle, his life now with Gus and Ada, and their experiences of lovemaking. A later volume, *The Painted Bed,* contains many poems about Kenyon, as well; it

FIGURE 14. Jane Kenyon's study,
Eagle Pond Farmhouse. Photo by
author.

opens with an epigraph from the Urdu poet Faiz: "The true subject of poetry
is the loss of the beloved."[2] For Donald Hall, the absence of Jane Kenyon
was immeasurable. A sign on her desk in her upstairs study now serves as
a reminder of his loss: "Sorry, we're closed."

In a fifteen-month period Hall endured the deaths of his wife, his mother,
and his mother-in-law. He had trouble sleeping, was besieged by nightmares, and lost twenty pounds. He claims to have screamed a lot and to
have fantasized about mowing down his audience at readings with a machine gun. He contemplated suicide and burning down the house.[3] In his
inimitable frankness the sixty-seven-year-old Hall admitted to being manic
and crazed by sexual desire. Solow intervened with medication to control
Hall's rage.[4]

At the center of his nightmares was one in which his wife had run off
with another man.[5] He explained that his outsized sexual needs and pro-
miscuity were in response to what he dreamed was Kenyon's adulterous
abandonment: "I had nightmares that she had left me for another man.
Maybe I was getting even?"[6] Two weeks after Kenyon's death he purchased
condoms.[7] He was sure that if she had outlived him, she would have taken
lovers.[8]

Ultimately, Hall was able to return to a normal life, enabled by what neighbors called "Hall's Harem," a constellation of women—Carole Colburn, housekeeper; Kendel Currier, office assistant; Pam Sanborn, trainer; and Louise Robie, postal carrier, carrying out all sorts of chores. Finally, Hall settled down with a long-term partner, Linda Kunhardt, who served as his editor, travel companion, and caregiver.[9] But he never ceased returning to his life with Jane, who remained for him the other poet who in their "double solitude" lived with him in his ancestral home, "the house of poetry," in rural New Hampshire.

Hall had unresolved, lingering questions about his and Kenyon's relationship. He worried whether her depression meant that she had not loved him as much as he loved her, but in the end, he thought she did.[10] Linked to that question was one about their intimacy. Hall confessed that their most intimate time was during her dying and admitted with shame that he would miss caring for her and her dependency on him.[11] It was this dependence that made them "a single soul."[12] It was a dependence she had struggled to break.

Finally, there was the question of their poetry. What had each contributed to the other? Kenyon credited her ambition and knowledge of the poetic craft to Hall,[13] and he admitted that his poetry improved after marrying her and moving to Wilmot. Reflecting on their life together, their friend Wesley McNair commented: "It is now clear to me, moreover, that whereas Hall's influence on the content of Kenyon's poetry was limited, Kenyon's influence on the content of his was profound. Only through his relationship with her in his ancestral farmhouse was he able to imagine the connection with Kate and Wesley Wells and their agrarian past that is essential."[14]

But Hall could not help viewing her as his dependent, his latter-day student. He recounted, "I watched in grateful pleasure as her poems became better and better,"[15] a pleasure that, while genuine, reflected pride in his teaching prowess. Gradually, as she developed her craft, she worked to create a separate identity from the poet husband, whom others assumed helped her in multiple ways. Although they worked to minimize competition, rivalry entered their relationship. He recognized that as she became more successful, his poetry deteriorated. He acknowledged that when he read "Let Evening Come," "Briefly It Enters and Briefly Speaks," "Having It Out with Melancholy," and "Twilight: After Haying," he was astounded by the "emotional abundance of her language."[16] In response he began to make his poems as unlike hers as he could.[17] He makes the extraordinary claim that it was only after her death that his poetry became as "potent" as hers: "In the months and years after her death, Jane's voice and mine rose as one, spiraling together images and diphones of the dead who were once the living. Our necropoetics of grief and love in the unforgivable absence of flesh."[18] Even in death Kenyon was bound to Hall. Her achievements were his achievements because in his mind they were a "single soul." For Hall, the myth of their oneness was irrefutable.

Kenyon's death had little impact on Hall's productivity. In the year of her death, he published two children's books and a book of essays, *Principal Products of Portugal,* which he dedicated to his doctor Don Clark. Hall went on to produce seven additional books of poetry, two of essays, three memoirs, and three children's books. He gave numerous readings and interviews and appeared five times on Garrison Keillor's *Prairie Home Companion.* In 2006 he was named Poet Laureate of the United States and in 2010 was awarded the National Medal of Arts. The achievements of the "Rockstar" of

FIGURE 15. Graves of Jane Kenyon and Donald Hall, Proctor Cemetery, Andover, New Hampshire, 2015. Photo by author.

the University of Michigan were undiminished. Donald Hall died on June 23, 2018, at the age eighty-nine. He was greatly mourned as a generous artist and respectfully honored for his diverse and prolific writing. He continued to write about Kenyon until the end. His last edited project was the slim, posthumously published *The Best Poems of Jane Kenyon*.[19]

What was the contribution of Donald Hall to the making of Jane Kenyon as a poet? She admitted that Hall taught her to be ambitious, and she was conscious that he financially supported her as she developed her craft. He introduced her to his many poet friends, and he served as her first reader and usually her sympathetic critic. He worked with her to compile her last volume, *Otherwise,* and after her death he sought continued publication of her work. Although their marriage was not the blissful relationship Hall projected, he was instrumental in making it possible for Jane Kenyon to be a poet. Nonetheless, she had to work to escape capture by his strong personality, celebrity, and needs.

24
ACCLAIM

I can't die until I have a reputation.
—Jane Kenyon

Jane Kenyon was clear: she wanted a reputation. At the time of her death, that reputation was emerging, and during subsequent decades, it expanded. The release of Moyers's "A Life Together," several late-life interviews, and the posthumous publication of *Otherwise* in 1996 worked to confirm her as an important contemporary poet. Publication of her new poems and selections from each of her previous books illustrated her development over time and raised the question of what she might have achieved had she lived. *Otherwise* sold seventy-five thousand copies, had eight editions, and was translated into Spanish. Its many reviews were uniformly positive, and the *New York Times* named it one of the notable books of 1997.[1]

In a review of *Otherwise*, poet and literary critic Adrian Oktenberg called Kenyon a "contemplative poet" who in plain language wrote gorgeous descriptions of the natural world, explored human emotions, and wrestled with Christian faith. Oktenberg claimed there was a stillness at the center of Kenyon's work and surmised that her sense of sorrow made her a poet. Her achievement was that she was able to write powerfully about both beauty and sorrow.[2] Emily Gordon in *The Nation* considered Kenyon a fearless and unsentimental poet who wrote with great generosity, even though some of her poems were mundane, and others, because of her many uses of ellipses, seemed unresolved. Her central struggle was how to reconcile her despair with the luminous realities she claimed could not be snuffed out.[3] Robert Richman rejected the notion that Kenyon's poetry could be categorized. She was not a confessional poet, as some claimed, because she transformed her experience rather than merely recapitulating it. She described what she saw in simple language and then took the reader beyond that description, transforming the particular into the "luminous and memorable."[4]

In the *New York Times*, Carol Muske commented that it is useless to compare Kenyon to other poets. Her words came from natural speech, Scriptures, and hymns, and as such her poetry was "singular psalm-like music." Muske argued that if Keats taught Kenyon anything it was the transience of all things.[5] Elizabeth Lund claimed that Kenyon's poetry was a "model of simplicity for an age that shuns adornment" and that she captured the "invisible force" underlying experience. Although seemingly calm, her poetry had a strong, unresolved "undertow" and gave evidence of what it was to struggle spiritually.[6]

A series of shorter reviews of *Otherwise* confirmed and expanded these evaluations. One notes that Kenyon was an unsentimental and honest poet, without airs, who used the language of "plainsong," paid attention to daily life, and offered images that stayed with the reader.[7] Poet Robert Hass suggested Kenyon with her plain style was like Robert Frost but more interior than he was.[8] This comparison with Frost is understandable given their pastoral subject matter and their dark meditations on universal themes. Constance Merritt noted Kenyon's ability to create an equilibrium between joy and pain and her unselfconscious use of personification, which like "the moon moves around the barn" brings Emily Dickinson to mind.[9] Another reviewer observed that Kenyon used neither rhyme nor meter but that her poems were tender and could be humorous and shockingly sexual.[10] Wes McNair saw that Kenyon's new poems were less autobiographical and more focused on the larger world than her earlier work; while acknowledging terror, she refused to be defeated, though there was always a sense of loss in her most joyful poems.[11]

Kenyon's reputation was also advanced in 1999 by the publication of *A Hundred White Daffodils*. It is a collection of mostly prose pieces, including an introduction by Hall, her *Twenty Poems of Anna Akhmatova*, twenty-six articles written for the *Concord Monitor* and other periodicals, four pieces about the craft of poetry, three interviews, a bibliography, and "Woman Why Are You Weeping?" which appeared for the first time. This volume gives texture and insight into Kenyon's life and work. As one reviewer said, it allows readers "a chance to walk around in the poet's mind at the leisurely pace prose allows."[12]

Tributes to Kenyon's life and work continued to proliferate. Remembrances were held at Harvard University with eight hundred people attending and at Friends meetings in Manhattan and in Boston. Graywolf Press sponsored a commemoration in Minneapolis, at which composer J. Mark Scearce's *American Triptych* premiered, and *New Letters* offered another commemoration at the University of Missouri. In New Hampshire, tributes were held in Concord City Auditorium, the Old Town Hall in Andover, Dean College in Franklin, and at the University of New Hampshire in Durham, with 150 people in attendance. The Association of Writers and Writing Programs offered a celebration of her life and work at its conference in Washington, DC, and William Bolcom, a Pulitzer Prize–winning composer, performed *Briefly It Enters: A Cycle of Songs from Poems of Jane Kenyon*. In India four tributes to her were given in the cities of Allahabad, Bombay, New Delhi, and Madras. Graywolf estimated that as early as July 1996 two thousand people had attended gatherings in her honor.[13] The entire issue of *Columbia: A Journal of Literature and Art* in spring 1996 explored her contributions to American literature. *Xylem*, the student literary journal at the University of Michigan, included a special section dedicated to her, and the *New Hampshire Arts Newsletter* published "Remembering Jane Kenyon," in which friends gave reminiscences.[14]

A major Kenyon retrospective, organized by Bert Hornback, was held in 1998 at Bellarmine College. The conference papers were issued as '*Bright Unequivocal Eye': Poems, Papers, and Remembrances from the First Jane Kenyon Conference*, and two years later the first book-length study of her work appeared.[15] Ten years after her death, Hall convinced Graywolf to publish her *Collected Poems*, which features on its cover a reproduction of a Dutch still life, *A Banquet with Cheese*, by seventeenth-century painter Roelof Koets; *Collected Poems* had nine editions. Dana Goodyear, a reviewer for the *New Yorker*, claimed this book was "the best argument for [Kenyon's] place in history," and while conceding she was an inconsistent poet, Goodyear insisted it showed Kenyon was, nonetheless, capable of "devasting clarity."[16] That same year, 2005, Hall's recollections of their life together, *The Best Day the Worst Day*, was published by Houghton Mifflin, and Joyce Peseroff edited a series of collected essays, *Simply Lasting: Writers on Jane Kenyon*, a kind of posthumous Festschrift. In honor of the twentieth anniversary of her death, the Association of Writers and Writing Programs again sponsored a panel on her life and work.

Donald Hall continued to give interviews and write essays about his life with Kenyon, and he established the Hall-Kenyon Prize to be awarded to major poets.[17] Alice James Books created a Jane Kenyon Chapbook Award, New Hampshire Public Radio established the Donald Hall–Jane Kenyon Prize in American Poetry, and the Massachusetts Cultural Council launched the Jane Kenyon Poetry Prize. Jane Kenyon had among her fans both ordinary poetry lovers and established poets. Poems memorializing Kenyon's life and work were written by David Ignatius, Sharon Olds, Hayden Carruth, Charles Simic, Maxine Kumin, Wendell Berry, Galway Kinnell, Joyce Peseroff, Gregory Orr, Marie Howe, Jean Valentine, Robert Bly, Linda Pastan, and Carol Finkelstein.

Since Kenyon's death, her poetry has been examined by scholars and made available in anthologies. But she would consider the most important accolade that her poetry is broadly available and accessible to the public. As she said, "Art is for everyone."[18] Approximately two hundred thousand copies of her books have been sold, and after her death, her poems have been read on Garrison Keillor's *Writers Almanac* fifty-five times.

The most common complaint of critics is that Kenyon had limited vision, was repetitive, and used mundane language to describe life.[19] But by using ordinary language and paying attention to the quotidian, Kenyon helps her readers experience the universal intertwining of joy and sorrow. In short, she democratized poetry. In her poems readers experience beauty transforming sorrow. More than anything else, an appreciative public has secured Jane Kenyon's reputation.

25
ADVOCATE FOR THE INNER LIFE

But I am, if nothing else, an
advocate for the inner life.
—Jane Kenyon

Jane Kenyon's untimely death raised many unanswerable questions about
her life and legacy. What if she had not married Donald Hall? Would she
have become a successful poet without his recognition and tutelage? If she
had lived, would she have written more prose and more essays on poetics?
Would her range of subject matter continue to expand? Would she have
augmented her repertoire beyond the short lyric? If her depression had
been brought totally under control, would she have continued to write
introspective poetry? Would her Christianity have been transformed by
her encountering the religion of India? Her early death ensured a limited
corpus, and because she lived outside academia, she trained no students to
carry on her work. Was she destined to have no lasting legacy?

Critics and fellow poets had a wide range of responses to her poetry.
While their comments are insightful and have validity, the reality is that
it is difficult to classify Kenyon's work. Ironically, that might democratize
her legacy and help it endure. Kenyon herself gives few hints of how she
evaluated the nature of her contribution, but her most revelatory statement
is contained in an unfinished, unpublished article:

> But I am, if nothing else, an advocate for the inner life. What do I mean by
> inner life? I mean the undefended insides—the aspect which will eventually

meet death with composure, or with regret and confusion. The inner life is under siege in our time, and everybody feels it. The requisites of inwardness are silence and idleness. . . . We almost never go about our lives in silence. . . . We deny ourselves stillness, too. . . . Our jobs and families make of us perpetual motion machines. The truth is we don't want to be still; it frightens us to be still. We don't want to think, and feel, to examine our hearts and ponder the great questions.[1]

Elsewhere, Kenyon spoke of the inner life as the foundation for the creation of all art: "Artists report on the inner life. In a way every piece of art, every performance is a state-of-the-soul address. We cannot afford to ignore our inner lives, our imaginations, for when we do, we become capable of extreme cruelty and destruction. 'Tenderness toward existence,' in the poet Galway Kinnell's lovely phrase, is what we lose when we lose art, or when we fail to value it properly."[2]

Depression was a major preoccupation in Kenyon's life, the subject of many of her poems, and a lure for readers who shared that disease. Nonetheless, she would not have wanted to be remembered solely as a poet of depression. She believed that because poets feel more deeply than others, their emotional lives are rich, complex, and often overwhelming.[3] When Bill Moyers queried whether "perhaps depression is itself a gift, a kind of garden in which ideas grow and in which experiences take root,"[4] she agreed that depression made her still, and stillness was the prerequisite for the creation of poetry, but she was quick to concede that depression was an "awful disease." Depression might create stillness, and it might allow for greater empathy for those who suffer, but it remained the "black bile of destruction."[5] She was clear: depression was not to be cultivated in the service of poetry.

It is instructive to survey how others evaluated her poetic contribution and how close they came to understanding her final legacy. Although Kenyon wanted a reputation as a poet, she was unable to see herself in the continuum of women's or any other poetry. The Pulitzer Prize–winner Charles Simic claimed that Kenyon's words came from silence, and, hence, the reader could trust her voice. She opened herself to everything, and yet her words eluded critical analysis.[6]

Joyce Peseroff noted there were two sides to Kenyon's vision, a great sensitivity to pleasure and eroticism and a great empathy for others. Peseroff wagered that Kenyon's poems would continue to be read because they were well crafted and offered what people needed—beauty, consolation, observation, and the gift of herself. Alice Mattison believed that Kenyon's legacy would endure because she was highly respected by fellow poets and her poetry served people who were less familiar with the genre.[7] Simplicity of language, focus on place, and timelessness of subject would appeal to the general reader. This evaluation is confirmed by Kenyon's friend and fellow writer Wendell Berry, who acknowledged that her poetry did not demand of the reader great intellect, learning, or sympathy but, rather, quiet and a capacity to listen. He found all her gifts were in her poems—"quietness, gentleness, compassion, elegance, and clarity, her awareness of mystery, her almost severe good sense." For Berry, she was "authentically a poet of inspiration."[8] Mattison and Berry confirm that her legacy is that it encourages the general reader to appreciate poetry.

Critic Dan Rattelle concurred, declaring Kenyon to be "plain-spoken and personal" but, above all, a poet of place. He hailed her as a "visionary" and a poet of "fine religious sensibilities," even though like most poets her work would be forgotten.[9] Liam Rector considered Kenyon a religious poet who had sympathy with everything that lived. She was simultaneously "lusty," "tolerant," "patient," and had a prayer in her heart for all things. She was a "rare Christian" and a "patron saint of writers."[10]

In this same vein, Gregory Orr, her longtime friend from Michigan days, called her "Our Lady of Sorrows," distinguishing her from "Our Lady of Rages," Sylvia Plath. For Orr, Kenyon was a poet of great vulnerability, openness, innerness, and subjectivity. She had the power of personal depth and the passion to create meaning She was a poet capable of transforming subjectivity and producing poems of healing. Hence, she was not the traditional "confessional" poet. For her the act of writing was an act of survival.[11]

Paul Breslin considered Kenyon the poet who wrote about depression more eloquently than anyone since Plath, even though their life outcomes were different. Plath chose oblivion while Kenyon chose to live. Unlike Plath, Kenyon's poetry had a quality of emotional generosity; it was not self-pitying. Compared to Plath, Kenyon's language was quieter and had greater subtlety, and she had better moral and poetic judgment.[12] Especially in her later poems she paid attention to the physical world not merely as description for description's sake but as a deterrent to the power of depression.[13]

Some critics thought Kenyon was a poet who wrote for women, which implied she was emotional, superficial, narrow in range, repetitive, and focused on the mundane. It is more appropriate to see her as a poet who valued being a woman and who wanted to make the creative work of women more available,[14] as she did through founding *Green House*, allying herself with Alice James Books, and encouraging women to critique and perfect their poetry. While not a feminist poet, her friend Jean Valentine attested that Kenyon was a pioneer as a woman poet, one who early on gave courage to other women poets who lived in a world that excluded and dismissed and did not take women seriously. Valentine understood that Kenyon's life was made even more complicated because she was married to a man who both helped her and from whom she had to separate herself.[15]

Others have called Kenyon a visionary poet and pointed to the sacramentality of her art. Lynn Strongin referred to her as a mystic poet and compared her to Emily Dickinson. She argued that Kenyon's poetry had a translucency, almost transparency, which saw the world as an icon to which she gave her undivided attention.[16] Carol Muske agreed that Kenyon wrote about ordinary life and saw the world as a kind of "threshold" through which one could enter God's wonder.[17] Robert Bly described her as "a woman of spirit who directed her spirit, infused by love, to everyday objects. . . . Her natural gaze was upward, but she remembered to bend down and give a blessing to earth-bound things."[18] Wesley McNair, good friend and later poet laureate of Maine, called Kenyon a visionary poet whose poetry pointed toward "the great goodness."[19] He acknowledged her imperfections but suggested that while her poems about pleasure and happiness were among her most moving, her religious poems might be her most enduring.[20] Kenyon's friend and poet Marie Howe declared Kenyon was a poet whose trust is based on an abiding love of the world, a world that is ordinary, precious, and terrible.[21]

These myriad critics and fellow poets each confirms in disparate ways what Kenyon herself asserted: she was "an advocate for inner life." From an early age she was drawn to solitude, her lifelong depression deepened her stillness and inwardness, and later she was given a fresh understanding of religion that offered consolation and meaning. Christian metaphors and allusions appeared in her poetry, but she was never sentimental or didactic in her treatment of spiritual reality.[22] Her life was grounded not in credal belief, dogmas, or moral strictures but on trust in what she named the mystery of the "great goodness." It was the "great goodness" that made life endurable and love, kindness, and beauty possible. It was this trust that the poet Lionel Basney argued she enacted in her poetry.[23] Whether writing about nature, love, death, or depression, all these themes were understood through the prism of the "great goodness." In this sense Kenyon wrote in the spirit not of religious poetry but contemplative poetry, in short as an "advocate of the inner life."

The distinction between belief and trust may help explain Kenyon's traumatic experience of religious doubt recorded in "Woman, Why Are You Weeping?" a poem Hall insisted she did not want included in *Otherwise* but which others have called "brave."[24] Her experience in India revealed foreign gods who meant nothing to her and challenged the God she knew, who lived within her and blessed her. She was left with the conviction of the "absurdity of all religious forms" while steadfastly expressing in her poetry insights rooted in Christianity.

This fracture between institutional religion and trust in the "great goodness" seems not to have been resolved in her lifetime, even though she continued to write poems with spiritual content and maintain a connection to her local church. Near her death she confessed to Hall and this was confirmed to Mattison that she believed in God and had no fear of punishment.[25] If she had lived, the challenge of doubt might have been a portal for new growth, producing a more capacious trust.

It was Kenyon's love of the natural world and trust in the "great goodness" that she translated with devastating transparency into her "intense, musical cries of the spirit." She came to this achievement from her ordinary life, the seedbed of her art, full as it was with contradictions and conundrums. She created her poems from her being, crippled by depression and yet gifted with a vision of light as mercy. She put universal feeling into beautiful words, offering poems of solace and consolation to the world. It is this that will secure her reputation as a poet and advocate for the inner life, endearing her to readers, and ensuring her legacy as an important contemporary poet.

NOTE ON SOURCES

The source material for this biography of Jane Kenyon is complicated. Most of what is known of Kenyon's life is based on commentary by Donald Hall, her husband of twenty-three years. Hall wrote poetry and prose about her, including *The Best Day the Worst Day*, and gave many interviews, written and digital, about their lives together. Most of their friends knew them jointly. Publicly, they presented themselves as a couple and were understood as such.

After Kenyon's death, Hall curated and established her archive at the University of New Hampshire, where his own archive is housed. Her archive contains fifty-five boxes: the majority consists of nineteen boxes of multiple drafts of her poems, five boxes are of correspondence from others to Kenyon, two boxes hold journals and day-timers, seven boxes are materials about her interests—Alice James Books and Green House—and thirteen boxes are reviews by others of her books, tributes, and writing. Ironically, the archive does not give extensive insight into her personal reflections and inner thoughts. With a very few exceptions her journals and notebooks record events but do not offer her reactions to them. The archive contains letters from others but not her letters. This makes the letters between Kenyon and her women friends Joyce Peseroff and Alice Mattison very important. Many of these letters are held privately.

It is in her poetry that Kenyon reveals her inner reflections. In her trove of poetry she speaks of her family, her depression, the beauty of nature, her love of animals, the importance of community, her visions and spirituality, the suffering life brings with it, her favorite mentors and muses, and her late-life interest in the larger world. Although in interviews she sometimes speaks of her writing life and her relationship to Hall, she does not write extensively about poetics.

This biography is an attempt to weave together these disparate sources to reconstruct Jane Kenyon's life, her development as a poet, and her liberation from the shadow of her well-known husband.

NOTES

Prologue

The epigraph is from Christian Wiman, *My Bright Abyss*, 47.

1. The show was televised in December 1993.

2. Jantsch, "Briefly It Enters," 11. It was William Bolcom, American composer and winner of a Pulitzer Prize and a Grammy, who compared Hall and Kenyon to the Brownings. He set several of Kenyon's poems to music.

3. Hall, *Best Day*, back cover.

4. Donald Hall, "Life after Jane," *Northeast Hartford (CT) Courant*, August 27, 1995, 11.

5. For more information on available sources, see "Note on Sources" in the current volume.

6. Kenyon, "An Interview with David Bradt," in *A Hundred White Daffodils*, 183. Hereafter this volume is referred to as *Daffodils*.

Chapter 1. Turning Inward

The epigraph is from Kenyon, "Evening Sun," in *Collected Poems*, 84. *Collected Poems* is hereafter referred to as *CP*.

1. When queried, both her adult friends Joyce Peseroff and Alice Mattison attested Kenyon almost never spoke of her childhood.

2. Timmerman, *Jane Kenyon*, claims Kenyon recalled her childhood with "fondness" and that she was part of a "frolicking" family household. This conclusion does not follow from extant evidence.

3. Journal 1961, folder 1, and journal 1962, folder 2, both in box 33, MC 164, Jane Kenyon Papers, Milne Special Collections and Archives, University of New

Hampshire, Durham. Hereafter Kenyon's papers are referred to as JKP. Donald Hall curated the collection.

4. Timmerman wrote a literary study not a biography and said that the facts in his study were checked by Donald Hall. However, Jane's brother, Reuel Kenyon, has no recollection of his father's prior marriage. Reuel Kenyon to author, email, June 1, 2020. This may have been a topic undiscussed in the family.

5. Reuel Kenyon to author, email, June 1, 2020.

6. Kenyon, "The Box of Beads," *CP*, 25–26.

7. Kenyon, "The Stroller," *CP*, 220.

8. Kenyon, journal 1961, November 16, 1961, folder 1, box 33, JKP.

9. Kenyon, journal 1961, November 16, 1961, folder 1, box 33, JKP.

10. Kenyon, "Two Poets," *Concord (NH) Monitor*, April 16, 1985, folder 25, box 41, JKP, 17–18.

11. Kenyon, "Catching Frogs," *CP*, 148, and "Insomnia," *CP*, 166.

12. Kenyon, "In the Grove: The Poet at Ten," *CP*, 149.

13. Kenyon, journal 1961, September 19, 1961, folder 1, box 33, JKP.

14. Kenyon, "A Boy Goes into the World," *CP*, 178.

15. Kenyon, "Drawing from the Past," *CP*, 280. Her brother, Reuel Kenyon, became an accomplished artist.

16. Kenyon, journal 1, September 9, 1961, and October 26, 1961, folder 1, box 33, JKP.

17. Reuel Kenyon (brother), phone interview with author, February 6, 2020.

18. Donald Hall alludes to this in his later poem "Blues for Polly" in *Without*, 31–32.

19. Kenyon, "An Interview with Bill Moyers," *Daffodils*, 154, 159. Reuel Kenyon Jr. agreed that both parents were depressed. Reuel Kenyon Jr., phone interview with author, February 6, 2020.

20. Kenyon, "The Stroller," *CP*, 221.

21. Kenyon, "Having It Out with Melancholy," *CP*, 231.

22. Kenyon, "Notes for a Journal," hospice journal, folder 10, box 40, JKP.

23. Kenyon, "My Mother," *CP*, 22. This concern that her mother might not return was mentioned in notebook, Michigan, early 1970s, folder 13, box 33, JKP.

24. Kenyon, "An Interview with Bill Moyers," *Daffodils*, 154.

25. Kenyon, journal 1961, October 2, 1961, folder 1, box 33, JKP.

26. Kenyon, "Childhood, When You Are in It . . . ," *Daffodils*, 61. This is an unfinished essay, probably written about 1970. A draft with the same title is in folder 26, box 19, JKP.

27. Kenyon, "Staying at Grandma's," *CP*, 175.

28. Kenyon, "The Argument," *CP*, 224.

29. Kenyon, "Staying at Grandma's," *CP*, 175, and "The Argument," *CP*, 224.

30. Kenyon, "Childhood: When You Are in It . . . ," *Daffodils*, 63.

31. Kenyon "Waking in January before Dawn," *CP*, 147.

32. Kenyon, journal 1961, September 19, 1961, folder 1, box 33, JKP.

33. Kenyon, "Childhood: When You Are in It . . . ," *Daffodils*, 64.

34. Kenyon, "Childhood: When You Are in It . . . ," *Daffodils*, 65.

35. Kenyon, "Learning in the First Grade," *CP*, 181.

36. Kenyon did not base her poems on invented events, but neither were they always strictly factual in small details.

37. Kenyon, "Trouble with Math in a One-Room Country School," *CP*, 116. See Emily Archer, "Trouble with Math."

38. Kenyon, journal 1961, September 19 and September 24, 1961, folder 1, box 33, JKP.

39. Kenyon, journal 1961, September 24, 1961, folder 1, box 33, JKP.

40. These comments and self-descriptors are drawn from Jane Kenyon's journal kept during fall 1961 with a brief addendum in January 1962.

41. Kenyon, "The Little Boat," *CP*, 117–18.

42. Kenyon, "Having It Out with Melancholy," *CP*, 231.

43. Kenyon, "Having It Out with Melancholy," *CP*, 231.

44. Kenyon, "Everything I Know about Writing Poetry," *Daffodils*, 139.

Chapter 2. Enlivened by Poetry

The epigraph is from Kenyon, "An Interview with Bill Moyers," *Daffodils*, 145.

1. Ann Arbor High School is now called Pioneer High School.

2. Kenyon, journal 1962, January 4, 1962, folder 2, box 33, JKP.

3. Kenyon, "A Gardener of the True Vine," *Daffodils*, 94.

4. At some point the family, except for Reuel Kenyon Sr., stopped visiting Dora. Reuel Kenyon (brother) to author, email, June 1, 2020.

5. Kenyon, "Childhood When You Are in It . . . ," *Daffodils*, 66.

6. Kenyon, "Childhood When You Are in It . . . ," folder 26, box 19, JKP. This was later published as "Childhood When You Are in It . . . ," *Daffodils*, 68, but the original has more information.

7. Mary Dawn Selvius, obituary, *Ann Arbor (MI) News*, July 20, 2010.

8. Larry Russ, seminar participant, phone interview with author, January 9, 2020.

9. Jane Kenyon to Alice Mattison, February 27, 1989, privately held. Correspondence from Alice Mattison to Jane Kenyon is housed in folders 3–16, box 27, and folders 1–7, box 28, JKP; see "Notes on Sources" in the current volume.

10. Kenyon, "The Needle," *CP*, 21.

11. David Tucker, Larry Russ, and Mary Baron, seminar participants, individual phone interviews with author, December 3, 2019, January 9, 2020, and February 21, 2020, respectively. See also writings by other seminar participants: Laurence Goldstein, "Remembering Jane Kenyon"; Jean Feraca, *I Hear Voices*, 118–29.

12. Tucker interview; Russ interview.

13. Kenyon, "The Socks," *CP*, 33, and "The Shirt," *CP*, 34.

14. Baron interview.

15. Kenyon, "Kicking the Eggs," *Daffodils*, 133–35.

16. Lammon, "Something Hard to Get Rid Of." This material was sent to the author by Robert Bly.

17. Kenyon, "Kicking the Eggs," *Daffodils*, 133.

18. Reuel Kenyon to author, email, October 24, 2021.

19. Kenyon, notebook 1970, folder 11, box 33, JKP.

20. Kenyon writes about this experience in the hospice journal, winter 1981, folder 3, box 33, JKP.

21. Kenyon, notebook 1970, folder 11, box 33, and notebook 1970, folder 1, box 34, JKP. Some of this essay is fictional or only semi-lucid. Hall, *Best Day*, 52.

22. I have written to four persons named John Briggs in Ann Arbor, Michigan, but have been unable to locate the correct John Briggs. In *The Best Day* Hall refers to him as "Bill" to protect his identity, but his name was revealed during the course of interviews. Kenyon refers to a love affair with "John" in notebook 1970, folder 11, box 33, JKP.

23. Kenyon, "Notes for a Journal," hospice journal 1981, folder 3, box 33, JKP.

24. See especially folders 1–5, box 19, JKP.

25. Szynol, "Poet Donald Hall."

26. Hall, *Carnival of Losses*, 127.

Chapter 3. Donald Hall, "Rockstar"

I am grateful to David Tucker for this designation. David Tucker, phone interview with author, December 3, 2019.

1. Pride, "Donald Hall, US and NH poet laureate dies at 89," *New Hampshire Union Leader (Manchester, NH), June 24, 2018,* https://www.unionleader.com/.

2. Alice Mattison, in-person interview with author, February 12, 2019, New Haven, Connecticut.

3. Kenyon to Alice Mattison, December 16, 1993, privately held.

4. Stevenson, "Intimacy and Solitude," 12.

5. The name of the town changed over time. When Hall and Kenyon lived there, they associated with South Danbury, had a phone number that was in Andover, received mail in Danbury, and paid taxes in Wilmot. Finally, the house was designated as in Wilmot. I am grateful to Mary Lyn Ray for this explanation. See also Kenyon, "Edna Powers," *Daffodils*, 75.

6. Goldstein, "Poets at the University of Michigan"; Tillinghast, "Poetry in Ann Arbor."

7. Hall would later conduct an interview with Ezra Pound for the *Paris Review*. Pound was a poet Hall much admired. Hall also interviewed poet Marianne Moore.

8. Pride, "Remembering Donald Hall."

9. Hall, *Carnival of Losses*, 127.

10. Hall, *Yellow Room*.

11. Feraca, *I Hear Voices*, 129.

12. See Hall on *Web of Stories*, www.webofstories.com/play/donald.hall/1, especially no. 51, Bisiewicz, "The End of My First Marriage and Psychoanalysis," in which Hall describes these years. *Web of Stories* has 111 segments on Hall discussing all aspects of his life.

13. Hall, "Falling in Love." Hall gives a more favorable review of her in *Best Day*, 51.

Chapter 4. Marriage by Default

The epigraph is from Kenyon, "Thinking of Madame Bovary," *CP*, 103.

1. Kenyon, hospice journal, Winter 1981, folder 3, box 33, JKP. She is reflecting on this difficult period in her life.
2. Martin-Joy, "Poetry, Aging, and Loss."
3. Feraca, *I Hear Voices*, 129.
4. Hall, *Best Day*, 54, 56.
5. Hall, *Best Day*, 52.
6. Hall, *Best Day*, 54.
7. Kenyon, notebook, early 1970s, folder 14, box 33, JKP.
8. Marian Blue to Jane Kenyon, April 22, 1993, folder 17, box 20, JKP.
9. Kenyon, "Interview with Marian Blue," *Daffodils*, 194–95.
10. J. S. Cramer, "With Jane and Without," 495.
11. Hall, *Best Day,* 54.
12. Reuel Kenyon, interview with author, October 26, 2021.
13. Kenyon, "Childhood, When You Are In It . . . ," *Daffodils*, 67.
14. Joyce Peseroff, interview with author, August 20, 2020.
15. Hall, *Best Day*, 56.
16. Lucy Hall to Jane Kenyon, 1972, folder 2, box 24, JKP.
17. Hall published *Dock Ellis in the Country of Baseball* in 1976.
18. Pride, "Conversation with Jane Kenyon," 107.
19. Hall, "The Long White House That Holds Love and Work Together," 53.
20. Valentine, "Jane Kenyon, 1947–1995," in Peseroff, *Simply Lasting*, 60.
21. Martin-Joy, "Poetry, Aging, and Loss."
22. Farrow, "Into the Light."
23. Kenyon, "An Interview with Marian Blue," *Daffodils*, 190.
24. Orr, "Our Lady of Sorrows," 32.
25. Kenyon, "Starting Therapy," *CP*, 35.
26. Kenyon, "Cages," *CP*, 38–40. Kenyon did not want this poem included in *Otherwise*. It was added to her posthumously published *Complete Poems*.
27. Lyman, "Jane Kenyon."
28. Hall details this process in *Best Day*, 58–62.
29. Rector, "About Donald Hall," 270–74.
30. Ultimately, *Writing Well* would have nine editions.

Chapter 5. House of the Ancestors

The epigraph is from Kenyon, "From Room to Room," *CP*, 7.

1. Hall, "When the Fine Days," in *Museum of Clear Ideas*, 70.
2. McDonald, "Donald Hall."

3. Kenyon, "Interview with Marian Blue," *Daffodils*, 200.

4. Kenyon, "Interview with Bill Moyers," *Daffodils*, 145.

5. Kenyon, hospice journal, 1981, folder 3, box 33, JKP.

6. Kenyon, "Here," *CP*, 8.

7. Hall, *Best Day*, 18. Kenyon used "gene pool" to apply to the church, but it was applicable to the community, as well.

8. Originally, this was a Congregational church, but it now is affiliated with the United Church of Christ.

9. Kenyon, "Childhood, When You Are In It . . . ," *Daffodils*, 68.

10. Kenyon, "Two Days Alone," *CP*, 9.

11. Kenyon, "Two Days Alone," *CP*, 9.

12. Berry, "Sweetness Preserved," 56–57.

13. Farrow, "Into the Light," 9; Hall, *Best Day*, 18.

14. Hall, *Best Day*, 17.

15. Kenyon, "Finding a Long Gray Hair," *CP*, 14.

16. Kenyon, "The Clothes Pin," *CP*, 17.

17. Kenyon, "Now That We Live," *CP*, 57.

18. Kenyon, "The Suitor," *CP*, 52.

19. Kenyon, "Leaving Town," *CP*, 6.

20. For a reference to yellow, see Hall's poem "Gold," https://poets.org/poem/gold.

21. Kenyon, "February: Thinking of Flowers," *CP*, 97.

22. Kenyon "The Moment of Peonies," *Daffodils*, 47. This first appeared in *Yankee Magazine* in June 1991.

23. See Kenyon's essays "The Moment of Peonies," 46–47; "The Phantom Pruner," 48–50; and "Season of Change and Loss" 85–87, all in *Daffodils*.

24. Pride, "Conversation with Jane Kenyon," 104.

25. Harrison Smith, "Donald Hall, Former U.S. Poet Laureate Wrote about Nature and Loss, Dies at 89," *Washington Post*, June 24, 2018, 9.

26. Patti Hartigan, "Happy for Now Donald Hall and Jane Kenyon, Poets at Their Peak," *Boston (MA) Globe*, December 12, 1993, 10.

27. Hall, *Principal Products*, 225–29.

28. Kenyon, "The Five-and-Dime," *Daffodils*, 91–93.

29. Hall, *Best Day*, 118.

Chapter 6. The Community of Wilmot

The epigraph is from Kenyon, "American Triptych," *CP*, 53–56.

1. Pride, "Conversation with Jane Kenyon," 108, and Pride, "All That a Poet Could Ask For," *Concord (NH) Monitor*, June 6, 1990, D-1, 6.

2. Pride, "Conversation with Jane Kenyon," 102.

3. Hall, *Here at Eagle Pond*, 145–69, 120–33.

4. Kenyon, "South Danbury Church Fair," *Daffodils*, 58–60.

5. Warford, *Becoming a New Church*, 88–94.

6. Kenyon, "A Gardener of the True Vine," *Daffodils*, 95.

7. Kenyon, "Interview with Bill Moyers," *Daffodils*, 162.

8. Hall, *Best Day*, 223.

9. Kenyon, "A Gardener of the True Vine," *Daffodils*, 96.

10. Kenyon, "Every Year the Light," *Daffodils*, 88–90.

11. Kenyon, "Interview with Bill Moyers," *Daffodils*, 161.

12. Kenyon, "Childhood, When You Are in It . . . ," *Daffodils*, 68.

13. Wynn, "Lord, you know that I love you"; Waldron, "Poet Jane Kenyon"; Booty, "Christian Poetry"; Chad Wriglesworth, "Re-presenting Life Back to God"; Timmerman, *Jane Kenyon*, treats this subject throughout.

14. Kenyon, "Interview with Marion Blue," *Daffodils*, 195.

15. Parini, "Jane Kenyon," 162. This is also found in Hill, *Simply Lasting*.

16. Kenyon, "Interview with David Bradt," *Daffodils*, 181.

17. Pride, "Conversation with Jane Kenyon," 102.

Chapter 7. The Muses

The epigraph is from Kenyon, "Interview with David Bradt," *Daffodils*, 183.

1. Kenyon, "Interview with Marian Blue," *Daffodils*, 191.

2. Kenyon, "Interview with Marian Blue," *Daffodils*, 191.

3. Kenyon to Alice Mattison, October 20, 1989, privately held.

4. Kenyon, "Interview with David Bradt," *Daffodils*, 180.

5. McNair, "Government of Two," 171–76.

6. Hall, *Essays after Eighty*, 71. Hall explains the origins of this name in *Best Day*, 223. The story of Hall's acquisition of the name goes back to when they first moved to Wilmot. On a trip to Maine they passed through Perkins Cove, a small fishing community and artist colony. Many enterprises and streets were named Perkins, which led Kenyon to say this Perkins must have been "quite a fellow."

7. Bly, "Few Memories about Jane," 69.

8. Mattison, "Let It Grow in the Dark," 17–18.

9. Kenyon, "At the Spanish Steps in Rome," *CP*, 172.

10. Mattison, "Let It Grow in the Dark," 17.

11. Kenyon, "Having It Out with Melancholy," *CP*, 231.

12. Kenyon, "Having It Out with Melancholy," *CP*, 231.

13. Oktenberg, "In Solitude and Sorrow," 27–28.

14. Kenyon, "Ice Storm," *CP*, 76.

15. Kenyon, "Interview with David Bradt," *Daffodils*, 178.

16. Orr, "Our Lady of Sorrows," 32–33.

17. Joyce Peseroff, phone interview with author, August 20, 2020, and Wes McNair, phone interview with author, April 9, 2020, and April 14, 2020.

18. Hall, introduction, x.

19. Valentine, "Jane Kenyon," 61.

20. Kenyon, "Interview with David Bradt," *Daffodils*, 175.

21. Kenyon, "Interview with David Bradt," *Daffodils*, 175.

22. Kenyon, "Introduction (1984)," *Daffodils*, 3–6.

23. Kenyon, "Kicking the Eggs," *Daffodils*, 134.

24. McDonald, "Donald Hall."

25. These poems are untitled and are distinguished by their first lines: "The memory of sun wakens in my heart;" "I know, I know the skies," "There is a sacred, secret line in loving," "Like a white stone in a deep well," "Everything promised him to me."

26. Kenyon, "Introduction (1984)," *Daffodils*, 3–6. These poems were first published by Eighties Press and Ally Press in 1985. They were republished posthumously in *Daffodils*, 3–39, and again in *CP*, 307–43. Kenyon included six of Akhmatova's poems in *From Room to Room*, which were revised later for inclusion with the Eighties Press and Ally Press edition.

27. Farrow, "Into the Light," 9.

28. A. J. Hogg, "Poet Kenyon Proves Constance Is a Virtue," (Ann Arbor) *Michigan Daily*, October 8, 1991, 5.

29. Harbilas, "Beautiful Clarity."

30. Kenyon, "Introduction (1984)," *Daffodils*, 3.

31. Kenyon, "Interview with David Bradt," *Daffodils*, 180.

Chapter 8. Finding Her Way

The epigraph is from Pride, "Conversation with Jane Kenyon," 108–9.

1. Heuving and Hogue, "American Women Poets."

2. Peseroff, "Green House"; Hayes, "After the Fact." Many of Peseroff's letters to Kenyon deal with the details of publication. Folders 8–20, box 36, JKP. It is clear from the letters that Kenyon is the junior partner in this venture; through the letters, Peseroff kept Kenyon apprised of all she was doing. Correspondence from Joyce Peseroff to Jane Kenyon is housed in folders 8–10, box 29, JKP.

3. Peseroff to Kenyon, folder 8, box 29, JKP.

4. Kenyon, "Review of New Shoes by Kathleen Fraser," 67.

5. Pride, "Conversation with Jane Kenyon," 107.

6. Peseroff, "Luminous Particular."

7. Peseroff to author, email responses to interview questions, January 30, 2019; Dinnerstein, *Mermaid and the Minotaur*.

8. Kenyon, "Falling," *CP*, 47.

9. Hall, *Best Day*, 228–29.

10. Peseroff to author, email responses to interview questions, January 30, 2019.

11. Adrienne Rich to Kenyon, July 18, 1978, folder 5, box 30, JKP.

12. Kenyon, "Now That We Live," *CP*, 57.

13. Kenyon, "Full Moon in Winter," *CP*, 49.

14. "Notes on Current Books."

15. Oktenberg, "Review of *From Room to Room*."

16. Stoneburner, "Review of *From Room to Room*"; Carruth, "Poets on the Fringe," 227.

17. One later reviewer, Robin Latimer, gave a positive review, calling the book "the poetic diary of a honeymoon," that in coming to grips with her new reality she moves between the personal to the universal, and her poems are saved from triteness by her craft. Latimer, "Jane Kenyon."

18. Rector, "Remembering Jane Kenyon," 75.

19. Breslin, "Four and a Half Books."

20. McNair, "Craft and Technique."

Chapter 9. A Double Solitude

The epigraph is from *Twenty Poems of Anna Akhmatova* in Kenyon, *CP*, 334, and is Jane Kenyon's translation.

1. Hall, "The Third Thing," *Best Day*, 118.

2. Kenyon, "Interview with David Bradt," *Daffodils*, 176.

3. McNair, "A Government of Two," 169–82.

4. Alice Mattison, in-person interview with author, February 12, 2019.

5. An Alice James Books representative confirmed total sales through 2020 were 600.

6. Kenyon to Joyce Peseroff, August 6, 1982, privately held.

7. Peseroff, phone interview with author, August 20, 2020.

8. Kenyon to Peseroff, August 6, 1982, privately held.

9. Hostetler, "Food as Sacrament." See Kenyon, "At the Town Dump," 64; "Briefly It Enters and Briefly Speaks," 137; "The Pear," 150; "Man Eating," 274; "Eating the Cookies," 184; and "Dutch Interiors," 290; all in *CP*.

10. Kenyon, "Man Eating," *CP*, 274.

11. Hall, "The Third Thing," *Best Day*, 107–18. This is a slightly different version of "The Third Thing."

12. Kenyon's passport, 1978–83, folder 11, box 40, JKP.

13. Kenyon, introduction to *Twenty Poems of Anna Akhmatova*, *CP*, 313.

14. Henry Raymont, "Poetry Translations: Literal or the Mood and Art?" *New York Times*, March 19, 1969, 40.

15. Kenyon, introduction to *Twenty Poems of Anna Akhmatova*, *CP*, 313.

16. Pound, "I Gather the Limbs of Osiris 2," 25.

17. Hall, introduction, *Daffodils*, x.

18. Hall, Afterword, *Otherwise*, 217–20.

19. "A Few Don'ts by an Imagiste" was first published in *Poetry Magazine* in 1913.

20. Kenyon, "Everything I Know about Writing Poetry," *Daffodils*, 140.

21. "Poem 15" in *Twenty Poems of Anna Akhmatova*, *CP*, 334.

22. Kenyon, "Interview with David Bradt," *Daffodils*, 180.

23. Hall, introduction, *Daffodils*, ix–x.

24. Kenyon, "Lines for Akhmatova," *CP*, 183.

25. Kenyon, "Interview with David Bradt," *Daffodils*, 179.

Chapter 10. Streaming Light and Death

The epigraph is from Kenyon, "Things," *CP*, 139.

1. Kenyon, "The Mailbox," *Daffodils*, 82–83.

2. Gwen Lyman, presentation, Museum of Fine Arts, April 20, 1980, folder 12, box 28, JKP.

3. Hall, *Best Day*, 12.

4. Kenyon, "Childhood, When You Are in It . . . ," *Daffodils*, 69.

5. Paulist Press to Kenyon, folder 6, box 29, JKP. This letter is evidence that she ordered a book by Richard of St. Victor.

6. Kenyon, "Childhood, When You Are in It. . . . " *Daffodils*, 69.

7. Kenyon, "Interview with Bill Moyers," *Daffodils*, 160.

8. Hall, introduction, x.

9. Hall, introduction, x.

10. Peseroff to Kenyon, June 24, 1980, folder 8, box 29, JKP.

11. Kenyon, "Who," *CP*, 136.

12. Kenyon, "The Bat," *CP*, 114.

13. Kenyon, "Gabriel's Truth," *Daffodils*.

14. Pride, "Conversation with Jane Kenyon," 105.

15. Kenyon, hospice journal, 1981, folder 3, box 33, JKP.

16. Alice Mattison, in-person interview with author, February 12–13, 2019.

17. Kenyon, hospice journal, training materials, 1981, folder 10, box 40, JKP. Kenyon also wrote poems that were illustrated by artist Loa Winter and made into cards to raise money for hospice. Folders 1–7, box 40, JKP.

18. Kenyon, hospice journal, 1981, folder 3, box 33, JKP.

19. Mattison to Kenyon, September 9, 1980, folder 3, box 27, JKP.

20. Kenyon, hospice journal, 1981, folder 3, box 33, JKP.

21. Kenyon, hospice journal, 1981, folder 3, box 33, JKP.

22. Kenyon, "Teacher," *CP*, 89.

23. Kenyon, "Frost Flowers," *CP*, 90–91.

24. His character is evident in the letters he sent to Kenyon and to Hall. Folder 6, box 26, JKP.

25. Kenyon tells Peseroff of administering morphine to her father. July 22, 1981, folder 9, box 29, JKP.

26. Kenyon to Mattison, March 29, 1982, privately held.

27. Kenyon, "Travel: After a Death," *CP*, 129–30.

28. Nabokov, *Speak, Memory*.

29. Kenyon, "Reading Aloud to My Father," *CP*, 291.

30. Kenyon, "We Let the Boat Drift," *CP*, 163–64.

31. Kenyon, "The Stroller," *CP*, 220–23.

32. Hall, *Best Day*, 137–38.

33. Several attempts to contact Solow have been unsuccessful.

34. The National Institute of Mental Health defines bipolar II as episodes of depression and hypomania, which is not as severe as bipolar I.

35. Hall, "Ghost in the House," 85.

36. Hall, "Ghost in the House," 87–88.

37. Hall, *Best Day*, 224.

38. Soon after they began to workshop together, Mattison switched from writing poetry to fiction. Kenyon and Peseroff happily critiqued that genre.

39. Mrs. Bomblatt is a cartoon housewife who wrote poetry on the side.

40. Peseroff, interview with author, January 30, 2019.

41. Pride, "Conversation with Jane Kenyon," 109.

42. Hall, *Life Work*, 44.

43. Mattison, "Let It Grow in the Dark," 12–13.

Chapter 11. The Boat of Quiet Hours

The epigraph is from Keats, "A Poetic Romance," *Endymion, Book I.*

1. Muske, review of *The Boat of Quiet Hours.*

2. Unterecker, "Shape-Changing."

3. Two reviewers make this point. Michael Milburn in reviewing the translation of Akhmatova refers to the poems of *The Boat of Quiet Hours*, indicating the sympathy between the two. David Harbilas makes a similar point in his paper "Beautiful Clarity."

4. Kenyon, "Ice Storm," *CP*, 76.

5. Kenyon, "The Pond at Dusk," *CP*, 82.

6. Kenyon, "Siesta: Barbados," *CP*, 115.

7. Kenyon to Alice Mattison, October 24, 1987, privately held.

8. Lyman, "Jane Kenyon 1984 & 1994 Series." Earlier, in 1976 and 1981, she also read on this program, *Poems to a Listener.*

9. Kenyon to Mattison, October 18, 1985, privately held.

10. Tree Swenson, phone interview with author, March 19, 2020.

11. Adrienne Rich to Kenyon, September 2, 1990, folder 5, box 30, JKP.

12. In May 1981 Andrew Hall had a car accident.

13. Kenyon, "Evening at a Country Inn," *CP*, 63.

14. Kenyon, "Rain in January," *CP*, 73, and "Bright Sun after Heavy Snow," *CP*, 75.

15. Kenyon, "Depression in Winter," *CP*, 74.

16. Kenyon, "Walking Alone in Late Winter," *CP*, 77, and "Portrait of a Figure near Water," *CP*, 98.

17. Kenyon, "Back from the City," *CP*, 67.

18. Kenyon, "Apple Dropping into Deep Early Snow," *CP*, 71.

19. Kenyon, "Mud Season," *CP*, 99.

20. Kenyon, "Depression," *CP*, 93.

21. Kenyon, "Thinking of Madame Bovary," *CP*, 103.

22. Kenyon, "April Walk," *CP*, 104.

23. Kenyon, "The Appointment," *CP*, 111.

24. Kenyon, "Philosophy in Warm Weather," *CP*, 106.

25. Kenyon, "No Steps," *CP*, 107, and "Wash," *CP*, 108; Kenyon to Mattison, June 15, 1984, privately held. Hall did not like "No Steps." "Wash" appeared in the *New Yorker* in May 1984.

26. Kenyon, "Song," *CP*, 121. See Jackman, "Metre and Meaning."

27. Kenyon, "Things," *CP*, 139.

28. Their trip to Rome, Milan, and Florence for a week is chronicled in "Siesta: Hotel Frattina," *CP*, 133, and "After Traveling," *CP*, 134. It is on this trip that they visited the room where Keats died. Kenyon, "At the Spanish Steps in Rome," *CP*, 172.

29. Kenyon, "Briefly It Enters, and Briefly Speaks," *CP*, 137–38.

30. Kenyon, "Twilight: After Haying," *CP*, 135.

31. Kenyon, "Coming Home at Twilight in Late Summer," *CP*, 123; Nourse, "Interior Garden."

32. Kuzma, review of *The Boat of Quiet Hours*.

33. Boruch, "Comment/Memory Theater."

34. Kumin, "Three's Company."

35. Gregerson, review of *The Boat of Quiet Hours*.

36. Katrovas, "History and the Transpersonal Talent"; Muske, review of *The Boat of Quiet Hours*, 232–33.

37. White, "It could be for beauty," 47.

Chapter 12. Waiting

The epigraph is from Kenyon, "Waiting," *CP*, 173–74.

1. Kenyon wrote about this event in an article for the *Concord (NH) Monitor*, "South Danbury Church Fair," *Daffodils*, 58–60.

2. Kenyon, "As Bread Must First Be Broken," folder 5, box 22, JKP. A copy of this 1983 composition was given to the author by Mary Lyn Ray.

3. Kenyon memorialized this event in "Breakfast at the Mount Washington Hotel," *CP*, 303–4. Both Andrew Hall and Philippa Hall Smith were asked by the author for an interview, but there has been no response.

4. Grant information, folder 18, box 39, JKP.

5. Hall, "Ghost in the House," 90.

6. Hall, "Ghost in the House," 90–91.

7. Kenyon to Alice Mattison, December 11, 1990, privately held.

8. Hall, "Ghost in the House," 89–91.

9. Hall, "Ghost in the House," 89.

10. Kenyon, "Sun and Moon," *CP*, 94–95.

11. Brown, "Jane Kenyon."

12. Mattison to Kenyon, June 1, 1985, folder 4, box 27, JKP.

13. Kenyon, "An Interview with Bill Moyers," *Daffodils*, 169.

14. Hall, *Best Day*, 235–36.

15. Kenyon, "The Blue Bowl," *CP*, 160.

16. Hall, *Essays after Eighty*, 71.

17. Hall has a lengthy discussion of their animals in "Animals inside the House." *Best Day*, 84–95.

18. Kenyon, "Interview with David Bradt," *Daffodils*, 182.

19. Kenyon, "Biscuit," *CP*, 226; "After an Illness, Walking the Dog," *CP*, 200–201; "With the Dog at Sunrise," *CP*, 214; and "The Physics of Long Sticks," *Daffodils*, 101–3.

20. Kenyon, "An Interview with Marian Blue," *Daffodils*, 193.

21. Hall, "Two Poets in One House," 2.

22. Kenyon's numerous recorded readings are available: "Jane Kenyon and Judith Moffett Reading Their Poems," *Library of Congress*, https://www.loc.gov/item/89741337/; Bill Moyers, "A Poet a Day: Jane Kenyon," *Vimeo*, https://vimeo.com/407706624, and "A Life Together," https://billmoyers.com/.

23. Mattison to Kenyon, June 18, 1984, folder 3, box 27, JKP.

24. Hall, *Best Day*, 164–71. This is the fullest description of the trip, but Kenyon wrote postcards to Mattison and Peseroff, expressing her delight, especially in China.

25. Kenyon, "Cultural Exchange," *CP*, 204.

26. Kenyon, "Childhood, When You Are in It . . . ," folder 26, box 19, JKP. This manuscript iteration contains additional information on her China trip that is not included in the printed version in *Daffodils*.

27. Kenyon, "Homesick," *CP*, 205.

28. Kenyon to Peseroff, March 1986, privately held.

29. Berry, "Sweetness Preserved," 52–57.

30. Philip Levine to Kenyon, February 7, 1988, folder 11, box 26, JKP.

31. Kenyon to Mattison, May 28, 1985, privately held.

32. Pride, "Still Present," 96.

Chapter 13. A Moment in Middle Age

The epigraph is from Kenyon, "The Pear," *CP*, 150.

1. Kenyon told Peseroff about her depression on August 6, 1987, and September 14, 1987, saying she is not in good shape. In a July 27, 1989, letter, she indicates she is still struggling. Privately held.

2. Kenyon, "Twilight after Haying," *CP*, 135.

3. The poems in *Ploughshares* are "Staying at Grandma's," *CP*, 175, and "With the Dog at Sunrise," *CP*, 214. The ones in *Ploughshares Poetry* Reader are "Frost Flowers," *CP*, 90; "Camp Evergreen," *CP*, 110; and "What Came to Me," *CP*, 87.

4. Kenyon, "At the Feeder," and "Reading Poetry."

5. Robertson, "Parnassus-on-Potomac," 13; Kenyon and Moffett, "Jane Kenyon and Judith Moffett." The *New York Times* reports this event in March 1987, but the Library of Congress records the event in March 1988, which may be incorrect.

6. Kenyon, "Estonia and New Hampshire," *Daffodils*, 77–81; Virginia Higgins, participant in Bridges of Peace Project, interview with author, November 11, 2019.

7. Kenyon, "While We Were Arguing," *CP*, 186.

8. Kenyon, "Now Where?" *CP*, 197.

9. Kenyon to Mattison, June 10, 1988, privately held. The only poem of this period that refers to an argument is "While We Were Arguing," *CP*, 186.

10. Kenyon to Mattison, August 29, 1988, privately held.

11. Kenyon to Mattison, September 2, 1988, privately held. Kenyon's planner indicates she saw Clark nine times in 1988.

12. Kenyon, "At the I.G.A.: Franklin, New Hampshire," CP, 305–6. This was first published in the *Ontario Review* in 1989.

13. Kenyon, "At the Public Market Museum, Charleston, S.C.," *CP*, 182. This first appeared in the *New Yorker*.

14. Kenyon gives a very brief description of the trip in Russian journal, October 1988, folder 4, box 33, JKP. Hall gives a fuller description in *Best Day*, 237.

15. Kenyon, "Lines for Akhmatova," *CP*, 183.

16. Hall, *Best Day*, 237.

17. Kenyon to Mattison, November 1, 1988, privately held.

18. Mattison to Kenyon, November 3, 1988, folder 8, box 27, JKP.

19. Hall, *Best Day*, 238.

20. Kenyon to Mattison, March 13, 1989, privately held.

21. Kenyon to Mattison, November 1, 1988, privately held.

22. Kenyon to Mattison, January 14, 1992, privately held.

23. Kenyon to Mattison, April 16, 1989, privately held.

24. Kenyon to Mattison, August 29, 1990, privately held.

25. Kenyon to Mattison, March 5, 1993, privately held.

26. Mattison, "Let It Grow in the Dark," 11.

27. Mattison, email to author, March 9, 2021.

28. Marie Howe, phone interview with author, February 18, 2020; Howe, "Jane Kenyon's *Constance*," 245–46.

29. Kenyon to Mattison, March 13, 1989, privately held.

30. Mattison to Kenyon, March 16, 1989, folder 9, box 27, JKP.

31. Kenyon, "Ice Out," *CP*, 195; "Poets Laureate."

32. Mattison to Kenyon, March 13, 1989, folder 9, box 27, JKP.

33. Mattison to Kenyon, March 13, 1989, folder 9, box 27, JKP.

34. Kenyon to Mattison, June 23, 1989, privately held.

35. Mattison to Kenyon, June 27, 1989, folder 9, box 27, JKP.

36. Kenyon, "A Modest Proposal," folder 41 (originally, folder 39), box 19, JKP.

37. Kenyon, "Estonia and New Hampshire," *Daffodils*, 77–81.

38. Pride, "Still Present," 98.

39. Pride, "Conversation with Jane Kenyon," 106.

40. Kenyon, "Edna Powers," *Daffodils*, 75–76.

41. Joyce Peseroff participated in "A Tribute to Jane Kenyon" at the Association of Writers and Poets, April 11, 2015, where she discussed the various forms of Kenyon's civic engagement. She called her a "literary citizen of the Republic." Peseroff, "Jane Kenyon's Civic Engagement."

42. Of the many drugs Kenyon was prescribed, only Wellbutrin might have increased libido, but she appears only to have begun taking that drug in 1990.

43. Kenyon to Mattison March 5, 1993, February 1, 1993, and January 14, 1992, privately held.

44. Kenyon to Mattison, October 11, 1991, privately held.

45. This lover is now ninety-two years old and residing in a care center. When contacted he indicated through his daughter that he recognized the name Jane Kenyon and he had some of her books of poetry, but he had no memory of her. Phone interview, August 2020.

46. Kenyon might have told Solow about her affair, but I have not been able to communicate with him.

47. Mattison, email to author, September 5, 2020.

48. Kenyon to Mattison, December 16, 1993, privately held.

49. Kenyon to Mattison, December 16,1993, privately held.

50. Kenyon to Mattison, December 27, 1993, privately held.

51. Kenyon to Mattison, January 7, 1994, privately held.

Chapter 14. The Coming Evening

The epigraph is from Kenyon, "Let Evening Come," *CP*, 231.

1. Kenyon, "Chrysanthemums," *CP*, 237–39.

2. Kenyon, journal, Italy, February 11–12, 1990, folder 5, box 33, JKP.

3. Kenyon, "A Gardener of the True Vine," *Daffodils*, 96.

4. Kenyon, "A Gardener of the True Vine," *Daffodils*, 96.

5. Hall writes about Jensen in *Best Day*, 230–31.

6. Pride, "Still Present," 99.

7. Kenyon, "In Memory of Jack," *CP*, 251.

8. Kenyon, "Moving the Frame," *CP*, 242.

9. Kenyon to Mattison, January 1, 1990, and Kenyon to Mattison, March 11, 1991, both privately held.

10. Kenyon to Mattison, April 16, 1989, privately held.

11. Kenyon, "An Interview with Bill Moyers," *Daffodils*, 171.

12. Kenyon, "Let Evening Come," *CP*, 213.

13. Pride, "Conversation with Jane Kenyon," 105.

14. Pride, "Conversation with Jane Kenyon," 103.

15. "Let Evening Come," drafts, folder 3, box 11, JKP.

16. Kenyon to Mattison, May 2, 1989, privately held.

17. Peseroff to Kenyon, April 27, 1989, folder 9, box 29, JKP.

18. Corn, "Plural Perspectives, Heightened Perceptions," 234.

19. Kenyon, "Looking at Stars," *CP*, 210.

20. Kenyon, "Last Days," *CP*, 209. This may have been inspired by the death of a hospice patient.

21. Kenyon, "With the Dog at Sunrise," *CP*, 214.

22. Kenyon, "Let Evening Come," *CP*, 213. See Peacock, "Comfort Poem," 183–90. "Let Evening Come" was included in *The Best American Poems 1991*, edited by Mark Strand.

23. Peacock, "Comfort Poem," 184.

24. Baker, "Culture, Inclusion, Craft."

25. Kaganoff, review of *Let Evening Come*, 13.

26. Kitchen, "Auditory Imagination."

27. Howe, review of *Let Evening Come*.

28. Matson, review of *Let Evening Come*.

29. McKee, review of *Let Evening Come*.

30. Harris, "Vision, Voice, and Soul-Making."

31. Pride, "All That a Poet Could Ask For."

32. Kenyon to Mattison, June 7, 1990, privately held.

33. Mike Pride, phone interview with author, November 11, 2019.

34. Hall, *Carnival of Losses*, 142–43.

35. Kenyon to Mattison, November 15, 1990, privately held. "The Honey Wagon" was published in the *Concord (NH) Monitor* and reprinted in *Daffodils*, 104–6.

36. Kenyon to Mattison, January 28, 1990, privately held.

37. Mattison to Kenyon, December 31, 1990, privately held.

38. Mattison to Kenyon, November 13, 1990, folder 12, box 27, JKP.

39. Mike Pride, phone interview with author, November 11, 2019.

40. Pride, "Conversation with Jane Kenyon," 108.

41. Pride, "Conversation with Jane Kenyon," 105.

Chapter 15. Widening Vison

The epigraph is from Kenyon, "A Proposal for New Hampshire Writers," *Daffodils*, 137.

1. Kenyon, "Back," *CP*, 241. This poem was the last stanza of a longer poem "Having It Out with Melancholy." The stanza was accepted by the *New Yorker* for publication, but this caused Kenyon to write another final stanza, "Wood Thrush."

2. Pride, "Conversation with Jane Kenyon," 106.

3. Kenyon, "August Rain, after Haying," *CP*, 219.

4. Kenyon, "The Clothes Pin," *CP*, 17.

5. Mattison, email to author, November 5, 2010.

6. Kenyon, "Coats," *CP*, 250; Mattison, "Let It Grow in the Dark," 4–5.

7. Kenyon to Mattison, August 9, 1989, privately held.

8. Kenyon, "Notes of a Novice Hiker," *Daffodils*, 51–57.

9. Kenyon, "Lord I Believe That You Are Closer . . . ," July 1991, folder 31, box 19, JKP. This was given to the author by Mary Lyn Ray.

10. Kenyon, "Spring Changes," *CP*, 165, and "The Stroller," *CP*, 220.

11. Kenyon to Mattison, June 28, 1990, privately held.

12. Kenyon, "The Argument," *CP*, 224.

13. Mattison, email to author, September 5, 2020.

14. Kenyon, "Childhood, When You Are in It . . . ," *CP*, 61–69.

15. Hall, *Best Day*, 171–73. Kenyon included some small details from the trip in India journal notebook, November 6–25, 1991, folder 16, box 33, JKP. An India notebook, folder 16, box 33, is largely about logistics, not her reflections.

16. Kenyon, "Woman, Why Are You Weeping?" *CP*, 292–96.

17. Kenyon, India journal, November 20, 1991, folder 6, box 33, JKP.

18. Kenyon, "Woman, Why Are You Weeping?" folder 27, box 16, JKP, and in *CP*, 292–96.

19. Kenyon to Mattison, March 30, 1992, privately held; Mattison to Kenyon, March 30 1992, folder 15, box 27, JKP; Kenyon to Mattison, April 2, 1992, privately held; Mattison, "Let It Grow in the Dark," 18–20.

20. Kenyon to Mattison, March 30, 1992, privately held.

21. Kenyon to Mattison, September 21, 1992, privately held.

22. Hall, introduction, *Daffodils*, xii. The poem was first published in the *Atlantic Monthly* in April 1999.

23. Kenyon, "Kicking the Eggs," *Daffodils*, 133.

24. Kenyon, "Sleepers in Jaipur," *CP*, 262.

25. Kenyon, "Gettysburg: July 1, 1863," *CP*, 263. This poem was written in 1991 and published in the *New Yorker* the following year.

26. Kenyon to Mattison, March 11, 1991, privately held.

27. Kenyon, "Top Dog," *Concord (NH) Monitor*, [ca. January 1991], folder 6, box 18, JKP.

28. Kenyon, "Three Small Oranges," *CP*, 259.

29. Kenyon, "An Interview with Marian Blue," *Daffodils*, 195–96.

30. Kenyon, "Potato," *CP*, 261.

Chapter 16. The Poet Laureate of Depression

I owe this chapter title to Joyce Peseroff.

The epigraph is from Kenyon, "Having It Out with Melancholy," *CP*, 231.

1. For analysis, see Breslin, "Jane Kenyon's 'Manners toward God'"; Olsen, "Unholy Ghost."

2. Kenyon, "Having It Out with Melancholy," *CP*, 231–35.

3. Waldron, "Poet Jane Kenyon." He points out that melancholy is the mutilator of souls, not of minds.

4. Hall suggests that the figure of depression raped her. See Martin-Joy, "Poetry, Aging, and Loss."

5. Hall, "Ghost in the House," 86–87, for a fuller listing of her drugs.

6. Kenyon, "Interview with Bill Moyers," *Daffodils*, 160.

7. Orr, "Postconfessional Lyric."

8. "Having It Out with Melancholy" appeared in *Poetry*, November 1992, 86–89.

9. Sheehan, *Grace of Incorruption*, part I. Sheehan claims Kenyon's reading of "Having It Out with Melancholy" occurred in 1992; Hall puts the date in 1991, which is probably correct.

10. Kenyon, "Interview with Bill Moyers," *Daffodils*, 154.

11. Kramer, "Unequivocal Eye."

12. Kenyon "Interview with Bill Moyers," *Daffodils*, 159.

13. Breslin, "Jane Kenyon's 'Manners toward God'"; Orr, "Our Lady of Sorrows," 39–41.

14. Rich to Kenyon, October 2, 1990, folder 5, box 30, JKP.

15. Kenyon, "Otherwise," *CP*, 266.

16. Orr, "Our Lady of Sorrows," 32.

17. Mattison, email to author, January 21, 2021.

18. Kenyon, "Have Faith, and the Mud Will Dry," *Concord (NH) Monitor*, April 18, 1992, 13. Reprint, "The Mud Will Dry," *Daffodils*, 114–16. Citation is to the original.

19. Kenyon, "Interview with Bill Moyers," *Daffodils*, 166.

20. Kenyon, "Litter," *CP*, 236, describes Lucy Hall's apartment after she was taken to the hospital.

21. Kenyon, "Joys amid the Shadows of Sadness: A Struggle with Illness Can Lead You to Pursue Life Simply and Fully," *Concord (NH) Monitor,* July 6, 1992. Reprint, "The Shadows," *Daffodils*, 117–19. Citation is to the original.

22. Hall, *Best Day*, 144.

23. Kenyon, "Pharaoh," *CP*, 265.

24. Kenyon, "Notes from the Other Side," *CP*, 267.

25. Kenyon to Thom Schramm, February 13, 1991, folder 5, box 20, JKP.

26. Hall, *Best Day*, 138; Kenyon, "An Interview with Bill Moyers," *Daffodils*, 161.

27. Kenyon, "An Interview with Bill Moyers," *Daffodils*, 161.

28. Kenyon "An Interview with Bill Moyers," *Daffodils*, 163.

29. Kenyon, "Reflections on a Roadside Warning," *Daffodils*, 126–27.

30. Kenyon to Mattison, October 24, 1992, privately held.

31. Kenyon to Mattison, January 14, 1992, privately held.

32. Kenyon to Mattison, January 14, 1992, privately held. Kenyon was referring here to a draft of a children's book she was writing.

33. Hall, *Carnival of Losses*, 142–43.

Chapter 17. Poetry Matters

The epigraph is from Kenyon, "Interview with David Bradt," *Daffodils*, 175.

1. Invitation from Jean Nordhaus, 1991, folder 6, box 23, JKP.

2. Kenyon, "Poems to a Listener." This was incorrectly listed as 1994. It occurred in 1993.

3. Kenyon, "An Interview with David Bradt," *Daffodils*, 172.

4. Geraldine R. Dodge Foundation Poetry Festival, brochure, 1992, folder 17, box 39, JKP.

5. These lectures and interviews were given between 1991 and 1993.

6. Auden, "In Memory."

7. Kenyon, "Kicking the Eggs," *Daffodils*, 133–35.

8. Kenyon served on this council from 1991 to 1993.

9. Kenyon, "A Proposal for New Hampshire Writers," *Daffodils*, 136–37.

10. Kenyon, "Thoughts on the Gifts of Art," *Daffodils*, 138.

11. Kenyon, "Everything I Know about Writing Poetry," *Daffodils*, 139–41.

12. Kenyon, "Interview with David Bradt," *Daffodils*, 174.

13. Kenyon, "Interview with Bill Moyers," *Daffodils*, 164.

14. Kenyon, "Interview with David Bradt," *Daffodils*, 173.

15. Kenyon, "Interview with David Bradt," *Daffodils*, 183–84.

16. Moyers, "Life Together."

17. Pride, "Conversation with Jane Kenyon," 104.

18. Kenyon, "Interview with David Bradt," *Daffodils*, 173; Kenyon, "Thoughts on the Gifts of Art," *Daffodils*, 138.

19. Kenyon, "Interview with Bill Moyers," *Daffodils*, 162.

20. Edgerton, "Attention as a Palliative," 82.

21. Pride, "Conversation with Jane Kenyon," 105.

22. Kenyon, "Interview with Bill Moyers," *Daffodils*, 171.

Chapter 18. The Busiest Year

The epigraph is from Kenyon, "Interview with Marian Blue," *Daffodils*, 195.

1. *The Best American Poetry 1993*, ed. Louise Glück, 1993.

2. Jantsch, "Briefly It Enters," 11. Nancy Jantsch claims it was William Bolcom who compared Hall and Kenyon to the Brownings.

3. Hartigan, "Happy for Now."

4. Kenyon to Mattison, May 4, 1993, privately held.

5. Mattison to Kenyon, May 10, 1993, folder 1, box 28, JKP.

6. Kenyon to Mattison, April 3, 1993, privately held.

7. Kramer, "Unequivocal Eye," 251–55.

8. Hartigan, "Happy for Now."

9. Kenyon to Mattison, August 19, 1993, privately held.

10. Kenyon to Mattison, February 1, 1993, privately held.

11. Kenyon to Mattison, March 5, 1993, privately held.

12. Kenyon, "An Interview with Marian Blue," *Daffodils*, 185, 198.

13. Kenyon to Mattison, January 7, 1994, privately held. Kenyon probably burned only a few letters. The bulk of Mattison's letters to Kenyon remains in the archives.

14. These included "From Rome to Room," "Finding a Long Gray Hair," "Suitor," "Briefly It Enters, and Briefly Speaks," and "Back."

15. Pride, "Still Present," 99.

16. Town of Wilmot, New Hampshire, "Words for a Warrant," 6. I am grateful to the Town of Wilmot for sharing this poem.

17. Moyers, "Life Together."

18. Hall, *Best Day*, 208.

19. Tree Swenson, interview with author, March 19, 2020, and March 25, 2020.

20. Kenyon, "Afternoon at MacDowell," *CP*, 287.

21. Kenyon, "An Interview with Bill Moyers," 145–71.

22. Kenyon, "An Interview with David Bradt," 172–84.

23. Kenyon, "An Interview with Marian Blue," *Daffodils*, 185–201.

24. Gross, "Donald Hall and Jane Kenyon."

Chapter 19. Deciding to Live

The epigraph is from Hartigan, "Happy."

1. Kenyon, India journal, 1993, folder 8, box 33, JKP. Hall also writes about this trip in *Best Day*, 171–73.

2. Kenyon to Alice Mattison, March 7, 1992, privately held; Kamal Kamar to Kenyon, folder 8, box 26, JKP.

3. No copy of her notes from this seminar appears to exist.

4. Kenyon to Joyce Peseroff, September 1993, India, postcard, privately held.

5. Hall also published *Life Work* in 1993.

6. Peseroff to Jane Kenyon, October 18, 1993, folder 19, box 29, JKP.

7. Hartigan, "Happy."

8. Hartigan, "Happy."

9. Kenyon, "Interview with Bill Moyers," *Daffodils*, 158.

10. Kenyon, "Interview with Bill Moyers," *Daffodils*, 166.

11. Basney, "Trust in *Otherwise*," 103. In this chapter he argues that faith for Kenyon is a form of trust.

12. Kenyon, "Watch Ye, Watch Ye," *CP*, 257.

13. Barber, "Constance," 256–59.

14. Howe, "Jane Kenyon's *Constance*," 238–46.

15. Davis and Womack, "Settling into the Light," 87–96.

16. Hall, *Best Day*, 209–10.

17. Kenyon to Mattison, September 28, 1993, privately held.

18. Rector, "About Donald Hall."

19. Victoria Clausi, phone interview with Dana Greene, August 27, 2020.

20. Rector, "Remembering Jane Kenyon," *New Hampshire Arts Newsletter*.

Chapter 20. Annus Horribilis

The epigraph is from Kenyon, "Interview with Bill Moyers," *Daffodils*, 166.

1. Mattison to Kenyon, February 3, 1994, folder 3, box 28, JKP.

2. Merton, "Prayer of Unknowing," *Thoughts in Solitude*, 79. This was confirmed in a phone interview with Alice Ling with the author, March 26, 2020. Ling provided a copy of the prayer.

3. Kenyon, "The Call," "How Like the Sound," "In the Nursing Home," and "Eating the Cookies," *CP*, 281, 283, 282, 284.

4. Hall, "Song for Lucy," *Without*, 6–7.

5. Kenyon, "Happiness," *CP*, 271–72, and "Mosaic of the Nativity: Serbia, Winter 1993," *CP*, 273.

6. Kenyon, "Dutch Interiors," *CP*, 290.

7. Finkelstein, "The Beacon." *Simply Lasting*, 64–68.

8. This poem was included in *The Best American Poetry 1996*, edited by Adrienne Rich.

9. Kenyon, "Reading Aloud to My Father," *CP*, 291.

10. Kenyon, "The Way Things Are in Franklin," *CP*, 289.

11. Kenyon, "Afternoon at MacDowell," *CP*, 287.

12. Hall, "Life after Jane."

13. Carruth, *Letters to Jane*.

14. Mattison to Kenyon, March 21, 1994, folder 3, box 28, JKP.

15. Hall, "Her Long Illness," *Without*, 1–52, continued at intervals.

16. Hall, "Blues for Polly," *Without*, 31–32.

Chapter 21. "Please Don't Die"

The epigraph is from Kenyon, [False Start] "By Now You Have Noticed That I Write Peculiar Editorials," folder 39, box 19, JKP.

1. The principal sources for this are numerous YouTube interviews, especially, Hall, "Jane Kenyon's Last Days and Death" and "Planning for Jane Kenyon's Death"; and Hall, *Best Day*, 146–61, 176–98; afterword, *Otherwise*, 217–220; and *Without*, 1–32.

2. Alice Ling, untitled prayer, November 15, 1994, folder 9, box 33, JKP; Alice Ling, phone interview with author, January 8, 2021.

3. Joyce Peseroff to author, January 10, 2021, email.

4. Stephen Merrill to Kenyon, 1995, folder 9, box 28, JKP.

Chapter 22. Falling into Light

The epigraph is from Kenyon, "Afternoon at MacDowell," *CP*, 287. These lines are inscribed on the gravestone of Jane Kenyon and Donald Hall.

1. This narrative of her final days is drawn from Hall, *Best Day*, 14; "Planning Jane Kenyon's Death." Kenyon left no record of this time.

2. Kenyon, "The Sick Wife," *CP*, 297.

3. Kirby Hall to Kenyon, April 15, 1995, folder 1, box 24, JKP.

4. Hall, "Her Long Illness," *Without*, 42.

5. This book of new and selected poems published in 1996 shares a title with her earlier poem "Otherwise" published in *Constance*.

6. Kenyon, "Woman, Why Are You Weeping?" *Daffodils*, 205–9, and *CP*, 292–96; Joyce Peseroff, phone interview with author, January 21, 2021.

7. Caroline Finkelstein gave Kenyon this art book.

8. Gross, "Donald Hall Pays Tribute."

9. Kenyon, "Things," *CP*, 139.

10. Hall, "Life after Jane."

11. Reuel Kenyon to author, January 14, 2021, email.

12. Alice Ling, interview with author, March 26, 2020. I am grateful to Ling for details of the funeral.

Chapter 23. The Aftermath

The epigraph is from Hall, "Life after Jane."

1. Hall, "Weeds and Peonies," *Without*, 81.

2. Hall, *Painted Bed*.

3. Martin-Joy, "Poetry, Aging, and Loss."

4. Hall, "Mid-winter Letter," *Without*, 78.

5. Martin-Joy, "Poetry, Aging, and Loss"; Hall, *Carnival of Losses*, 90.

6. Hall, "Ghost in the House," 92; Martin-Joy, "Poetry, Aging, and Loss."

7. Hall, *Unpacking the Boxes*, 154.

8. Walters, "Conversations."

9. Pride, "Donald Hall's Late Burst of Creativity."

10. Glass, "Interview"; Gross, "Donald Hall Pays Tribute."

11. Glass, "Interview"; Gross, "Donald Hall Pays Tribute"; Hall, *Best Day*, 213.

12. Hall, "Life after Jane."

13. Kenyon, "An Interview with Marion Blue," *Daffodils*, 191.

14. McNair, "Government of Two," 174.

15. Hall, *Best Day*, 112.

16. Hall, *Carnival of Losses*, 144–45.

17. Hall, "Poetry of Death."

18. Hall, *Carnival of Losses*, 146.

19. Kenyon, *Best Poems*.

Chapter 24. Acclaim

The epigraph is from Kenyon to Mattison, July 16, 1986, privately held.

1. "Notable Books of the Year 1997."

2. Oktenberg, "In Solitude and Sorrow," 27.

3. Gordon, "Above an Abyss."

4. Richman, "Luminous Particulars," 76.

5. Muske, "In the Heart of the Heart."

6. Lund, "Poems of an Age."

7. Garrison, "Simply Lasting."

8. Hass, "Poet's Choice."

9. Merritt, "Jane Kenyon, *Otherwise*."

10. Dirda, "Gift of Being Simple." A previous and longer article appeared in 1996 in the *Washington Post*.

11. McNair, "Government of Two," 181; Lewis, review of "Otherwise."

12. E. Davis, review.

13. Maryles, "Behind the Best Sellers."

14. Rector, "Remembering Jane Kenyon," *New Hampshire Arts Newsletter*.

15. Timmerman, *Jane Kenyon*.

16. Goodyear, "Hundred-Proof Water."

17. Poets who have received this prize include Ted Kooser, Kay Ryan, Jane Hirschfield, Jill Collins, Sharon Olds, Charles Simic, Mark Doty, Frank Bidart, and Tracy K. Smith.

18. Kenyon, "A Proposal for New Hampshire Writers," *Daffodils*, 137.

19. Phillips, "Poems, Mostly Personal." Phillips claims Kenyon had limited vision, is imprecise, and is repetitive, but she creates striking images.

Chapter 25. Advocate for the Inner Life

The epigraph is from Kenyon, [False Starts] "By now you have noticed I write peculiar editorials . . . ," undated, folder 39, box 19, JKP.

1. Kenyon, [False Starts] "By now you have noticed I write peculiar editorials . . . ," undated, folder 39, box 19, JKP.

2. Kenyon, "Thoughts on the Gifts of Art," *Daffodils*, 138.

3. Pride, "Conversation with Jane Kenyon," 104.

4. Kenyon, "Interview with Bill Moyers," *Daffodils*, 166.

5. See K. R. Jamison, *Touched by Fire* and "Mood Disorders," and N. Jamison, "Creativity and Mental Illness," both of whom discuss the prevalence of depression among writers, especially poets. They maintain that while depression does not cause creativity, it provides material poets can use, as they perceive reality in new ways.

6. Simic, "Jane Kenyon."

7. Adams, "Friends Pay Tribute."

8. Berry, "Sweetness Preserved," 55, 57.

9. Rattelle, "Exile as Resettlement." See also Pride, "Review of *The Best Poems of Jane Kenyon*," *Concord (NH) Monitor*, April 19, 2020, https://www.concordmonitor .com/.

10. Rector, "Remembering Jane Kenyon," *New Hampshire Arts Newsletter*, 6–7.

11. Orr, "Our Lady of Sorrows," 41, 38.

12. Breslin, "Four and a Half Books," 230–33.

13. Breslin, "Jane Kenyon's 'Manners toward God,'" 203.

14. Kinnahan, "Critical Mapping."

15. Jean Valentine, phone interview with author, February 8, 2020.

16. Strongin, "A Faith That Blessed through Sorrow," 214, 221.

17. Muske, "In the Heart."

18. Robert Bly, "Essay on Jane Kenyon," no date, unpublished, folder 53, box 307, Robert Bly Collection, University of Minnesota Archives. See also Bly, "Few Lines about Jane."

19. Wesley McNair, phone interview with author, April 9, 2020.

20. McNair, "Craft and Technique."

21. Howe, "Jane Kenyon's *Constance*"; Marie Howe, phone interview with author, February 18, 2020.

22. Wynn, "Lord, you know that I love you."

23. Basney, "Trust in *Otherwise*," 103.

24. Hall, introduction, *Daffodils*, xii; Taylor, "Presence of Jane Kenyon."

25. Gross, "Donald Hall Pays Tribute"; Mattison, "Let It Grow," 22.

BIBLIOGRAPHY

Adams, Noah. "Friends Pay Tribute to the Late Jane Kenyon." *All Things Considered. National Public Radio*, May 3, 1996. www.npr.org/.

Akhmatova, Anna. *Twenty Poems of Anna Akhmatova*. Translated by Jane Kenyon with Vera Sandomirsky Dunham. Saint Paul, MN: Eighties, 1985.

Allen, Jessica. "Jane Kenyon." In *Contemporary American Women Poets: An A-to-Z Guide*, edited by Catherine Cucinella, 194–98. Westport, CT: Greenwood, 1998.

Archer, Emily. "Trouble with Math in a One-Room Country School." In *Poetry for Students*, edited by Ira Mark Milne, 9, 236–50. Detroit: Gale, 2000.

Auden, W. H. "In Memory of W. B. Yeats." In *Another Time*. New York: Random.

Baker, David. "Culture, Inclusion, Craft." Review of *Let Evening Come. Poetry* 158, no. 3 (1991): 161–64.

Barber, David. "*Constance.*" In Peseroff, *Simply Lasting*, 256–59.

Basney, Lionel. "Trust in *Otherwise*." In Hornback, *Bright Unequivocal Eye*, 99–104.

Berry, Wendell. "Sweetness Preserved." In Peseroff, *Simply Lasting*, 47–59.

Bisiewicz, Susan. "The End of My First Marriage and Psychoanalysis." January 21, 2018. *Web of Stories*. www.webofstories.com/.

Bly, Robert. "A Few Lines about Jane." In Peseroff, *Simply Lasting*, 69–73.

———. Papers. Folder 53, box 307. University of Minnesota Archives, Minneapolis.

———. "The Yellow Dot." In Peseroff, *Simply Lasting*, 73.

Booty, John. "Christian Poetry: Three Modern Women Poets." *Sewanee Theological Review* 44, no. 3 (2001): 267–68.

Boruch, Marianne. "Comment/Memory Theater." *American Poetry Review* 16, no. 2 (1987): 22.

Breslin, Paul. "Four and a Half Books." *Poetry*, 179, July 4, 1997, 226–39.

———. "Jane Kenyon's 'Manners Toward God': Gratitude and the 'Anti-urge.'" In Peseroff, *Simply Lasting*, 203–11.

Brown, Robyn. "Jane Kenyon: A Poet in Quiet Hours." *Enterprise*, January 14, 1987, 1–2.

Carruth, Hayden. *Letters to Jane*. Keene, NY: Ausable, 2004.

———. "Poets on the Fringe." In Peseroff, *Simply Lasting*, 227–28.

Cookson, Sandra. Review of *Otherwise: New and Selected Poems*. In *World Literature Today* 71, no. 2 (1997): 390.

Corn, Alfred. "Plural Perspectives, Heightened Perceptions." In Peseroff, *Simply Lasting*, 234–35.

Cramer, Jeffery S. "The Long White House That Holds Love and Work Together: An Interview with Donald Hall at Eagle Pond Farm." *Meridian* 4 (1999): 42–66.

———. "With Jane and Without: An Interview with Donald Hall." *Massachusetts Review* 39, no. 4 (1998): 493–510.

Cramer, Stephen. "Home Alone: Self and Relation in Part I of *The Boat of Quiet Hours*." In Peseroff, *Simply Lasting*, 160–68.

Davis, Ellen. "*A Hundred White Daffodils* by Jane Kenyon." Review. *Metamorphoses*. *Harvard Review* (Spring 2000): 133–34.

Davis, Todd F., and Kenneth Womack. "Settling into the Light: The Ethics of Grace in the Poetry of Jane Kenyon." In Hornback, *Bright Unequivocal Eye*, 86–97.

Dinnerstein, Dorothy. *The Mermaid and the Minotaur: Sexual Arrangements and the Human Malaise*. New York: Harper and Row, 1976.

Dirda, Michael. "The Gift of Being Simple." In Peseroff, *Simply Lasting*, 267–69.

Doty, Mark. "Life Lines: Jane Kenyon's Shimmering Poems Illuminate the Profound in the Everyday." *O, the Oprah Magazine* 6, September 2005, 182.

Edgerton, Becky. "Attention as a Palliative for Depression: The Poems of Jane Kenyon." In Hornback, *Bright Unequivocal Eye*, 77–85.

Farrow, Anne. "Into the Light All Things Must Fall." *Northeast: The Hartford (CT) Courant*, August 27, 1995, 9.

Feraca, Jean. *I Hear Voices: A Memoir of Love, Death, and Radio*. Madison: University of Wisconsin Press, 2007.

Finkelstein, Caroline. "The Beacon." In Peseroff, *Simply Lasting*, 64–68.

Garrison, Deborah. "Simply Lasting." In Peseroff, *Simply Lasting*, 260–64.

Glass, Ira. "Interview with Donald Hall." February 13, 1998. Audio, 18 mins. *This American Life. National Public Radio*. www.thisamericanlife.org/.

Goldstein, Laurence. "Poets at the University of Michigan, 1925 to 1980." *Michigan Quarterly Review* 57, no. 1 (2018): 52–68.

———. "Remembering Jane Kenyon." *Xylem* 12 (Winter 1996): 55–58.

Goodyear, Dana. "Hundred-Proof Water." Review of *Collected Poems*. *New York Times Book Review*, November 20, 2005, 20.

Gordon, Emily. "Above and Abyss." Review of *Otherwise*. *Nation* 262, April 29, 1996, 29.

Gregerson, Linda. Review of *The Boat of Quiet Hours*. *Poetry Review* 151, February 1988, 421–23.

Gross, Terry. "Donald Hall and Jane Kenyon Discuss Their Marriage and Work." September 1, 1993. Audio, 22:34 min. *Fresh Air, 1975–2022. National Public Radio.* https://freshairarchive.org/.

———. "Donald Hall Pays Tribute to His Late Wife Jane Kenyon." April 25, 1996. *Fresh Air, National Public Radio.* https://freshairarchive.org/.

Gundy, Jeff. "Darkness and Light: Jane Kenyon's Spiritual Struggle." *Christian Century* 123, January 24, 2006, 26–29.

Hall, Donald. Afterword. In *Otherwise: New & Selected Poems of Jane Kenyon*, 217–20. Saint Paul, MN: Graywolf, 1996.

———. *The Best Day the Worst Day: Life with Jane Kenyon.* Boston: Houghton Mifflin, 2005.

———. *A Carnival of Losses: Notes Nearing Ninety.* Boston: Houghton Mifflin Harcourt, 2018.

———. *Essays after Eighty.* New York: Houghton Mifflin, 2014.

———. *Exiles and Marriages.* New York: Viking Press, 1956.

———. "Falling in Love and Getting Married to Jane Kenyon." July 28, 2017. *YouTube.* www.youtube.com/watch?v=2nO0paG1aRI.

———. "Ghost in the House." In *Simply Lasting*, 83–93.

———. *Here at Eagle Pond.* New York: Ticknor and Fields, 1990.

———. "An Interview with Donald Hall." Interview by David Hamilton. *Iowa Review* 15, no. 1 (1985): 1–17.

———. Introduction to *A Hundred White Daffodils*, by Jane Kenyon, ix–xii. Saint Paul, MN: Graywolf, 1999.

———. "Jane Kenyon's Last Days and Death." July 28, 2017. *Youtube.* Youtube.com.

———. "Life after Jane." *Northeast: Hartford (CT) Courant*, August 27, 1995, 11.

———. *Life Work.* Boston: Beacon, 2003.

———. *The Museum of Clear Ideas.* Boston: Houghton Mifflin Harcourt, 1994.

———. *The Old Life.* Boston: Houghton Mifflin Harcourt, 1996.

———. *The Painted Bed.* Boston: Houghton Mifflin Harcourt, 2002.

———. "Planning for Jane Kenyon's Death." July 28, 2017. *Youtube.* Youtube.com.

———. "The Poetry of Death." *New Yorker*, September 12, 2017. www.newyorker.com/.

———. *Principal Products of Portugal.* Boston: Beacon, 1995.

———. *String Too Short to Be Saved: Recollections of Summers on a New England Farm.* New York: Viking Press, 1961.

———. "Thank You Thank You." *New Yorker*, October 26, 2012. https://www.newyorker.com/.

———. "The Third Thing." *Best Day*, 107–18. Originally published October 30, 2005. https://www.poetryfoundation.org/poetrymagazine/articles/60484/the-third-thing.

————. "Two Poets in One House." In Hornback, *Bright Unequivocal Eye*, 1–2.

————. *Unpacking the Boxes*. Boston: Houghton Mifflin Harcourt, 1997.

————. *Without*. Boston: Houghton Mifflin, 1998.

————. *The Yellow Room: Love Poems*. New York: Harper and Row, 1971.

Harbilas, David. "Beautiful Clarity: Jane Kenyon, Anna Akhmatova, and the Luminous Particular." Paper delivered at the Association of Writers and Writing Programs, September 2007.

Harris, Judith. "Discerning Cherishment in Jane Kenyon's Poetry: Psychoanalytic Approach." In *Simply Lasting*, 191–202.

————. "Vision, Voice, and Soul-Making in 'Let Evening Come.'" In Hornback, *Bright Unequivocal Eye*, 63–68.

Hass, Robert. "Poet's Choice." In Peseroff, *Simply Lasting*, 265–66.

Hayes, Boyd. "After the Fact: Donald Hall and Jane Kenyon, July 1977." Interview with Boyd Hayes, July 1977. Audio recording, 1:02:25. https://soundcloud.com/afterthefact-1/donald-hall-and-jane-kenyon-july-1977.

Heuving, Jeanne, and Cynthia Hogue. "American Women Poets, 1950–2000." In *A History of Twentieth-Century American Women's Poetry*, edited by Linda A. Kinnahan, 289–303. New York: Cambridge University Press, 2016.

Hill, Laban. "Jane Kenyon." In Peseroff, *Simply Lasting*, 113–44.

Hornback, Bert G., ed. *'Bright Unequivocal Eye': Poems, Papers, and Remembrances from the First Jane Kenyon Conference*, edited by Bert G. Hornback. New York: Lang, 2000.

Hostetler, Ann. "Food as Sacrament in the Poetry of Jane Kenyon." In Hornback, *Bright Unequivocal Eye*, 105–13.

Howe, Marie. "Jane Kenyon's *Constance*." In Peseroff, *Simply Lasting*, 238–46.

————. Review of "Let Evening Come." *Ploughshares* 16, no. 4 (90–91): 283–84.

Jackman, Michael. "Metre and Meaning in Jane Kenyon's 'Song.'" *New Writing: The International Journal for the Practice & Theory of Creative Writing* 14, no. 1 (2016): 80–85. doi:10.1080/14790726.2016.1248981.

Jamison, Kay Redman. "Mood Disorders and Patterns of Creativity in British Writers and Artists." *Psychiatry* 52, no. 2 (1989): 125–34.

————. *Touched by Fire: Manic-Depressive Illness and the Artistic Temperament*. New York: Free Press, 1993.

Jamison, Nancy. "Creativity and Mental Illness: Prevalence Rates in Writers and Their First-Degree Relatives." *American Journal of Psychiatry* 144, no. 10 (1987): 1288–92.

Jantsch, Nancy Jennings. "Briefly It Enters: A Song Cycle by William Bolcom from Poems by Jane Kenyon." PhD diss., Ohio State University, 2001.

Kaganoff, Penny. Review of "Let Evening Come." *Publishers Weekly*, March 30, 1990, 237.

Katrovas, Richard. "History and the Transpersonal Talent, or 'I'm Just Tired of Reading Guys.'" *New England Review* 11, no. 3 (1989): 345–46.

Kenyon, Jane. "At the Feeder." Date unknown. Audio. 1:21 min. "Phone-a-Poem: A Selection of Archival and Newly-Commissioned Answering Machine Poems

(2013)." Woodberry Poetry Room, *Harvard University*. https://library.harvard
.edu/sites/default/files/static/poetry/listeningbooth/poets/phone-a-poem
.html.

———. *The Best Poems of Jane Kenyon*. Compiled by Donald Hall. Minneapolis,
MN: Graywolf, 2020.

———. *The Boat of Quiet Hours*. St. Paul, MN: Graywolf, 1986.

———. *Collected Poems*. Minneapolis, MN: Graywolf, 2005.

———. *Constance*. Saint Paul, MN: Graywolf, 1993.

———. *From Room to Room*. Cambridge, MA: Alice James Books, 1978.

———. "Having It Out with Melancholy." In *The Best American Poetry 1993*, edited
by Louise Glück, 287. New York: Macmillan, 1993.

———. *A Hundred White Daffodils*. Saint Paul, MN: Graywolf, 1999.

———. *Let Evening Come*. Saint Paul, MN: Graywolf, 1990.

———. "Let Evening Come." In *The Best American Poetry 1991*, edited by Mark
Strand, 119. New York: Scribner's, 1991.

———. *Otherwise: New & Selected Poems*. Saint Paul, MN: Graywolf, 1996.

———. Papers. MC 164. Milne Special Collections and Archives. University of
New Hampshire, Durham, New Hampshire.

———. "Reading Aloud to My Father." In *The Best American Poetry 1996*, edited by
Adrienne Rich. New York: Scribner's, 1996. Repr., *The Best of the Best American
Poetry*, edited by Robert Pinsky. New York: Scribner's, 2013.

———. "Reading Poetry." *New Letter*, May 15, 1987, Kansas City, Missouri. Radio.
Catalogue No. 19870515.

———. Review of *New Shoes* by Kathleen Fraser. *Green House* 2, no. 2 (1979): 67.

———. "Three Songs at the End of Summer." In *The Best American Poetry 1989*,
edited by Donald Hall. New York: Collier, 1989.

Kenyon, Jane, and Judith Moffett. "Jane Kenyon and Judith Moffett Reading
Their Poems." Gertrude Clarke Whittall Poetry and Literature Fund, and Archive
of Recorded Poetry and Literature. *Library of Congress*, 1988. Audio.

Kinnahan, Linda. "Critical Mapping: An Introduction." In *A History of Twentieth-
Century Poetry* by Women, edited by Linda Kinnahan, 3–25. New York: Cambridge University Press, 2016.

Kinnell, Galway. "How Could She Not," In Peseroff, *Simply Lasting*, 43–44.

Kitchen, Judith. "Auditory Imagination: The Sense of Sound." *Georgia Review* 45,
no. 1 (1991): 154–60.

Kramer, Peter D. "Bookend: The Anatomy of Melancholy." *New York Times*, April
7, 1996, sec. 7, 27.

———. "Unequivocal Eye." In Peseroff, *Simply Lasting*, 251–55.

Kumin, Maxine. "Dinner at Jane and Don's." In Peseroff, *Simply Lasting*, 45–46.

———. "Three's Company." *Women's Review of Books* 4, no. 10–11 (1987): 6.

Kuzma, Greg. Review of *The Boat of Quiet Hours*. *Iowa Review* 19, no. 1 (1989):
167–70.

Lammon, Martin. "Something Hard to Get Rid Of: An Interview with Robert
Bly." *Ploughshares* 8, no. 1 (1982): 11–23.

Latimer, Robin. "Jane Kenyon." In *American Poets since World War II*, edited by R. S. Gwynn, 172–75. *Dictionary of Literary Biography*. 3rd series. Detroit, MI: Gale Research, 1992.

Lewis, Leon. Review of "Otherwise." *Magill's Literary Annual*, June 1997, 1–3.

Lucas, Rose. "'Into Black Air': Darkness and Its Possibilities in the Poetry of Jane Kenyon." *Plumwood Mountain Journal*, February 2014. https://plumwood mountain.com/.

———. "Poetry in the Cut: Harvests of Loss and Consolation in the Poetry of Jane Kenyon." *Studio Journal* 1, 2 (2007). http://studiojournal.ca/vo1no2/studio 5b1.html.

Lund, Elizabeth. "Poems of an Age that Shuns Adornment: Review of *Otherwise*. *Christian Science Monitor* 88, 193, August 29, 1996, B1.

Lyman, Henry. "Jane Kenyon 1984 & 1994 Series." *Poems to a Listener*, 2022. https://poemstoalistener.org/ interview/jane-kenyon.

Martin-Joy, John. "Poetry, Aging, and Loss: An Interview with Donald Hall." September 13, 2016. *TriQuarterly*. Northwestern University, 2022. www.triquarterly.org.

Maryles, Daisy. "Behind the Best Sellers." *Publishers Weekly*, July 15, 1996, 19.

Matson, Suzanne. Review of "Let Evening Come." *Harvard Book Review* 17–18 (Summer–Fall 1990): 23–24.

Mattison, Alice. "Beyond Memory and Reportage." Paper presented at Association of Writers and Writing Programs conference, Austin, Texas, 2006.

———. "Jane Kenyon's Diction." Paper presented at Association of Writers and Writing Programs conference, Minneapolis, Minnesota, 2015.

———. "Let It Grow in the Dark like a Mushroom: Writing with Jane Kenyon." In Peseroff, *Simply Lasting*, 3–22.

McCann, Janet. Review of *Collected Poems*. *Magill's Literary Annual*, June 2006, 1–3.

McDonald, David. "Donald Hall." *The Free Library*, January 1, 2002. https://www .thefreelibrary.com/donald+hall-a082535303. Originally in *American Poetry Review* 31, no. 1 (2002): 17–20.

McKee, Louis. Review of *Let Evening Come*. *Library Journal*, May 15, 1990, 80.

McNair, Wesley. "Craft and Technique: Four Poets." *Michigan Quarterly Review* 36, no. 4 (1997). http://hdl.handle.net/2027/spo.act2080.0036.422.

———. "A Government of Two." In Peseroff, *Simply Lasting*, 169–82.

———. "Taking the World for Granite, Four Poets in New Hampshire." *Sewanee Review* 104, no. 1 (1996): 70–81.

Merritt, Constance. "Jane Kenyon, *Otherwise*." In Peseroff, *Simply Lasting*, 270–76.

Merton, Thomas. *Thoughts in Solitude*. New York: Farrar, Straus, and Cudahy, 1958.

Milburn, Michael. Review of *Twenty Poems of Anna Akhmatova*. Special issue, Eroto. *Harvard Review* 4 (April 1987): 4.

Moyers, Bill. "A Life Together." December 17, 1993. *Bill Moyers. Doctoroff Media Group*. https://billmoyers.com/content/a-life-together-donald-hall-jane -kenyon/.

Muske, Carol. "The Boat of Quiet Hours." In Peseroff, *Simply Lasting*, 232–33.

———. "In the Heart of the Heart of the Country." Review of Otherwise. *New York Times*, January 5, 1997, BR 12.

Nabokov, Vladmir. *Speak, Memory: An Autobiography Revisited*. New York: Putnam, 1966.

"Notable Books of the Year 1997." *New York Times*, December 7, 1997. www.nytimes .com/.

"Notes on Current Books, Winter 1979: *From Room to Room*." Review. *Virginia Quarterly Review* 55, no. 1 (1979). https://www.vqronline.org/recent-books/notes -current-books-winter-1979.

Nourse, Marsha. "The Interior Garden in Jane Kenyon's Poetry." In Hornback, *Bright Unequivocal Eye*, 119–20.

Obituary. Mary Dawn Selvius. *Ann Arbor (MI) News*, July 20, 2010.

Oktenberg, Adrian. "In Solitude and Sorrow." *Women's Review of Books* 13, no. 10–11 (1996): 27–28.

———. "Review of *From Room to Room*." *Ploughshares* 8, no. 1 (1982): 168–71.

Olsen, Trenton B. "'Unholy Ghost': Jane Kenyon and the Religious Binaries of Depression." *Intermountain West Journal of Religious Studies* 2, no. 1 (2010): 93–108.

Orr, Gregory. "Our Lady of Sorrows." In Peseroff, *Simply Lasting*, 32–42.

———. "Postconfessional Lyric." In *The Columbia History of American Poetry*, edited by Jay Parini, 667–72. New York: Columbia University Press, 1993.

———. "Two Chapters from *Poetry as Survival*." *American Poetry Review* 31, no. 3 (2002): 24–27.

Peacock, Molly. "A Comfort Poem." In Peseroff, *Simply Lasting*, 183–90.

Perillo, Lucia. "Notes from the Other Side." In Peseroff, *Simply Lasting*, 247–50.

Peseroff, Joyce. "Green House." In Hornback, *Bright Unequivocal Eye*, 5–10.

———. "Jane Kenyon's Civic Engagement." Paper presented Association of Writers and Writing Programs, April 11, 2015, Minneapolis, Minnesota.

———. "The Luminous Particular." Review of *Collected Poems*. *Women's Review of Books* 25, no. 5 (2006): 22–23.

———, ed. *Simply Lasting: Writers on Jane Kenyon*. Saint Paul, MN: Graywolf, 2005.

Phillips, Robert. "Poems, Mostly Personal, Some Historical, Many Unnecessary." Review of *Otherwise*. *Hudson Review* 49, no. 4 (1997): 661–62.

Pinsky, Robert. "Tidings of Comfort and Dread: Poetry and the Dark Beauty of Christmas." In Peseroff, *Simply Lasting*, 236–37.

"Poets Laureate." Readings by Donald Hall, Jane Kenyon, Maxine Kumin, and Charles Simic. *New Hampshire Public Radio*, September 15, 1989. https://www .nhpr.org/post/archives-poets-laureate#stream/0.

Pound, Ezra. "A Few Don'ts by an Imagiste." *Poetry: A Magazine of Verse*, March 1913, 200–208. *Poetry Foundation*, 2023. Poetryfoundation.org.

———. "I Gather the Limbs of Osiris 2." In *Selected Prose of Ezra Pound (1909–1965)*, edited by William Cookson, 25. London: Faber, 1973.

Pride, Mike. "The Abiding Presence of Jane Kenyon." *Sewanee Review* 113, no. 3 (2005): 458–62.

———. "A Conversation with Jane Kenyon." In Peseroff, *Simply Lasting*, 100–109.

———. "Donald Hall's Late Burst of Creativity." *New Yorker*, October 31, 2018. https://www.newyorker.com/.

———. "Donald Hall, US and NH Poet Laureate Dies at 89." *New Hampshire Union Leader*, June 24, 2018. https://www.unionleader.com/.

———. "Remembering Donald Hall 1928–2018." *The Pulitzer Prizes*, 2023. www .pulitzer.org/.

———. "A Review of *The Best Poems of Jane Kenyon*." *Concord (NH) Monitor*, April 19, 2020. https://www.concordmonitor.com/.

———. "Still Present." In Peseroff, *Simply Lasting*, 94–99.

Rattelle, Dan. "Exile as Resettlement: A Review of *The Best Poems of Jane Kenyon*." *Front Porch Republic*, July 8, 2020. www.frontporchrepublic.com.

Raymont, Henry. "Poetry Translations: Literal or the Mood and Art?" *New York Times*, March 19, 1969, 40.

Rector, Liam. "About Donald Hall." *Ploughshares* 27, no. 2–3 (2001): 270–74.

———. "Remembering Jane Kenyon." *New Hampshire Arts Newsletter* 12, no. 2 (1995): 6–7.

———. "Remembering Jane Kenyon." In Peseroff, *Simply Lasting*, 74–82.

Richman, Robert. "Luminous Particulars." Review of *Otherwise*. *New Criterion* 14, no. 9 (1996): 76–80.

Roberts, Gary. "Jane Kenyon." In *Contemporary Women Poets*. Detroit, MI: St. James, 1998.

Robertson, Nan. "Parnassus-on-Potomac: Poets Celebrate English." *New York Times*, March 31, 1987, 13.

Ruderman, Anne. "Jane Kenyon: A Poet's Life Cut Short." *Concord Monitor,* September 18, 2005, D4.

Sheehan, Donald. *Grace of Incorruption: The Selected Essays of Donald Sheehan*. Edited by Xenia Sheehan. Orleans, MA: Paraclete, 2015.

Simic, Charles. "Jane Kenyon." *Columbia: A Journal of Literature and Art* 26 (Spring 1996): 172–73.

Smith, Harrison. "Donald Hall, Former U.S. Poet Laureate Wrote about Nature and Loss, Dies at 89." *Washington Post*, June 24, 2018, 9.

Spirko, Robert. "Affective Disorders: The Treatment of Emotion in Jane Kenyon's Poetry." In Hornback, *Bright Unequivocal Eye*, 121–26.

Stevenson, Peter. "Intimacy and Solitude." Review of Donald Hall's *Unpacking the Boxes. New York Times Book Review*, November 7, 2008, 12.

Stoneburner, Tony. "Review of *From Room to Room*." *Religion and Intellectual Life* 3 (Spring 1988): 105–9.

Strongin, Lynn. "A Faith That Blessed through Sorrow: Meditations on Jane Kenyon's Poetry." In Peseroff, *Simply Lasting*, 212–23.

Szynol, Paul. "Poet Donald Hall: 'Old Age Is a Ceremony of Losses.'" September 24,

2018. *Atlantic*. YouTube video, 13:14. www.theatlantic.com/video/index/571141/donald-hall.

Tate, Haines Sprunt. "Intimations of Mortality." In Peseroff, *Simply Lasting*, 277–78.

Taylor, Keith. "The Presence of Jane Kenyon." *Michigan Quarterly Review* 45, no. 4 (2006): 702–12.

Tillinghast, Richard. "Poetry in Ann Arbor: The Early Days of the M.F.A." *Michigan Quarterly Review* 57, no. 1 (2018): 103–4.

Timmerman, John H. "In Search of the Great Goodness: The Poetry of Jane Kenyon." May 16, 2003. *Reformed Journal*. https://reformedjournal.com/.

———. *Jane Kenyon: A Literary Life*. Grand Rapids, MI: Eerdmans, 2002.

Town of Wilmot, New Hampshire. "Words for a Warrant." Annual Report, 1993.

Unterecker, John. "Shape-Changing in Contemporary Poetry." *Michigan Quarterly Review* 27 (1988): 490–92.

Valentine, Jean. "Elegy for Jane Kenyon." In Peseroff, *Simply Lasting*, 63.

———. "Interview with Jean Valentine." With Kaveh Akbar. *DiveDapper*, 2014. https://www.divedapper.com/interview/jean-valentine.

———. "Jane Kenyon 1947—1995." In Peseroff, *Simply Lasting*, 60–62.

Waldron, Robert G. "Poet Jane Kenyon: A Modern Christian Voice." *Spiritual Life* 53, no. 2 (2007): 99–107.

Walters, John. "Conversations with Poet Donald Hall, New Hampshire's Adopted Native Son." Audio, 1:18:09. Interview by Walters, May 13, 2002. *The Front Porch. New Hampshire Public Radio*, June 25, 2018. http://www.nhpr.org/.

Warford, Malcolm. *Becoming a New Church: Reflections on Faith and Calling*. Cleveland, OH: Pilgrim, 2000.

White, Roberta. "'It could be for beauty. . . .': Poetics in *The Boat of Quiet Hours*." In Hornback, *Bright Unequivocal Eye*, 47–54.

Wiman, Christian. *My Bright Abyss: Meditations of a Modern Believer*. New York: Farrar, Straus, and Giroux, 2013.

Wriglesworth, Chad. "Re-presenting Life Back to God: Contemporary Poetry and the Complexity of Human Experience." Paper presented to Regent College, Vancouver, Canada, July 2019.

Wynn, Pam. "'Lord, you know that I love you': An Examination of Christian Language in the Poetry of Jane Kenyon." *Arts: The Arts in Religious and Theological Studies* 16, no. 1 (2004): 14–19.

INDEX

DANA GREENE is Dean Emerita of Oxford College of Emory University. Her books include *Denise Levertov: A Poet's Life* and *Elizabeth Jennings: "The Inward War."*

The University of Illinois Press
is a founding member of the
Association of University Presses.

————————————————————

Composed in 10.25/14 Chaparral Pro
with Frutiger LT Std display
by Lisa Connery
at the University of Illinois Press
Manufactured by Sheridan Books, Inc.

University of Illinois Press
1325 South Oak Street
Champaign, IL 61820-6903
www.press.uillinois.edu